SHADOW
CITIES

SHADOW CITIES

A BILLION SQUATTERS,
A NEW URBAN WORLD

ROBERT NEUWIRTH

Routledge
New York • London

Published in 2005 by
Routledge
270 Madison Avenue
New York, NY 10016
www.routledge-ny.com

Published in Great Britain by
Routledge
2 Park Square
Milton Park, Abingdon,
Oxon OX14 4RN U.K.
www.routledge.co.uk

Routledge is an imprint of the Taylor & Francis Group.
Printed in the United States of America on acid-free paper.

10 9 8 7 6 5 4 3 2

Library of Congress Cataloging-in-Publication Data

Neuwirth, Robert.
  Shadow cities : a billion squatters, a new urban world / Robert Neuwirth.
    p. cm.
  Includes bibliographical references and index.
  ISBN 0-415-93319-6 (hardback : alk. paper)
  1. Squatter settlements. 2. Urban poor—Housing. I. Title.
  HD7287.95.N48 2004
  307.3'36—dc22
                                    2004011849

FOR SQUATTERS EVERYWHERE

TABLE OF CONTENTS

Prologue
Crossing the Tin Roof
Boundary Line

Let the wall crumble on which another wall is not growing.
— César Vallejo

Tema said it with a sigh. He spoke softly, with great fatigue, as if he was confiding something inexpressible, something sad, something he feared an outsider might never understand. I made him repeat the words: "Ai, Robert, o terceiro mundo é um jogo de video." "The third world is a video game."

It was around midnight. We were sitting in Beer Pizza, a restaurant halfway up the Estrada da Gávea, the main drag of the illegal neighborhood called Rocinha, the largest squatter community in Rio de Janeiro. The neighborhood was boogying. There was a convivial crowd at the outdoor tables of the pizzeria, and a guitarist had set up at one side of the courtyard. He sang bossa nova, Motown, and rock 'n' roll standards. Inches away, just beyond the curb, cars and buses and motorcycles jammed the roadway. A continual flow of people moved along the street. Scores of stores were still open, despite the hour. Just down the hill, six men were drinking *cachaça* and singing *pagode* at a small bar. One strummed a banjo while the others hammered the soft syncopated beat on their chairs as they sang. A few hundred paces farther up the slope, a dozen kids were playing soccer on a floodlit field, oblivious of everything around them except the black and white ball.

And then there were the homes. Little more than a decade ago, people here lived in waterlogged wooden barracks. When they wanted electricity, they stole it, looping long strands of wire through the trees and pilfering weak current from faraway poles. They hauled water up the hill in buckets and wheelbarrows and sometimes on the back of a burro.

But that is all in the past. Today there are thirty thousand homes in Rocinha spread across the sharp incline of Two Brothers Mountain. Most are two, three, or four stories tall, made from rein-forced concrete and brick. Many boast shiny tile facades or fantastic Moorish balustrades or spacious balconies, which look out over the endless waves crashing on the beach at São Conrado, far down the hill. Electricity and water have come to this illegal city, and with them a degree of consumerism. Most families have a refrigerator, a color television (Jerry Rubin would approve), and a stereo. Rocinha today is a squatter village 150,000 people strong—the largest in Rio de Janeiro. It occupies its hilltop redoubt between the wealthy neigh-borhoods of Gávea and São Conrado with the confidence of a mod-ern, self-built Renaissance hill town.

One-fifth of Rio lives like this. A million people. They don't own the land, but they hold it. And no one contests their possession. Their communities are called favelas.

I reveled in the contrasts. Smokey Robinson and samba. A sidewalk cafe in the squatter neighborhood. Illegal houses with the best views in town. Permanent buildings in an impermanent community.

Yes, it is a video game: the Marvelous City presented as a city of marvels, with a play of images and sounds as bright and diverting as in any Play Station or X-Box program. But for Tema, for the hordes on the hill, it was life, not display. They built their illegal homes simply because they couldn't afford anyplace else to live. And from that humble origin, against all odds, they produced something complex and sometimes harsh and unruly. They produced a new city.

The hut was made of corrugated metal set on a concrete pad. It was a 10-by-10 cell. Armstrong O'Brian, Jr., shared it with three other men.

Armstrong and his friends had no water (they bought it from a nearby tap owner), no toilet (the families in his compound shared a single pit latrine), and no sewers or sanitation. They did have electricity, but it was illegal service tapped from someone else's wires and could power only one feeble bulb.

This was Southland, a small shanty community on the western side of Nairobi, Kenya. But it could have been anywhere in the city, because more than half the city of Nairobi lives like this—1.5 million people stuffed into mud or metal huts, with no services, no toilets, no rights.

Armstrong explained the brutal reality of their situation. They paid 1,500 shillings in rent—about $20 a month, a relatively high

The tin roof boundary in Kenya.

price for a Kenyan shantytown—and they could not afford to be late with the money. "In case you owe one month, the landlord will come with his henchmen and bundle you out. He will confiscate your things."

"Not one month, one day." His roommate Hilary Kibagendi Onsomu, who was cooking *ugali*, the spongy white cornmeal concoction that is the staple food in the country, cut into the conversation.

"We kneel before the landlord and his agent all the time," Armstrong said.

They called their landlord a *wabenzi*—meaning that he's a person who has enough money to drive a Mercedes-Benz. He lives in a wealthy area, a community called Karen, in honor of Danish Baroness Karen Blixen, who once owned a coffee farm there. Blixen left Kenya better than 70 years ago, when it was still a British holding, but her memory lives on in a book—*Out of Africa*, written under the pen name Isak Dinesen—and in that shaded grove of colonial entitlement on the edge of the Ngong Hills where her manor was located.

Hilary served the *ugali* with a fry of meat and tomatoes. The sun slammed down on the thin steel roof, and we perspired as we ate. After we finished, Armstrong straightened his tie and put on a wool sports jacket. We headed into the glare.

Outside, a mound of garbage formed the border between Southland and the adjacent legal neighborhood of Langata. It was perhaps 8 feet tall, 40 feet long, and 10 feet wide, set in a wider watery ooze. As we passed, two boys were climbing the Mt. Kenya of trash. They couldn't have been more than 5 or 6 years old. They were barefoot, and with each step their toes sank into the muck, sending hundreds of flies scattering from the rancid pile. I thought they might be playing King of the Hill. But I was wrong. Once atop the pile, one of the boys lowered his shorts, squatted, and defecated. The flies buzzed hungrily around his legs.

When 20 families—one hundred people or so—share a single latrine, a boy pooping on a garbage pile is perhaps no big thing. But it stood in jarring contrast to something Armstrong had said as we were eating—that he treasured the quality of life in his neighborhood. For Armstrong, Southland wasn't constrained by its material conditions. Instead, the human spirit radiated out from the metal walls and garbage heaps to offer something no legal neighborhood could: freedom.

"This place is very addictive," he had said. "It's a simple life, but nobody is restricting you, nobody is controlling what you do. Once you have stayed here, you cannot go back." He meant back beyond that mountain of trash, back in the legal city of legal buildings with legal leases and legal rights. "Once you have stayed here, you can stay for the rest of your life."

Sartaj Jaipuri was evicted in 1962, pushed out of Bombay's seaside Worli neighborhood because the government had determined that it would be the city's next commercial center.

He vowed he would never be booted from his home again. So he relocated to a place he thought would be safe. It was a dozen miles further out of town, far from the sea, far from the center of the city. He moved his family to a steep unused plot near the tracks of the Western Railway in a scantily developed area called Malad.

It was rough living, but it was home. Sartaj and his fellow land invaders built their houses from bamboo topped with grass mats. The jungle was their toilet. They carried water from the public taps near the train station, a kilometer or so away. They christened their new community with an admirably straightforward name: Squatter Colony.

Squatter Colony developed with caution. The residents maintained a low profile for nine years before they took the risk of laying permanent foundations for their homes. Those who had money ripped out their original wood and mud platforms and laid down a brick base for their bamboo huts. Then they were quiet again for another decade, before they finally pooled their savings and paid a contractor to run water pipes and open communal taps. A few years later, they made another investment, again hiring the contractor to run the pipes directly into each home. In 1989, 27 years after they seized the land, they finally built something more permanent than their bamboo homes. They tore down the structures and the foundations and built anew with steel and concrete. They waited seven more years for the final piece of the puzzle—electricity.

Today there are perhaps a thousand families in Squatter Colony. Their homes are permanent and some are quite spacious. Most have water and toilets built inside. Sartaj's townhouse is on the upper end of a narrow lane that is paved with tiles and cement. His home, though on a tiny plot, is built to maximize space. The ground floor does quadruple duty as kitchen, living room, bedroom, and bath. There's a steep staircase that leads to a mezzanine, used for storage or an extra bed, and on to a top floor where his youngest son, Aasif, bunks. Another son, Aarif, lives a few blocks down the hill, in a spacious, airy second-floor studio apartment. He's also a squatter.

"These houses are all illegal," Sartaj said. "Even where you are sitting right now is illegal." A slight, soft-spoken man who, among other professions, is a poet and lyricist, he sat cross-legged on the floor of his son's room and swiped one hand through his twist of white hair. He seemed, suddenly, too fragile and fatigued to be a homesteader. He sensed my skepticism and confronted it head-on: "These houses are made by us, by money of our own, and not by the government," he declared.

Mumbai, as the city has been called since 1996, is India's richest city. The city's metropolitan area accounts for 40 percent of the tax revenues of the entire nation. Yet approximately half the inhabitants—more than six million people—have created their homes the same way Sartaj Jaipuri did. They built for themselves on land they don't own. Mumbai is a squatter city. Still, Malad has gentrified over the years and land has become valuable. After more than 40 years in the home he built with his own hands, Sartaj Jaipuri finds himself wondering whether the future could be like 1962 all over again.

Yahya Karakaya came to Sultanbeyli in 1969. He was 4 years old, and all he remembers is a sleepy community of two dozen families in a wooded valley on the Asian side of Istanbul. The villagers raised cows, sold the milk to passing city-dwellers, and harvested lumber from the vast forest around them.

Today, Sultanbeyli is an independent squatter metropolis—population 300,000—and Yahya Karakaya is its popularly elected Mayor. From an oversized desk in a cavernous office on the seventh floor of the massive squatter City Hall, he presides over an empire that includes everything you thought squatters could never achieve: a planning department, a department of public works, a sanitation department, even a municipal bus service.

In Sultanbeyli, nobody owns, but everybody builds. Fatih Boulevard, the main drag, is 5 miles long and boasts a strip of four-, five-, and six-story buildings complete with stores, restaurants, banks, and real estate brokerages. This illegal city even has its own post office.

With this level of development, Sultanbeyli has taken the quaint notion of squatter construction to a new level. For years, Turkey's squatters built at night to take advantage of an ancient legal precept that said, essentially, that if they started construction at dusk and were moved in by sunrise without being discovered by the authorities, they gained legal standing and could not be evicted without a court fight. That's why squatter housing in Turkey is called *gecekondu* (the "c" in Turkish is like "j" in English, thus: geh-jay-kon-doo), meaning "it happened at night." Half the residents of Istanbul —perhaps six million people—dwell in gecekondu homes.

In Sultanbeyli, the squatters are no longer furtive. Gone are the nights of anxiety and sweat as families built under cover of darkness.

Gone are the tiny homes, designed to be erected quickly and to be hidden in sunken lots in order to escape official notice. Squatters in Sultanbeyli boldly proclaim their existence. Construction goes on in the open, 24 hours a day. "We are not gecekondu," the Mayor said with a smile. "We are gunduzkondu"—happening during the day.

Four cities. Four countries. Four continents. Four cultures. One reality: squatters.

Estimates are that there are about a billion squatters in the world today—one of every six humans on the planet. And the density is on the rise. Every day, close to two hundred thousand people leave their ancestral homes in the rural regions and move to the cities. Almost a million and a half people a week, seventy million a year. Within 25 years, the number of squatters is expected to double. The best guess is that by 2030, there will be two billion squatters, one in four people on earth.

As you might expect, with numbers like these, squatters are a pretty diverse bunch. There are those we are used to in the developed world, who intrude into buildings that are abandoned by their owners. There are those who build cabins in remote areas, farming land they don't own. There are those whose invasions are organized by a political outfit, like the Movement of Landless Workers, which is challenging the rule of the land barons in rural Brazil.

But these people are not the mass of squatters. The overwhelming majority of the world's one billion squatters are simply people who came to the city, needed a place to live that they and their families could afford, and, not being able to find it on the private market, built it for themselves on land that wasn't theirs. For them, squatting is a family value.

These squatters mix more concrete than any developer. They lay more brick than any government. They have created a huge hidden economy—an unofficial system of squatter landlords and squatter tenants, squatter merchants and squatter consumers, squatter builders and squatter laborers, squatter brokers and squatter investors, squatter teachers and squatter schoolkids, squatter beggars and squatter millionaires. Squatters are the largest builders of housing in the world—and they are creating the cities of tomorrow.

Three hundred people a day make the trek to Istanbul, three hundred more to Mumbai, and three hundred also to Nairobi. Nicodemus Mutemi was one of them. He came to Kenya's capital in 1996 from his family's home in the Mwingi district. The Mutemi family cultivates corn and millet on their small holding in the parched hills an hour's walk from the nearest village. The land is dry in Mwingi—locals call it semiarid—and the air is still and hot. Growing crops in the cracked earth is a struggle. The family supplements its subsistence agriculture with a small herd of goats and a group of chickens and roosters.

Nicodemus' father poured some home-made honey beer from his gourd into a well-used plastic container. The brew was slightly sour and amazingly refreshing in the heat. As the sun tilted toward the horizon, slipping behind the silhouette of a baobab tree, Nicodemus explained why he left his homeland and clan and moved to Nairobi.

The problem, he said, is economic: You can grow enough to eat, but you can't grow enough to live.

Nicodemus hefted a burlap bag half filled with corn. That bag, he told me, would fetch five shillings at a local wholesale market. But to buy the corn back, in the form of *unga*, the flour used to make *ugali*, would cost 45 shillings at the local store.

The farm economy doesn't work. A farm family can raise enough to eat, but the crops alone will not generate an income. So how will the family members buy clothes or water or school books? How will they pay for kerosene or paraffin so they can light a lamp at night? How will they get tea for breakfast? And what about greater expenses? How will they repair the ancient mud and thatch huts that have served for generations but are beginning to crumble? And, if someone in the family gets sick, how will they pay for a doctor when medicine is a cash business.

The Mutemi family struggled to give Nicodemus an education. He graduated from Form 4—the equivalent of gaining a high school diploma. He would have liked to go to college, but there was no more money. Thus it became his turn to provide for his family, to repay his parents' investment, to secure a future for his own children. So he came to the city.

To be fair, Nicodemus's story is nothing new. This massive migration from rural regions to the urban centers of the world has been going on for thousands of years. And always, once they got to the cities of their dreams, the migrants have become squatters.

In Ancient Rome, despite the astounding government investment in public works, waterways, and infrastructure, squatters took over the streets, occupied fountains, and erected crude lean-tos called *tuguria*, tucked up against the sides of buildings. They were brazen and often seemed to dare authorities to remove them, but there were so many of them that the government couldn't keep up. And it has been like this in almost every city. Some sections of London were squatter zones until the mid-1800s. Paris, too, had its squatters, and historians suggest that the Court of Miracles, immortalized by Victor Hugo in *The Hunchback of Notre Dame*, was originally a squatter colony. Even New York, the definition of the modern real estate city, was a squatter metropolis until the early years of the twentieth century. In fact, the word *squatter* is an American term, originating in New England around the time of the revolutionary war as a popular term for people who built their homes on land they didn't own. The first use of the word in writing came in 1788, by the man who would become the fourth president of the United States—James Madison.

At the same time Nicodemus was establishing himself in Nairobi, I was beginning my own journey.

It was 1996 and the United Nations Commission on Human Settlements—Habitat, for short—the world body that studies and works on housing issues, was holding a major conference in Istanbul. Habitat holds these meetings once every decade, giving bureaucrats and nonprofit organizations a chance to compare notes and promote enlightened policies.

Preparing for that meeting, the statistics fell into place. If seventy million people are coming to the cities every year, and neither governments nor private builders are prepared to handle the onslaught, then all the government bureaucrats and staffers from nonprofits who were gathered in the fancy hotels overlooking the Bosphorus were in the wrong place. They should have been in Sultanbeyli and other squatter neighborhoods, learning from the land invaders.

I began to wonder about the morality of a world that denies people jobs in their home areas and denies them homes in the areas where they have gone to get jobs. And I began to think about my responsibility. I have written scores of articles on real estate, housing, architecture, design, business, planning. Wasn't I guilty, too? Hadn't I focused too much on developers and tycoons and architects, people who, despite the soaring ambition and ego contained in their buildings, have produced relatively little? Why wasn't I writing about the world's squatters, who have journeyed so far and produced so much without any noticeable self-aggrandizement?

After all, if society won't build for this mass of people, don't they have a right to build for themselves? And if they do, then isn't there merit in their mud huts? If they are creating their own homes and improving them over time, then isn't there something good—at least potentially—about a community without water and sanitation and sewers? And if that's true, then shouldn't the comfortable class stop complaining about conditions in the shantytowns and instead work with the squatters to improve their communities?

They have created tiny ridges in the earth, outlines that indicate what is yours, what is mine. The dividing lines are nothing—scarcely more than an inch high, but pounded hard so they cannot be easily erased. Each seam delineates a living space. This is where people cook, read, eat, wash, sleep. This is where they store their food and their clothes. For the past three years, Laxmi Chinnoo, her mother, and her three daughters, have lived in one of these imaginary homes, under a bridge that crosses the tracks of the Harbor Line Railway not far from the Chuna Bhatti station in Mumbai.

Aside from those lines in the dirt and a few rugs hung on ropes so her daughters have a private place to change clothes, she has not built anything. There are a dozen other families living here in the same circumstances.

Are these people squatters?

Or how about Gita Jiwa, a construction laborer who has lived with her three daughters in a makeshift bamboo and plastic tent on the median strip of Mumbai's Western Expressway for the past five years? Fifteen families live alongside her. Are they squatters?

Or how about Washington Ferreira, who lives with his mother and younger sister in a two-room rental in Rocinha. They are tenants, not invaders. Are they squatters?

To me, they are all squatters. But their experiences reveal that there are many different types of squatters, with different needs, different incomes, different aspirations, different social standing, different stories.

I'm standing on a wasteland. Several hundred acres, vacant, home only to scrub and weeds and illegally dumped trash. In the fall, the wind whips across these desolate blocks and the air turns tart against your skin. In winter, the flat expanse becomes a tundra as ice crusts the top of the construction debris. In springtime, butterflies squat on the tufts of sand grasses, and the land seems alive with possibilities. On bright summer days, dragonflies sprint above the cracked pavement, seeming to be racing their own shadows. This is beachfront property, perhaps ten miles from the tip of Manhattan, a bit more than an hour away by subway—Sprayview Avenue on the Rockaway Peninsula in Queens. Fifty years ago, it was a bungalow community—a summer resort for the lower middle class. Then, in the 1960s, the government took it for urban renewal. It has been vacant ever since. The paved streets, the rusting hydrants, the sewers, the streetlights—all the services people could need—have been in suspended animation, waiting for someone, anyone, to see the possibility.

Every time I visit Sprayview Avenue, I think of the third world. I think of Rio and Nairobi and Mumbai and Istanbul. In each of those cities, Sprayview Avenue would have life. People who needed it would have seized the land and built their rustic homes. They would not be anarchists or radicals or hotheads. They would not be people with a political ax to grind or an ideological agenda. They would, rather, be regular people. Working people. People with families. With young children. People who came to the city to find work. Mechanics and waitresses, laborers and salesclerks, teachers and taxi drivers. These city-builders would construct using the crudest materials—mud, sticks, scavenged cardboard, wood, plastic, and scrap metal. At the start, their Sprayview Avenue would be a severely unhygienic place. No water. No toilets. No sewers. No electrical connections.

Eventually, though, one resident would have seen the potential and opened a bar by the beach, selling beer out of buckets of chopped ice. Another enterprising squatter would have started a restaurant—perhaps a pizza joint. Various small-scale entrepreneurs would have fashioned home-made pushcarts and plied the nearby boardwalk, selling *churrascos* or *nyama choma* or *bhel puri* or *kofte*. A few years on, one canny fellow would realize that he could rent apartments at a nice markup (but still far less than in the surrounding legal neighborhoods) if he built with a degree of quality and style. So he would gather his neighbors, and they would rip down and build again, but this time with higher standards and nicer finishes. And then the neighborhood—self-built and self-governed but owned by no one—would have tenants, too.

Of course, we outsiders would find ways to discredit this free soil republic. We would call it a slum. We would warn our children: these are criminals, dirty people, thieves, muggers, prostitutes, gang leaders, disreputables, abusers. We would ignore the hard work it takes to build a community and argue instead that these are people trying to get something for nothing, sponging off the system, ripping us off because they don't pay taxes. We would decry the density, the lack of adequate sanitation, the cacophony of construction styles, the sad-sack structural engineering. Politicians and real estate investors would call for inspections. Wealthy neighbors would clamor for police action. Together, we would make Sprayview Avenue a world apart. And ultimately, we would wipe it out.

Why do we have this animus against squatters? Why do we insist that there is something deeply wrong with their communities?

Favela, kijiji, johpadpatti, gecekondu: Brazil, Kenya, India, and Turkey have specific, descriptive, evocative terms for their squatter communities—in their own languages. It's the same around the world. From the *aashiwa'i* areas of Cairo to the *barriadas* of Lima, the *kampungs* of Kuala Lumpur, the *mudukku* of Colombo, and the *penghu*, or straw huts, of Shanghai in the 1930s, most languages have specific and even poetic names for their squatter communities. But in English, there's come to be one dominant term: slum.

Why slum? By the dictionary, a slum is simply an overcrowded city neighborhood with lousy housing. But the term is laden with emotional values: decay, dirt, and disease. Danger, despair, and degradation. Criminality, horror, abuse, and fear.

Slum is a loaded term, and its horizon of emotion and judgment comes from outside. To call a neighborhood a slum immediately creates distance. A slum is the apotheosis of everything that people who do not live in a slum fear. To call a neighborhood a slum establishes a set of values—a morality that people outside the slum share—and implies that inside those areas, people don't share the same principles.

Slum says nothing while saying everything. It blurs all distinctions. It is a totalizing word—and the whole, in this case, is the false. So, though it is the generally accepted term for squatter communities in both Kenya and India, I will avoid the word as much as I can.

I decided to do my part, to investigate the squatter communities of the world. At that point, each city made a case for itself.

Rio de Janeiro demanded that it be a focus because squatters there have a long and noble history. Their communities have existed for better than a century, and they have created permanent high-quality neighborhoods with high-rise buildings made from poured concrete and brick. Some of the city's squatter communities are so well-established that squatter houses command prices similar to those in legal neighborhoods of the city. Also, Rio's squatter areas have an impressive, dark subtext. For decades, national, state, and local governments steadfastly refused to provide services to these communities. And with that neglect came criminality. So most of Rio's favelas are now controlled by highly organized and extremely well-armed drug gangs. These gangs are both criminal and communitarian. They offer squatters a trade-off. In a city where assaults and violence of all sorts can be common, there is no crime in the squatter communities—as long as people look the other way when the dealers are doing their business. This, I thought, was an interesting story.

Nairobi claimed its place because two-thirds of its residents live in shantytowns, and, in the 40 years since Kenya won independence from Britain, the city's shantytown communities have remained unrelentingly primitive. What's more, Nairobi is the world headquarters of the UN's Habitat group, and I wondered why the agency had been unsuccessful in working to improve conditions for the

1.5 million people who live in the city's shantytowns—without water, electricity, sewers, or sanitation—just a few miles from its comfortable headquarters.

Mumbai insinuated itself because of its massive squatter presence. So many squatters live in the city that they have distinct class differences. Pavement dwellers—people who live in shacks built right on the sidewalks—are at the lowest end of the economic spectrum. People like Sartaj Jaipuri are at the higher end. Mumbai also boasts the largest squatter community in Asia, a neighborhood called Dharavi, which is now being eyed by developers because of its central location. In addition, Mumbai is where Jockin Arputham lives. A generation ago, Jockin founded a small community organization of squatters. Today, that group has become a multinational nonprofit organization active in a dozen countries. No story of squatters can be complete without spending some time with Jockin.

Finally, Istanbul leaped to mind. I knew the city had been the location of the United Nations meeting on housing in 1996. But, I would come to learn, Turkey has two notable laws that give squatters legal and political rights, and thus the chance to build permanent communities. If Turkey's legal system were in place in all the countries I visited, squatters would be in much better shape around the world.

They all laughed. Six men laughing because I didn't understand their concept of land ownership. We were in a teahouse in a dusty patch of Istanbul called Paşaköy, far out on the Asian side of the city. Here, the streets were dusty cuts hacked into the scrubby hills. Each home, too, was dusty, caked, it seemed, with red earth. Even the giant blue plastic water barrels that stood in front of each house were coated with dust.

The tea, the men joked, was exotic—it had come from far away. Sadik Çarkir, the teahouse owner, had hauled the water from a spring several kilometers away. As we spoke, several women strode down the street with five buckets in a wheelbarrow. They were making the run to the source.

"Tapu var?" I asked. "Do you have title deeds?"

They all laughed. Or, more accurately, some laughed, some muttered uncomfortably, and some made a typical Turkish gesture. They jerked their heads back in a sort of half-nod and clicked their tongues. It was the kind of noise someone might make while calling a cat or a bird, but at a slightly lower pitch. This indicates, "Are you kidding?" or "Now that's a stupid question," or, more devastatingly, "What planet are you from, bub?"

I blundered on.

"So who owns the land?"

More laughter. More clicking.

"We do," said Hasan Çelik, choking back tears.

"But you don't have title deeds?"

This time they roared. And somebody—I forget who—whispered something to my translator: "Why is this guy so obsessed with title deeds? Does he want to buy my house?"

You can't talk about squatters without talking about property. But talking about property involves different issues depending on where you are in the world.

In the developed world—particularly in the United States—many people still view property in the same absolutist terms that William Blackstone, the famed legal commentator, sketched out in the eighteenth century: Property, he wrote, is "that sole and despotic dominion which one man claims and exercises over the external things of the world, in total exclusion of the right of any other individual in the universe." What a revealing statement: property and despotism standing shoulder to shoulder. It's a distressing thought. Still, the United States maintains a hard-core devotion to property rights and free markets, which, many economists contend, are the roots of all our liberties.

Alexis de Tocqueville recognized this feeling during his mid-nineteenth century trip around the new nation in North America. "In no other country in the world is the love of property keener or more alert than in the United States," he wrote, "and nowhere else does the majority display less inclination towards doctrines that threaten the way property is owned."

Peruvian economist Hernando de Soto has adopted this hard-core attitude and advanced a hypercapitalist argument in favor of squatters. De Soto suggests that the countries of the developing world should legalize their squatters just as the United States legalized the settlers throughout the western states under the Preemption Act of 1841 and the Homestead Act of 1862. De Soto argues that giving squatters individual title deeds will liberate what he terms the "dead capital" inherent in their homes, and will automatically give them a place in the market economy.

It sounds so simple: send some law school-trained Johnny Appleseeds to trek through the cities of the developing world, handing out title deeds. Then step back and watch the communities blossom.

I wish it would work.

No doubt, some squatters would be able to access more money if they had title deeds. But the folks I met in Brazil, Kenya, India, and Turkey didn't go through the tremendous struggles of building and improving their homes to liberate their dead capital. They went through incredible privation and deprivation for one simple reason:

because they needed a secure, stable, decent, and inexpensive home —one they could possibly expand in the future as their families grow and their needs change. And title deeds—so natural to those of us who live in the developed world—can actually jeopardize this sense of security by bringing in speculators, planners, tax men, and lots of red tape and regulations.

This is in part why they laughed at me all over the world when I spoke of private property. They laughed in Brazil, when I asked who owned the land in Rocinha. They laughed in Kenya, when I asked who owned the land under the mud and steel huts of the sprawling shanty communities. And they laughed in India, too, when I asked who owned the marshland that today is Dharavi. They didn't laugh because they would turn down a title deed if it was offered. They laughed because private ownership is not their most crucial concern.

When squatters feel secure in their homes, they build, invest, and prosper—and they don't need a title deed to do so. Squatters in Brazil and Turkey have erected permanent buildings without title deeds. Squatters in India have created whole neighborhoods while knowing that the land is not theirs. They have accepted the unofficial lines that divide one person's home from another's. They buy and sell and rent their buildings. They negotiate with each other over their future plans for their homes.

The medieval Jewish sage Rashi proclaimed that being (or what it means to be a human being—to act, to live, to do things, even the most mundane things, in this world) is essentially having a standpoint, a position, a base of operations. A massive number of people around the world have been denied that right. So they have seized land and built for themselves. With makeshift materials, they are building a future in a society that has always viewed them as people without a future. In this very concrete way, they are asserting their own being.

We can learn from their example. The world's squatters offer a different way of looking at land. Rather than treating it as an economic value, squatters live according to a more ancient notion: the idea that every person has a natural right, simply by virtue of being born, to have a home, a place, a location in the world. Their way of dealing with land offers the possibility of a more equitable city and a more just world.

Time Present

CHAPTER 1

Rio de Janeiro
City without Titles

Everything in the world began with a yes. One molecule said yes to another molecule and life was born.

— Clarice Lispector

Maria das Graças Freitas de Sousa said yes to Rocinha and Rocinha said yes back.

Maria came to Rocinha in 1989, when she was 17. She traveled to the big city from her family's home in the Ceara, the far northeastern province of Brazil. She came for economic reasons. She had left school after first grade and her family didn't have any money. There were no jobs upcountry. So she came to the city.

Initially, Maria stayed with her brother, who had come to Rio a few years before and had established himself in Rocinha. The favela was still primitive then. The main road was only partly paved and remained, in much of the squatter area, a dirt and gravel track. Many of the houses were still made of wood. Few people had electricity, and water had to be carried up the hill in buckets and barrels. But she stuck it out and grew as Rocinha grew.

Rocinha has been the center of Maria's adult life. She married in Rocinha. She raised a daughter in Rocinha. She divorced in Rocinha. She met a new man in Rocinha. She had a second child in Rocinha. She works in Rocinha. She owns one home in Rocinha and rents out another. And her dream is to open her own business in Rocinha.

Maria's story is one of commerce, as are so many stories in Rocinha. She has held a job almost since the first day she arrived in Rio. First, she was a housekeeper, working for a variety of middle-class families. Then she became a waitress, working in middle- and upper-class communities. She remains a waitress to this day, but she now works inside Rocinha, in the neighborhood's oldest restaurant, Pizza Lit (a "t" at the end of a word is soft in the Carioca brand of Portuguese, so "lit" sounds like "leech").

Within a few years of landing in Rocinha, she bought herself a kitchenette: a one-room apartment. In 1994, when she was still together with her husband and was pregnant with her daughter, she realized the small apartment was not big enough for her family. So she sold it and used the profit to buy a larger one. In 2001, with her daughter almost a teenager and a second child on the way, she decided to make another small step up the social ladder. She turned herself into a landlord, renting out the apartment she owns. She charges R$180 a month, around $72. (At the time, the Brazilian real—pronounced, ray-ahl—was worth about 40¢.) And she has used that money, plus her wages, to lease a larger, more modern apartment for her family, paying R$300 (around $120). Her new home looks out on Rocinha's Praça do Skate, a small urban playground with a concrete half-pipe for skateboard enthusiasts.

At first, she was a reluctant witness. She thought I shouldn't be interviewing her. "Why do you want to speak with me," she protested. "I'm a nobody. I don't know anything important. I'm just a waitress." Instead, Maria said, I should be talking with successful people in Rocinha: business owners, political leaders, not her.

Maria was still on the clock, still responsible for waiting on tables during the slight lull between lunch and dinner. Every time a customer walked in, she jumped up to do her job. "I am a person for whom everything is difficult," she insisted.

As Maria moved between the customers and the kitchen, I recognized that she had a point: not about herself, but about Rocinha and, indeed, all of Rio's favelas. Nothing is as easy for squatters as it seems to be from outside. Today, Rocinha seems to be a finished product, permanent and immovable, a neighborhood as a force of nature. But it wasn't always like this. The squatters' struggle to have a place to call their own required a lot of hard work. Living for long periods of time without water and electricity is no easy feat.

"It's much better now—much," she said. "We live better and there are more stores and jobs. For me, this is a great place to live. It's wonderful. I would rather live here than in any other neighborhood. There's everything here. You don't need to leave."

She dreams of renting a small storefront just opposite the Praça where she lives and opening her own restaurant. To do so, she said, would take at least R$10,000 (about $4,000), money she fears she will never have. But just having that dream marks a big change. When she arrived in Rocinha, it was hard to dream. Now, despite her worries, her dream doesn't seem so far away.

Maria's story is Rocinha's story. And Rocinha's story is hers, repeated and magnified 150,000 times. It is a story of success against very great odds.

Zezinho said yes to Rocinha and Rocinha said yes back.

Jose Geraldo Moreira is his full name, but no one calls him that. He is simply Zezinho—little Joey—the fruit and vegetable man. He has been in Rocinha for more than 30 years. For the first decade, he manned a push cart, roving up and down the dirt and gravel pathways known as *becos*, selling his wares. After 10 years of itinerant sales, he made enough money to purchase a kiosk on Rocinha's main street.

Zezinho was a child when he came to Rio. His parents were divorced and his mother went to the big city for work, and then returned years later to get the kids. Since 1971 he has lived in a small wooden house on the Rocinha street known as *Rua Dois* (Second Street). His mother still lives there.

Of old Rocinha, he said, "In general, 30 years ago, life was slower. It was better before because businesses were not as big as they are now."

Modern Rocinha, he said, is a place to make money, a place to become a success. "I am not a materialist," Zezinho insisted. "This is what I believe: if you do good, you get good. If you do bad, you get bad. I care that you like me for what I am, not what I have."

Still, Rocinha has been good to Zezinho. He moved out from his mother's house and purchased a small *barraca* (a wooden shanty) in the Rocinha neighborhood called Cachopa. And then he made enough money to tear down the shack and build a three-story house. "I don't rent apartments out. It's all for my family:" his wife, Ana Paula, and their two sons. Now he makes enough money to send his children to two good schools outside of Rocinha: one in the ritzy Barra de Tijuca, a few kilometers to the south, the other in wealthy Gávea, just over the top of the hill.

"I could live in fancy neighborhoods, like Copacabana or Ipanema," Zezinho explained. "But I like it here. Here I can live with my philosophy of life."

A woman passed by and he handed her a bag of fruit, free. "The poor," he said brightly, "are the foundation of society."

Márcio Ferreira, too, said yes to Rocinha and Rocinha said yes back.

Márcio grew up in Rocinha. His family had little money, so he had to go to work when he was young. As he recalls it, his aunt was selling things at street fairs around town and he accompanied her on some of her jobs. She told him he had a talent for sales, and he pursued it.

At first, he worked the trains in Central Station downtown, selling ice cream to commuters. But that put him in the middle of a fight between rival gangs who wanted to control the business. So he quit the trains and started manning a pushcart, selling cheap biscuits and candies. That propelled him to working fairs in wealthy neighborhoods not far from Rocinha. There, making money required high-quality goods, so for a while he peddled silver bracelets and necklaces from his mobile kiosk. But, he says, the up front costs were too great, and the business was cyclical—and profits were sometimes meager.

So he returned to Rocinha, the neighborhood where he grew up.

Twice a day, Márcio roves the main streets and alleys of Rocinha, moving up and down the steep hill, selling snack pastries and *cafezinhos*, the small, sweet, milky coffee concoctions that are a beloved Brazilian specialty.

Márcio prides himself on the quality of his ingredients. He keeps the coffee and hot chocolate he sells in thermos jugs that he sterilizes every day by soaking them in boiling water (he insists that this also removes any residual bitterness.) He uses what he considers the best ingredients: the most expensive coffee and premium cocoa. He brags that the proprietors of some local coffee shops won't drink their own coffee but wait for him to arrive, because they prefer the beverage he lovingly prepares in his home.

With crooked teeth, a wily but endearing Alfred E. Newman smile, an earring in one ear, and a colorful bandanna that he wears when he is working, he looks more like an urban pirate than a squatter/street kid. He is a Rocinha original. The job he has made his own helps pay for a stylish kitchenette apartment on the Estrada da Gávea, which he shares with his girlfriend, Claudia, who works as a hairdresser in the wealthy beachfront neighborhood of Copacabana.

Rio is a big city, with around 5 million inhabitants. It is a cosmopolitan place, but a beach town at heart. From midmorning until after dusk, if you drop by any of the city's beaches you will find groups playing soccer on the sand or displaying amazingly acrobatic scissor kicks in the sport called *futvolei* (volleyball played only with the feet) or simply lolling on the soft hot sand. Everyone here goes to the beach, rich and poor alike.

But behind the sprawl of white sand and soft surf, behind the glamorous waterfront drives and the old-world elegance of some of the five-star hotels, Rio is a city of intense contrasts. The hills start just three blocks inland from the beaches, and they dominate much of the city's geography. Two of the hills are sites of tourist attractions: Corcovado, with the famous Christ figure that rises from the heights, its arms encompassing the whole expanse of the big beach town; and Pão de Asucar, the double-humped mountain that juts into the foaming sea and separates Botafogo from Leme and Copacabana.

But those are just two of hundreds of hills. For centuries these mountains were uninhabited, too steep and rocky and densely forested to be developed. Later, they came to be considered ecologically important, and building on them was prohibited. But despite all the difficulties, when the need became great enough, the hills were the place where squatters first congregated.

Initially they built shanties: isolated *barracas* that could remain hidden under the dense jungle canopy. Today they create full cities— self-built and proud of it—all without a single title deed. When I arrived in Rocinha, I still had the idea that squatter communities had to be primitive. But Rocinha was like nothing I had ever imagined.

I entered Rocinha from the Passarella, an arcade of kiosks that borders the main highway dividing Rocinha from the middle-class enclave of São Conrado. In the Passarella, the first experience of Rocinha is a crowd of *camelôs* (street vendors). Most of them are illegal, but they do business openly, even though there's a police kiosk strategically placed on the edge of the favela. Newly issued CDs of Caetano Veloso, MV Bill, pop, oldies, and current rock 'n' roll are sold here for a buck or two. They are all illegal, pirated, their jackets simply color copies of the originals. Here, you can also buy *prohibidão*: music banned because of its explicit lyrics about sex and violence. Next to the CDs are candy bars and soccer jerseys, bikinis and bibles, flip-flops and floppy disks. Anything and everything you could imagine.

Just across the highway, in São Conrado, the pace was serene and slow. Being there, particularly in the aptly named Fashion Mall, the local shopping center, was like stepping into a Stepford existence, where everyone moves at a leisurely clip and exhibits an identical lack of passion. But in the Passarella, and beyond it inside Rocinha, life was exactly the opposite. Hundreds of people moved in all directions. Cars, trucks, and buses massed at each curve. Dozens of *moto-taxistas* (guys with motorcycles who ferry people up and down the favela for a modest price) zipped through the small spaces between the other vehicles and the people, coming agonizingly close to smashing arms, legs, torsos.

This was the first revelation: the squatter community was busier than the legal community right next to it. It had more life.

A short distance up the hill, we stopped on the patio of Pizza Lit to grab some lunch. We were in what most outsiders call a slum or shantytown. But it didn't look like any shantytown I could imagine. The buildings were all made of poured concrete and brick. They had water. They had electricity. Pizza Lit even had a computerized cash register (although Maria and the other waiters always added the bill on their own, perhaps preferring to give the customer a calming personal touch).

Pizza Lit, I soon learned, was the right place to go on my first day in Rocinha. It is a favela institution. It was the first real restaurant in the squatter community and its owner, Sérgio, is as close to royalty as Rocinha gets. Sérgio started Pizza Lit as a takeout place, a hole in the wall pizza joint, and was both pizza-maker and motorcycle delivery boy. The restaurant originally had a different name—Pizza Hit—but the American chain Pizza Hut threatened to sue, arguing that the business was deliberately using a name that would cause confusion among the *favelados*. Sérgio changed the name rather than face a court fight, but he had the newspaper clippings about the dispute framed and keeps them on the wall just outside the bathroom. The irony is that Sérgio now runs a full-fledged restaurant while Pizza Hut had problems with its franchisee and still has no stores in Rio. Sérgio's business is thriving and it supports a fine lifestyle. He lives in a stylish new townhouse farther up the hill in Rocinha.

The food came—an ample supply of grilled chicken, rice and beans, and french fries—and we ate with gusto.

Dining out is hardly the measure of a community. But it broke a stereotype. I had been led to expect poverty and criminality. Instead, I had walked into a normal neighborhood.

Maria at the counter in Pizza Lit.

After lunch, we resumed our climb. We followed the Estrada da Gávea through a tight uphill S-curve, then left the crowded main drag to enter a *beco*. The *becos* originally were dirt pathways hacked by the residents through the dense hillside jungle. Today, although often scarcely wide enough for two people to pass, they are the streets of the favela. Most houses in Rocinha can only be reached on foot, via the *becos*. Once when I was trekking the heights of the community, I passed a man carrying a new couch-bed on his back, squeezing his purchase up the twisting *beco*, trying desperately not to rip the fabric on the jutting bricks of the buildings on either side of the path. At other times, I saw people hefting refrigerators, stoves, buildings materials, sacks of flour, and cases of beer onto their shoulders and then humping them up these mountain trails. Today, most of the well-trodden *becos* are paved with concrete, although the rough surface has been worn slick by thousands of footfalls, and the steeper portions are like concrete staircases. They still wind their way up the hill, detouring around rock outcroppings or taking a sharp curve because someone's home blocks the way. Hiking them is like climbing a canyon on concrete steps.

On the larger *becos*, a pack of 20 or 30 white plastic pipes may follow the route, sometimes submerged in concrete, other times snaking across the pavement and veering into, underneath, and around peoples' houses. These, I discovered later, are the water supply.

I was covered in sweat when we emerged on a quiet side-street paved with well-worn concrete. This was Rua da Raia, the quiet centerpiece of the neighborhood called Cachopa.

This was another lesson. Rocinha was large and diverse enough to have its own neighborhoods. They have picturesque names: Ropa Suja (Dirty Clothes), Valão (Sewer), Vila Verde (Green Villa), Rua Um (First Street), Rua Dois (Second Street), Trampolim (Trampoline,

Up and down the canyon on concrete steps.

which is an anomaly in Rocinha: an old hotel was on the site many years ago, so there is private property ownership here, but the city never approved the informal subdivision of the land after the hotel was sold; so the homes here are privately owned but still technically illegal), Noventa e Nove (Ninety-nine), Laboriaux (the name doesn't seem to have a meaning, but Laboriaux has an interesting history: it was a separate favela hanging above the heights of Gávea until the houses of Rocinha sprawled over the top of the Two Brothers Mountain and overran it, in the squatter version of municipal annexation), and Cachopa. Cachopa is an old word meaning "beautiful young girl," but old-timers in the neighborhood claimed to have no memory of the original *garota* who gave their community its name.

We clambered through a metal doorway and into a spacious courtyard, and then up an uneven flight of concrete steps to the dark hallway that led to my apartment.

This was the next revelation. The building was not much from the outside: a haphazard-looking concrete and brick structure, left rough-hewn and unfinished. I expected equally raw fixtures inside. But when we opened the door, I came face to face with an airy three-room flat with tile floors, a full bathroom, a decent-sized kitchen, four electrical outlets in every room, and a balcony with a view of the ocean.

Standing there, I viewed the impressive panorama of a neighborhood of row houses piled on top of each other. Their form was dynamic: bricks jutting out at odd angles, partial floors framed in concrete, walls that rise only to end abruptly in the soft blue of the sky. Houses seemed to twist towards the sun, crowding each other for light and air. From a distance there seemed to be no roads, no yards, no restful space of any kind. Just a beehive of human habitations. I took it all in, wowed by the community's presence and permanence.

I would later discover that not all of the community shared that modern look. My landlord, Seu Antonio, had recently added on to his building and my apartment was almost new. But downstairs, my neighbors lived in units that were more like concrete prison cells. And the higher you got on the hill (and the further from the main drag), in the far reaches of Rua Um and Noventa e Nove, the smaller and more primitive the homes became and the more desperate

The view from my balcony in Rocinha.

people seemed. Some were so small that a single bed and a small table completely covered the floor space. At these frayed edges, the sleek stores of nouveau Rocinha disappeared, replaced by sparsely stocked groceries that looked like outposts in a rural backwater. Chickens strutted around (and sometimes in) the primitive homesteads. The older people seemed frailer and less vital. The young folk simply seemed out of it: drug users, perhaps, or simply much less hopeful than the people further down the hill.

The decline in construction quality resulted in part because the more far-flung areas of Rocinha require more hiking to get to each home, and thus are less valuable. They're where Rocinha's poorest people live. Also, they may be underdeveloped because of the difficulty in getting construction materials through the community. In Rocinha, everything needs to be hauled in by hand, and it's not easy to heft packs of steel reinforcing bars, dozens of bags of cement, and scores of wheelbarrows full of sand a kilometer uphill on pathways that sometimes don't have enough room for two people.

At the end of my first full day in Rocinha, Paul Sneed, who brought me into the community and lived in the flat next door to mine, took me down the hill to the *baile funk*: an all-night dance party. Many favelas have them, usually on the weekends. Rocinha's *baile* took place every Friday night in the Valão. We took a series of *becos* that brought us to the bottom of the hill in what seemed to me to be record time. The *becos* were quite active and several bars—little more than counters set into the ground floor of buildings, with stools set up on the lip of the pathway—were hopping.

In the Valão, a disc jockey had set up a wall of 50 speaker boxes alongside the 10-foot-wide channel of open sewage that ran down the neighborhood's main drag and that gave the area its name. He was spinning aggressive, assault-your-ears rap and hip hop. Although it was past midnight, it was still early for the *baile*. Hundreds of people were milling about. Three girls who must have been about 13 or 14 were doing synchronized dance steps at one end of the line of speakers. They had synchronized their outfits, too: white hotpants and glittery, gold strapless tube tops. Some younger boys had perched inside the speaker boxes and were simply sitting there, banging to the beat, and, no doubt, damaging their eardrums. Most of the stores were open. And why not: it was too loud to sleep and the party would continue till dawn. Far better to get some money out of the deal.

Competing with the free *baile* was a nightclub, Emoçoes (Emotions), located in a spartan cement structure along the Estrada da Gávea that seemed like it might have been built as a parking garage. There, the loud rap sounds echoed off the concrete. Entry was by paid admission—R$5 (about $2)—and, although women were let in with no trouble, any man entering was frisked by the sturdy bouncers. The frisk finished with a quick squeeze of the testicles, to ensure that no one had a concealed weapon.

It was crowded and humid inside. People pressed forward to dance or hung at the back, where there was a makeshift bar. Here, *caipirinhas* sold for less than a buck, and there seemed to be no check at all on underage drinking.

Rocinha had lots of these kinds of parties, and they were magnets for the thousands of teenagers who live in the community. Twice a month, Beer Pizza sponsored a massive free dance party called *Cien Porciento Bagunça* (One Hundred Percent Chaos), usually held on the dance grounds of the local samba school. Again, the music was hard-edged rap and hip hop, and the teenyboppers reveled in showing off their synchronized dance movements.

All across the favelas, few people listened to the music that outsiders think of as Brazilian. Everyone knows the samba, bossa nova, and Musica Popular Brasileira (MPB) hits. They're the soundtrack of the *telenovelas*—TV soap operas—and the ever-present background of everyday life. But the mass of favela dwellers have embraced hard core rap and funk (what Brazilians call funk is akin to what Americans know as hip hop) as their emblematic sound. This music can be raunchier than the West Coast variety that carries parental advisory labels in the United States, and is often blasting from various places in the favela at incredibly high volume.

Like all of the 600 favelas in Rio, Rocinha is an illegal community. It was created over decades through successive land invasions. The name is a friendly diminutive—*roça* means farm and *rocinha* is little farm—and this indicates what Rocinha was like when it was first settled. Indeed, just two decades ago, Rocinha was still like a small farm: a tiny outpost of *barracas* on an obscure hill south of the fancy tourist areas. Rocinha's early residents followed an unwritten rule (although Apolonio, who owned a two-story garage-like structure across the street from where I lived, took it seriously enough to call it a law): build nothing permanent. The early settlers assumed that building a stone or brick home would be so brazen that it might encourage the government to come out and demolish the homes, while making do with rickety mud and wood houses would not seem threatening to the government. In this manner, Rocinha could grew under the eyes of the bureaucrats and developers without really being seen. But, of course, it also meant that the first invaders survived with no water, no electricity, no gas, no toilets, nothing.

These original residents formed *mutiroes*—mutual construction societies—and helped each other build. Often, a *mutirão* would be made up of the members of one extended family or a few people who had migrated to the city from the same region. By now, though, the bonds of ethnicity, homeland, and language have started to break down. The era of the *mutirão* is largely over. Most current construction in Rocinha is done by wage laborers who congregate at various locations on the hill, looking to be hired by professional contractors. And, to address community-wide issues, each favela has a residents' association, with an elected leadership. Large favelas may have several residents' associations. Today, Rocinha has three residents' associations, which sometimes compete with each other but usually nervously coexist.

The issues the residents' associations face are not all that different from those any block or community association would take on in an American town or city. Amendoim (no one ever calls him anything but this—Peanut—although he's neither outrageously small nor reminiscent of a peanut), who is President of the *Associação de Moradores e Amigos de Bairro Barcellos*, the residents' association of the lower portion of Rocinha, has found that one of his major jobs is to organize a recreation program—swimming, volleyball, basketball, and more—for kids at a spa/health club just outside the favela in Gávea. Even with the beach just a few minutes away, Amendoim said, kids need structured recreation or they might get into trouble.

As the community developed, the residents were emboldened by their numbers. They seized services the same way they seized land. *Gatos*—which literally means cats but is Brazilian argot for people who pirate public services—ran wires to tap into the electric grid. For years, Rocinha was festooned with curving strands of lamp wire bringing feeble current to each house. Today, the power company has recognized that Rocinha is not 150,000 thieves but 150,000 potential customers, and has spun off a nonprofit to embark on a $R10 million ($4 million) plan to provide legal electricity in the favela, provided residents agree to install a meter. The company expects 25,000 households in Rocinha to sign up as legal account holders as the upgrade in service is completed. Over the first three years of the program, officials of the utility report that the firm has saved 210 gigawatts: enough to power 100,000 houses for a year. Today, there's only one throwback to the days of the *gatos*: almost every streetlight or electric pole in Rocinha still has illegal wires tapping into it. Some look like postmodern wire sculptures, with hundreds of cables branching out in all directions.

Once the electricity came, water was not far behind. A different crew of *gatos* tapped into the water mains that fed São Conrado and Gávea, and ran long lines of cheap plastic tubing to each squatter home. All a homeowner needed to take advantage of the new system was an inexpensive electric pump and a water tank (*caixa*) on the roof. In Rio, when you walk into a community and see blue plastic water tanks on each roof, you can be pretty sure that you're in a favela.

Part of Rocinha was a real estate development gone bust: the investors carved streets out of the jungle at the top of the mountain, intending to capitalize on the view and carpet the hill with private mansions. But costs mushroomed, the money ran out, and the developer abandoned the project. Little by little, squatters moved in, capitalizing on the rough roads that had been cut into the hillside and that made moving in relatively easy.

Today, those old roads are paved, and their existence makes Rocinha unique among Rio's favelas. It is the only squatter community with a municipal road within its boundaries. All other favelas, even large ones like Jacarezinho and Rio das Pedras, which rival Rocinha in size, are self-contained. The nearest public roads are just outside the favela. Rocinha's road has been a major engine of its success: it not only has car and truck access but two municipal bus lines also run straight through the favela.

Still, with the exception of the area called Trampolim, no one in Rocinha owns the property on which they have built. And, as squatters built bigger, more sophisticated buildings, the social relations of possession became complicated. Some buildings, like the one where Maria owns her kitchenette, have been sold as unofficial condominiums. Others include a combination of apartments that people have purchased and apartments that are rented out. And still others developed in a more organic way. A family would take land and build a two-story dwelling. Because they needed money to pay off the investment, the family would sell the *laje*, or roof rights, to a friend or acquaintance, who would build an additional two stories. And that person, in turn, might sell his or her roof rights too.

Today, most of those original land invaders are either elderly or have sold their self-built homes to newcomers. Indeed, Rocinha has a thriving housing market and the most common signs you see around the neighborhood are *aluga-se* and *venda-se*: for rent and for sale. There are even local real estate agents who operate in the community.

Rocinha has been such a commercial success that residents have coined a new word to describe the process they see unfolding in their neighborhood: *asfaltização* (asphaltization) It is the squatter city version of gentrification. It refers to businesses from outside the favela —from the asphalt city, the legal city—invading illegal turf.

Dante Quinterno's family was perhaps the pioneer of asfaltização. He runs a business located just outside Rocinha but nevertheless all over the favela: cable television. Quinterno's family is based in Argentina but they make investments in both countries. Quinterno's effort to wire Rocinha started in 1994, when his father came to Rio on a business trip and stayed in the Intercontinental Hotel, within shouting distance of Rocinha in quiet São Conrado. He looked out from the hotel's windows and saw something few others had ever believed existed in the favela: customers. For a while, the family toyed with the idea of doing an expensive installation for Internet, cable television and telephone service. Eventually, they chose to do a more modest $4 million installation, and the service debuted in 1997. Today, his firm, TV Roc, has 30,000 customers in Rocinha. The firm employs 32 technicians, half of whom live in Rocinha. The basic cable package costs R$20 a month (about $8). If a family wants premium movie channels, they have to pay R$32 (almost $13).

Business was slow at first. But it boomed when a state-run bank, the Caixa Economica, made a special offer to Rocinha's squatters. The bank opened an office in the favela and invited residents to get credit cards. The initial credit limit was only R$200 (about $80), but the cards were a big success. Having a cable account helped people establish an address and credit-worthiness, and thousands of people signed up.

"The first year we started here, nobody had a credit card or a bank account or even an address," Quinterno said. "But now there are more than 6,500 accounts totaling more than 2.5 million reais."

As for profits, Quinterno said they will come more slowly. "In the short term it is not a very good business," he conceded. "But as a long term thing, it's very good. We make money. The profit margin is not 45 percent or 20 percent. But 8 percent is pretty good."

Quinterno would like to expand to other favelas. But he knows he will face competition. His research shows that two-thirds of Rio's favelas have some form of pirated cable service, most frequently an unregistered firm that receives satellite TV transmissions and has built a small, illegal distribution network for the favela. Two such *pirata* channels exist in Rocinha.

Deplá, the largest film developing company in Brazil (with 160 franchises, larger even than Kodak), was the first major retail business from the asphalt world to open stores in the favelas. In 1996 Daniel Pla, who heads the firm that was founded by his parents half a century ago, had the same insight as Dante Quinterno's father. "There is a lot of prejudice about the favela population," Pla said. "They have income, despite what other people believe. They all have video players, they all have TVs—indeed they have more TVs than refrigerators. They don't pay taxes, so sometimes they have more disposable income than people in other neighborhoods. They have lots of children and they love to take photographs of those children. They see the Deplá brand as something sophisticated. We charge more than other places, and they prefer to pay a little more to get Deplá photo finishing."

Like any good entrepreneur, Pla understood that one of the keys to doing business in Rocinha was to tap into the pride residents feel about their communities. "When we opened the store, we gave candy to children," he recalled. "Also, we were the first store in Rocinha to have air conditioning." This, he said, gave the residents a feeling of accomplishment. What's more, his stores offered credit, which showed residents that despite their being squatters, he trusted them to pay their bills. And his faith was rewarded. "Everybody pays," Pla said. "They honor their debts. Credit is very important for the favela population."

Pla opened his first store in a small favela called Pavão–Pavãozinho (the name means Turkey–Little Turkey, from a combination of the two favelas that originally split the hillside) that occupies the steep slope that separates Copacabana and Ipanema. Now Pla has added two stores in Rocinha. He declares that there's so much business in the favelas that he'd like to open a third store in Rocinha, and hopes also to grab locations in both Jacarezinho and Rio das Pedras.

McDonald's followed Deplá into Rocinha. So far, the golden arches franchisee simply operates a kiosk. No burgers here, just water and soft ice cream. But statistics show that it's a tremendously successful operation despite its limited size.

The early years of the new millennium brought an explosion in asfaltização. Suddenly, businesses from all over discovered Rocinha.

In 2001, Mega Mate opened in the Passarella. A small chain of franchised outlets that sell mate, guarana, and specialized tropical fruit and protein blender drinks, this store is doing well in part because it's adjacent to the bus stops on the main route between Rocinha and the center of town.

In 2002, Bob's and Brasimac opened fancy stores in the heart of Rocinha, halfway up the hill on the Estrada da Gávea. Bob's is Brazil's homegrown answer to McDonalds: a burger, fries, and milkshakes joint (the firm's most popular meal, its answer to the Big Mac, is Bob's Big Boy.) Bob's wasn't content with a kiosk. It opened a full-fledged restaurant with all the accoutrements of its locations in the legal city. Next door to Bob's is Brasimac, the squatter outpost of a 150-store retail appliance and furniture chain based in São Paulo. Here, Brasimac offers an array of fancy appliances and cheap furniture in a spacious two-story air-conditioned store.

For the honor of being in Rocinha, Brasimac pays R$6,000 a month in rent (about $2,400). "Bom cara," branch manager Rizete Matuszo admitted, when I whistled at the price. "Pretty steep." But, she added, Rocinha is not a cheap neighborhood. Many Rocinha residents came into Brasimac the first week it opened simply to admire its style. With its clean plate glass windows and bright modern interior, the Brasimac store looked like it belonged in one of the city's fancy malls.

"The firm did a lot of research to check out Rocinha," she said. "Here you had a captive population that had to go to the center of the city or to Barra [the wealthy Barra de Tijuca neighborhood, a 20-minute bus ride to the south] to get appliances. Rocinha is not a poor community. I think there will be more such big stores. It has great potential." Like Deplá, Brasimac is looking to locate in other large favelas.

In a sense, asfaltização is nothing new. What's new is simply the scale. On a basic level, asfaltização has been around for quite a while. For more than a decade, Jofre Guerra, who runs Shook Video, a video rental store in Rocinha, has been a reverse commuter to the favela. He works in Rocinha but lives in the ritzy area called Copacabana.

When Jofre started in the video business, he located his store in the fancy area called Gávea. There, he faced a plethora of other *locaduras*: video rental competitors. One of his employees, who lived in Rocinha, suggested that he relocate to a community where his store would have a likely monopoly.

"It was a good business decision," Jofre said. "At one time, I rented out 300 or 400 tapes a day."

Shook is hardly Blockbuster. It's a small neighborhood video store, open from 10 A.M. to 10 P.M., 363 days a year (Jofre closes on Christmas day and Easter Sunday), with a limited and well-used stock of videos. Shook survived competition from other rental stores. But TV Roc and the two pirate satellite stations do cut into the business.

"They show all the new films," Jofre said. "Today I only rent out 90 to 100 tapes a day and I can only survive with a certain dignity." He shrugged, then added, "But in this country, survival is a big thing."

Some favela residents have fears about asfaltização. They believe the continuing invasion of *asfalto* businesses into the favela is killing the self-reliant spirit of the community. More asfaltização, they claim, less *mutirão*: the larger and more urbanized a favela gets, the more the businesses from outside come in, and the more power those businesses grab, at the expense of long-term residents and the community networks they have created.

But the process is moving too rapidly to stop. When I arrived in Rocinha in November 2001, a dozen small pharmacies owned by squatters were spread throughout the community. By the time I left, in February 2002, only three months later, two major asfalto chains had purchased buildings in the lower part of Rocinha and, after major renovations, opened large, modern 24-hour drug stores. One small drug store near my house closed the same night the big stores opened. Other druggists were worried that they would be driven out of business. "Go talk to the residents' association," one nervous storeowner commanded. "Ask Amendoim how he can protect me."

But Amendoim had no sympathy. Although a member of Brazil's Communist Party, Amendoim spoke the words of a hardened capitalist when I asked him about the plaintive druggist. "Let me tell you a story," Amendoim said. A few years back, he said, several dozen Chinese immigrants arrived in Rocinha. No one knows why they came to Brazil or why they arrived in the favela (and the Chinese themselves declined to answer when I asked them). "For years," Amendoim continued, "we ate *salgados* [greasy snack pastries reminiscent of ham and cheese croissants] and *caldo de cana* [sugar cane juice]. We always paid R$1 for one pie and 50 cents for the cane juice. Then the Chinese came and opened three big snack counters in Rocinha. They offered a special: one pie and one cane juice, both for R$1. Now, that's what everyone charges. When McDonald's came here, the number one *lancheonette* [snack bar] in the community had to get better."

Then he came to his message for Rocinha's small drug stores. "You know what those guys have to do?" Amendoim bellowed. "It's simple! Lower the price!" He sounded more like a Wal-Mart executive discussing the pressure his chain puts on Main Street America than a community leader discussing the fate of the businesses in his community. "Time passes and it's necessary to develop," he continued. "You know why these businesses come here? They come because they see several hundred thousand people. They see profits. Big profits."

Amendoim is in his 40s now. He has lived in Rocinha since he was 3 months old, and he sees these big consumer chains as a possibility, a way forward for Rocinha. But that journey may soon offer some increasingly dangerous trade-offs for the squatters.

I witnessed one of them. For most of my stay, there were only three foreigners living in Rocinha. Paul Sneed was an American anthropologist studying rap and funk music and working to create a community-based educational foundation. Corrine Davis, a University of Texas sociologist, was studying community development and dispute resolution within the favela and had married a wonderful fellow named Rogerio, who lived in the Valão. And there was me.

Then I ran into Mick. It was hard to miss him: a seriously sunburned fellow wearing Teva sandals, ill-fitting shorts, and a stained T-shirt walking down the Caminho dos Boiadeiros, in the lower portion of Rocinha. He stopped for a protein drink at Mega Mate in the Passarella and I had a chance to ask him some questions. He had come to Rio from Great Britain to spend a month studying parasailing. He had intended to live in a hotel in Copacabana, but had been mugged twice during his first week in town. He mentioned this to one of his instructors and the man offered an immediate solution: come to Rocinha. He was clear about the trade-off: You'll be living in an illegal community and you'll have to put up with the fact that there's no garbage pickup and no real sewers. But you'll never be the victim of a crime. Mick quickly agreed and a few days later moved into a kitchenette apartment in the Trampolim neighborhood. The owner charged him R$500 for the remaining 21 days he would stay. While this was clearly a rip-off (I was paying R$300 a month for my three-room flat, and I had been told the going rent for single rooms ran from R$150 to a little more than R$200) it was quite a bit cheaper than he would have paid for his hotel in Copacabana.

This was unprecedented: a tourist coming to live in the squatter community. I asked my friends what they thought of it. For the most part, people were positive. As one long-term resident told me, "If he lives here without being assaulted and pays too much in rent, that's good for him and good for the landlord. And his money and the landlord's money will be spent in Rocinha."

But Zezinho, as usual, saw the issue in more complicated terms. When he gets wound up in complex discourse, Zezinho likes to illustrate his points with his produce. He'll slide a mango forward, then a banana, and, when things get really crazy, he'll augment the argument with an avocado or even a cucumber.

With a carrot for the British fellow and a beet for the landlord, Zezinho let me understand that the relationship was beneficial for both of them. That much was clear. But then he brought out the bigger guns. "Let's say that you call me up and say, 'Zezinho, I have two friends who want to come down here for the carnival. Can you put them up?' [He introduced a small bunch of red-skinned bananas for me and an onion and a squash for my hypothetical friends.] And maybe I have some extra space. If they stayed in a hotel they might spend R$20,000 for four days, for room and breakfast and everything. Here, they can have the same thing for R$5,000. They save R$15,000. And how long would it take me, at R$300 a month to make R$5,000?"

It's easy math: the money he could draw in four days during Carnival from this new form of asfaltização would take more than a year to make at the normal rent.

For Zezinho, this was no abstract possibility. He was already dealing with the issue. A friend was losing his home elsewhere in Rocinha and was looking to move. Zezinho had contacted a neighbor who had a vacant flat, but the man refused to rent it because he thought he could make more by holding it vacant and leasing it to an outsider during Carnival.

Back where I came from, this was a familiar issue. Landlords in gentrifying neighborhoods in New York routinely hold apartments vacant in expectation of a future windfall. In those neighborhoods, the more vacant apartments in a building, the higher the price it can command if it's put up for sale. But in the illegal city, such speculation is the real estate equivalent of the new world order.

Zezinho put the fruit back on the appropriate piles. "As more Rocinha people have friends in the asfalto world or from abroad, the pressure will become greater to do more of these deals," he said. "As to whether it's good or bad, we'll just have to see."

Whenever I spoke with people like Zezinho, who had lived through the *barraca* and *gato* days, I asked whether asfaltização had improved Rocinha. The answer, resoundingly, was no. They all agreed that Rocinha today is better for making money. But, despite water and electricity and easily available consumer goods, they felt it had become a much worse place to live. Life, they said, was less enjoyable. Younger people, by contrast, who didn't know the neighborhood before asfaltização, answered differently. They couldn't imagine living in Rocinha without water and electricity and MTV.

But no matter what old-timers feel, if they reject asfaltização, others will accept it. A few days after I spoke with Zezinho, I visited Rumba Gabriel, the charismatic president of the residents' association in Jacarezinho. Jacarezinho is huge (about 100,000 people) but because it's in a tougher turf—a working class zone far from the beach—it has received much less investment than Rocinha. Asfaltização has hardly dented Jacarezinho. There's no cable TV station, and only one pirate network selling satellite downloads. There are no outside chain stores yet. And the Chinese immigrants have just arrived. Rumba was immediately intoxicated with the idea that Deplá was interested in a store in his community. He demanded that I give him Pla's email address and telephone number. He was ready to make a deal.

There's another, homegrown, aspect to asfaltização. In response to the interest from outside firms, local entrepreneurs have begun to try to preempt the arrival of asfalto businesses by copying some of the popular enterprises that exist on the outside and opening them in the favela. When I was in Rocinha, for instance, there were at least three health clubs. They all boasted the latest machinery for toning, exercising, and sculpting the muscles. They all offered classes in aerobics and weight training. They all gave discounted monthly memberships. And they all had the mirrored walls and booming disco music that seem to be the norm for fitness training. In a beach/body culture like Rio de Janeiro, there was no shortage of members. And there was also no need for a gym from the asfalto world to attempt to invade Rocinha.

A few other notable business efforts in Rocinha mirror the asfalto world. One is the favela version of the post office. Brazil's post office will deliver mail along the Estrada da Gávea, which is a legal city street. But the bulk of Rocinha's residents, who live along the *becos*, don't qualify for mail delivery. For a little more than a dollar a month, Correios Zig-Zag and Correios Amigos, rival private postal services, will accept your mail from the post office and deliver it directly to your door. They will also receive appliances and other deliveries and arrange to have the goods carted to your home. Another quasi-asfalto business is the Estação Futuro: the Station of the Future. This modern enterprise on the Caminho dos Boiadeiros, near the bottom of Rocinha, offers high-speed Internet browsing and computer training courses. It's not exactly an entrepreneurial effort in that it's funded by Viva Rio, a giant nonprofit formed to aid downtrodden communities. But Viva Rio believes that wiring the favela—connecting it not only with the asfalto parts of Rio but the international asfalto—will encourage commerce and entrepreneurship. Of course, many of the young boys who regularly occupied the terminals were interested in another portion of the wired world: hard core pornography.

Another example of local entrepreneurs responding to local demand are the *mototaxistas*. As Rocinha developed, more young people had disposable income. On most evenings there was steady traffic moving up and down the hill. People moved around Rocinha going to parties, clubs, and restaurants. People who did their shopping at the bottom of the hill needed to haul their groceries to the top. Some alert entrepreneurial residents organized taxi stands, where you will be guaranteed to find a guy with a motorcycle. For either 50 cents or R$1 (20 or 40 cents) you can get anywhere in Rocinha that a bike can go. The drivers own their own bikes. But they chip in monthly to the stand operator for the right to park and be part of the queue.

I was taking a shower in the nice tile bathroom in my flat when the water suddenly sputtered and then was gone. I wiped the soap from my eyes, toweled down, pulled on some clothes, and sought out my landlord, Seu Antonio.

Seu Antonio thought deeply. We went upstairs to look at the *caixa* on the unfinished third floor. It was perhaps two thirds full. We went back downstairs to all the other homes. Seu Antonio had water. Paul had water. The people on the ground floor had water.

Then we went back into my flat. Seu Antonio turned on all the faucets. Nothing happened.

He spoke slowly. "This is a very grave problem," Seu Antonio said. Seu Antonio plugged in his electric pump and filled the *caixa*. Still no water. He inspected all the pipe joints. He banged and tugged on the pipes. Still no flow.

He thought long and hard. After about 20 minutes, he came up with an answer. He shut off the water in the bathroom and went to the spigot in the kitchen. He leaned down and put his lips around the faucet and sucked. At first nothing happened. Then there was a gurgle, a few whooshes of air, and then there was water.

I was happy. But Seu Antonio was not.

He considered this all deeply and a few hours later pulled me aside. My apartment was the newest in the building. I was the first tenant to occupy it, and Seu Antonio told me he had misjudged the extra demand one more flat would create. The solution, he added, was to install larger water pipes, and to move the *caixa* up one more floor to the roof.

He would do this, he told me, when he had a bit more money. For now, he said, any time the water died, just plug in the pump to refill the *caixa* and then suck.

There were a few other design flaws in my flat. There was no window in the bathroom, only a vent panel into the apartment. So in humid weather my towels didn't dry and the tiles grew mildew. The kitchen had an odd shape, and there really wasn't enough room for a stove. And there was no drain on the balcony in case it rained.

But think about it: I was living in a three-room apartment with tile floors, running water, a full toilet and shower, and a balcony with a view of the ocean.

From the outside the building looked like nothing—like every other building in the squatter area—with bad-looking brickwork and rusting rebar sprouting from its roof, and a staircase so uneven that I kept tripping and bumping my head when I used it after dark.

But despite how things looked, Seu Antonio had built well. First, because he lived there. He wanted his home to be nice—as nice as anyone else's. And he could find all the materials he needed—the tiles, the windows, the plaster, the concrete—all within the favela at a price he could afford. And mostly he built this way because he knew he was secure.

This is how a squatter community develops. This is how a city develops: organically.

So I say: Thank God for mass production. Praise be to plastic pipe. All honor the prefab window. Bow down to sheets of old plywood, stock-model sinks, mass-produced tile. Three cheers for cement and cinderblock. Exalt the lowly rebar. Let's hear it for quick-drying concrete. Hooray for easy plastic wiring, easy plug outlets, and modular telephone service.

With these products, a mud or cardboard hut gives way to wood, and wood gives way to brick, and brick to reinforced concrete. Suddenly a community goes from small huts and barracks to stylish apartment blocks but without developers or builders. All built by the squatters themselves.

Of course, sometimes, they will make mistakes, and until they fix them, they will occasionally have to put their lips around the water pipes and suck.

With money from the Inter-American Development Bank, the city of Rio has been slowly investing in the favelas. A program called *Favela/Bairro* (favela/neighborhood) is designed to provide a certain amount of amenities in the illegal city. Through the program, the city has built soccer fields and child care stations, has paved roads and installed drainage ditches, and has brought the city government inside the illegal communities. *Favela/Bairro* has put money into hundreds of favelas—but not into Rocinha.

A parallel program, called *cellula urbana* (urban cell) is bringing the Bauhaus (the German architectural school that traces its lineage to the utilitarian/futurist movement of the 1930s) to Rio to create a plan to rebuild an overcrowded and unhealthy section of Jacarezinho, where some people live in rooms with no windows.

These are notable achievements but they remain top-down affairs, indeed city bureaucrats confessed to me that Jacarezinho residents didn't invite in Bauhaus, but had the plan sprung upon them with little notice. Other cities, notably Recife, Belo Horizonte, and Porto Allegre, have attempted more participatory programs. These involve having squatters vote on how the city's community development budget would be spent, and defining favelas into the local zoning code so that the city and residents can exert some control over development. Some Rio favelas have imposed their own restrictions on new construction and height limitations on new buildings, so as not to create overcrowding and infrastructure problems.

Rocinha, although it was not part of *Favela/Bairro*, does have some governmental involvement. Indeed, Rocinha has grown so large that, though it is an illegal neighborhood, it is a legal district of the city. The city maintains an office there, staffed by a regional administrator and many assistants. Rocinha has a city health clinic and several schools. The city has worked with the residents' associations to prevent the community from sprawling further across the hillside. But, although the city has brought in professional planners to work with residents, it still has not negated the old-fashioned system of planning in the illegal community. Rocinha homeowners still negotiate with their neighbors if they want to add onto their homes and, usually, will not go ahead with a plan if anyone objects.

With this level of exchange between government and the favelas, you might expect squatters to be deeply invested in city politics. But it's been slow going.

Only one person has made the jump from favela leader to political figure. Her name is Benedita da Silva.

Benedita's parents emigrated from the central state of Minas Gerais to Rio in the 1940s. They bought themselves a *barraca* in Praia do Pinto, a favela near the beach in the neighborhood now known as Leblon. They stayed there until the 1960s, when Praia do Pinto burned in a suspicious fire. They then moved to a small hillside favela above the beach at Leme (adjacent to the touristy neighborhood of Copacabana) called Chapéu Mangueira.

Benedita became a community leader in this small favela and then parlayed her activism into politics. She joined the left-leaning *Partido Trabalhadores* (the Worker's Party) and ultimately became a *vereador*, or member of the City Council. This, in itself, was an amazing achievement. Rio's City Council is elected on an at-large basis, which means Benedita could not simply depend on her home area for votes. She had to campaign across the whole city. Benedita's successful campaign for *vereador* showed the power that the people in the favelas can have if an outspoken and trusted leader emerges.

Later, Benedita became vice governor of the state of Rio de Janeiro. When the governor, Anthony Garotinho, ran for president of Brazil in 2001, he stepped down and Benedita briefly became acting governor. She ran for the office herself in 2002, but was soundly defeated by Garotinho's wife. (Garotinho himself, after losing his presidential bid, has returned to Rio as a minister in his wife's administration.) In 2003, Benedita went to Brasilia, to work under the country's progressive new president Luiz Ignacio Lula da Silva.

Her reputation, however, is diminishing. As Benedita broadened her appeal, her standing among favela dwellers dwindled. Many of my friends laughed openly at Benedita. They no longer considered her a *favelada*: a favela resident. To them, she had long since deserted her roots on the hills. And it is literally true. She no longer lives in the Chapéu Mangueira, but has moved down to her husband's house in the fancier Barra de Tijuca.

So far, no other favela leader seems prepared to follow in Benedita's footsteps. And until one does, one fifth of Rio's population will not have its interests fully represented in civic affairs.

The first favela was born of anger and betrayal. In the late 1890s, a group of slaves in Rio de Janeiro were freed and immediately drafted into the Brazilian army. They were sent to the north of the young country, to the spot where a charismatic preacher had challenged the power of the federal government by establishing a collectivist outpost on a farm called Canudos. The slaves-turned-soldiers massacred the revolutionaries, violently squashing all resistance. When they returned to the capital (Rio was Brazil's capital until the 1960s, when the government carved Brasilia out of the high jungle in the middle of the country), the former slaves expected to be treated like great conquerors and to be given quarters, as was the norm for victorious fighters. Instead, they were left to fend for them-selves. So a few of them built shanties out of mud and scrap wood on Morro da Providência, a hill within shouting distance of the army headquarters and not far from the city's center of mercantile wealth. They christened their hill *Morro da Favela*, in honor of a weed that thrived in the rough terrain near the rebel outpost they had overrun. The name also was a reference to a mountain that the Canudos rebels had used as a lookout point. In this way, the first squatters were letting the government know that it had a new rebel-lion on its hands.

Twenty years later, the early encampment had grown substan-tially. There were now 839 families on the hill. A decade later, the mountain stronghold boasted more than 1,500 homes. An American geographer who visited in 1930 was distressed by what he saw. "Here, almost within a stone's throw of the commercial core, clinging to the steep slopes is a community dwelling in the most prim-itive mud huts without light, water, or sewage, even without organ-ized streets—a squatter settlement without order or organization."

Morro da Providência may have appeared degraded to him. But it could not have seemed bad to the freed slaves and ill-fed farmers who journeyed to the big city to work in its factories. Anyone who arrived in Rio without a thick bankroll quickly found that an apart-ment—even in the most decayed and overcrowded *cortiço* (beehive: Brazilian slang for tenement buildings that often featured shared kitchens and bathrooms)—was far too expensive.

The staying power demonstrated by the residents of Morro da Providência drew new invaders who created new settlements. The hills made perfect hideouts for clandestine residents. Squatters quickly established colonies on other hills. And the name stuck: Wherever they located, the land invaders called their new outposts favelas.

The favelas were able to survive in part because of Brazil's murky position on property rights. Before European colonization, there was no consistent system of private property in the country. Then, when the Portuguese took over, all land was suddenly viewed as owned by the royal family, and private individuals could only own land if they received explicit grants from the king or queen. So there is not a long tradition of private ownership in the country, and almost no tradition of recorded title deeds. And in that vacuum, a home-grown industry has arisen: people who specialize in misleading or fabricated title deeds. They're called *grillos* (crickets) and they are to title deeds what the *gatos* are to pirated electrical power. For the right price, a *grillo* will find a way to get you a doctored title claim. Ownership of particular parcels is sometimes hotly contested by dozens of false or fraudulent claimants. In the midst of all this trickery, the squatters' claims—the modern equivalent of the ancient idea that actual possession is the preeminent right to be protected—seem reasonable.

In addition to the hillside hideouts, favelas sprang up where people found work. The larger favelas were in the city's industrial northern region (the *Zona Norte*), while the *Zona Sul* (home of Rio's famed beaches) had few squatter enclaves. By the 1940s, there were 36 principal favelas, but scores of other smaller self-built communities were shoehorned next to small factories all over the city.

A report from 1942, by Maria Horténsia do Nascimento e Silva, a city social worker, detailed two types of favelas: those on the mountain and those on flat ground. "Those of the hill are most numerous because they are less accessible and therefore cheaper," she wrote. The larger favelas on the hills of the *Zona Norte*—Morro do Salgueiro, Morro do Querozene, and Morro da Mangueira—had "already become part of the story of the city," she wrote, and even featured two and three story buildings. This level of development must have been the product of an extraordinary amount of hard work, but Maria Horténsia (Brazilians tend to use first names, even in formal contexts) couldn't resist stereotyping the residents anyway. "Life, for them, is organized as if the world below doesn't exist," she wrote. "Idleness is an esteemed profession and samba is a way of life."

But despite the few highly developed favelas, most remained quite crude. A city survey showed that three quarters of the houses in the city's favelas were made of wood or mud and fewer than 10 percent of all squatter families had direct access to water.

In the 1940s, Jacarezinho, a community set on a gently sloping plain near the Jacaré river, adjacent to a giant General Electric factory, was the city's biggest favela: 15,500 people strong. By contrast, Rocinha was a tiny settlement of fewer than 200 families hiding on the steep slopes of the densely forested Pedra Dois Irmaos.

The favelas grew quickly over the next few decades. In 1950 there were 105 favelas containing 44,000 houses. Ten years later the number of favelas had jumped 42 percent and there were now 147 separate squatter communities. The density had jumped even more dramatically—almost 300 percent—and there were 162,741 squatter houses. By 1970 there were 300 favelas with 185,000 houses.

Conditions improved as well. By the 1960s, half the squatter houses had three or more rooms, and almost three quarters had electric service (predominantly through the *gatos*). One in five even had indoor showers—although that doesn't necessarily mean that they had running water.

Despite the improvements, the favelas remained contentious areas. Rich people hated them, as did developers and people with property interests. And politicians worried that they were breeding grounds for radicalism. "The residents, certainly, are not militants, and few have a fixed ideology," a government survey of the "mental life of the *favelados* of the federal district" reported in 1958. "But treating them as a potential battle force, united by means of propaganda and myths that correspond to the misery of the *favelados* in contrast to the luxury of the city, they may favor communism." The writer excused the *favelados* for their wobbly political allegiances. "Their civilization only knows decadence," the report stated, "so it isn't their fault."

Jacarezinho, in particular, was a major target of the real estate industry. Nearby owners plotted to remove the squatters. The first wave of demolitions came in 1942, and the owners made repeated efforts to snuff out the favela over the following two decades. But the *favelados* fought back. In contrast to Maria Horténsia's description of indolence and lack of initiative, squatters almost always rebuilt their huts immediately after they were knocked down. And they played politics: trading votes for political power. It was a tough fight, but they were able to push successive governments at least to recognize their right to exist on their precarious invaded perch. By the 1960s, Jacarezinho was the first favela to reach an important watershed of respectability: more than 100,000 residents.

But Rio's economy soon began to change. Factories cut back, manufacturing slowly died off, and tourism grew to be the dominant industry. Today, the largest of the city's 600 favelas are in the *Zona Sul*: the tourist zone.

Back downtown, just behind Central Station, Rio's passenger rail depot, the first favela is still there, still atop the hill called Morro da Providência. Economic changes and real estate development have passed this favela by, although the *Favela/Bairro* program recently installed new concrete steps that lead to the barren rock outcropping at the top. Hiking this new staircase, you get the feeling you are on a mountain far from the city. Morro da Providência feels more like an impoverished country village than an inner city neighborhood. Two small chapels—built, most likely, when this was still an area to reckon with—are all that remains to indicate how old and important this place used to be. They are run down now, but still decorative, and preside gently over the rocks like unlikely jewels amid the prefabricated materials of the modern squatter homes.

Roberto Carlos da Silva (he goes by the moniker Carlinho, or little Carl), lives at the top, where he has his home and runs a grocery kiosk and bar. When I visited, Carlinho was finishing a construction project. He had rebuilt his *barraca* with concrete, steel, and brick, making it a spacious two-story dwelling. His roof offered a rare 360 degree view of the city—the view is a throwback to what the old community must have been like—and his house also benefits from the hilltop breezes.

When you leave Morro da Providência, descending on the opposite side toward an abandoned freight depot and the seedy portside neighborhood of Gamboa, you pass a 1960s-era *conjunto*: a city housing project. Here, the concrete apartment buildings are crumbling and shards of glass litter the trash-filled parking lots between them. The prospect of growing up in these Soviet-style apartment blocks seems infinitely worse than being a kid in the humble self-built structures just up the hill. The *conjunto* is a brutalizing place, and residents seem to have no incentive to make life better. By contrast, up in Morro da Providência, people are still building, improving, planning for the future. One hundred years after the favela's founding, without ownership, without authorization, without legal recognition, Carlinho has found that there's still hope on the hill.

In the favelas, people like Carlinho and Márcio and Zezinho and Maria have all found the means to survive and improve their lives. They have done this without the chance to own their property. And they don't need to. I learned this from Jorge Ricardo.

Jorge was a large, cryptic, funny man who by day is the financial director of Administradora de Imóveis Passárgada, a Rocinha real estate agency, and by night is a party animal and disc jockey who goes by the name Kadinho. (He must also be a sort of blithe spirit intellectual, for the name of his unofficial realty office seems to be a misspelling inspired by *Vou-me Embora Pra Pasárgada*, a poem by Manuel Bandeira (1886–1968), about a dreamworld utopia where he goes when he gets sad or stressed; *Pasárgada* is also the name sociologist Boaventura de Sousa Santos chose to apply to an anonymous favela he profiled in a 1977 essay.) Jorge didn't divulge his last name: he didn't refuse to, he simply didn't respond to my repeated questions. We sat in his office, on the second floor of an odd-shaped little building (450 Estrada da Gávea), next to the garage that is the last stop for the 192 and 193 bus routes. He called out to an assistant, who dug into a brand new filing cabinet and handed him several papers. He waved them in the air for a moment, then handed them to me. One was called "Private Instrument for the Purchase of Improvements and the Assignment of Possession." The other, "Instrument for the Promise of the Assignment of Possession and Sale."

They were august-looking forms, printed in the flowing type styles typical of important legal papers. But, essentially, they were title deeds that weren't title deeds. They were an attempt to memorialize something that might seem ineffable to an outsider: the sale of possession rather than property. These nontitle deeds can be signed, notarized, and filed with the various residents' associations of Rocinha to memorialize transactions that are not quite land sales.

Jorge acknowledged that financing was a more complex problem. "Banks don't lend money for buildings here," he told me. This is true: although the federal *Caixa Economica* and *Banerj*—a formerly state-run bank that was recently privatized—have offices in Rocinha, they offer savings accounts and credit cards but no loans. "There are local lenders. But if you don't pay, you might pay with your life."

That may change, however. Just before I left Rocinha, a company named ASB Financial opened a store on the Via Ápia. "Dinhiero em uma hora," the sign promised. Money in an hour. "It actually isn't true," Oliviero, the office director, told me. "It's actually money in 20 minutes." The firm wasn't yet offering large or long-term loans. The highest amount a person could receive was R$6,000 (about $2,400) and the maximum payment term was nine months. Oliviero admitted that the *juros* (interest rate) was high, although he refused to divulge the exact amount. Still, even for short-term, high-interest money, 10 or 15 people a day were stopping by. And the rumor was that other banks were setting their sights on Rocinha.

But the perils of finding financing didn't deter Jorge in his attempt to sell his nontitle deeds. Rocinha doesn't need title deeds or *asfalto* banks to improve, he told me. His pieces of paper offered everything the community needed to grow.

"Negotiation of buying and selling always has been a case of words," Jorge said with a laugh. "Brazil has passed from Third World to Second. And the reality of Brazil is Rocinha. We are a community that serves as a model for other communities. We are the future."

CHAPTER 2

Nairobi
The Squatter Control

Well, independence did indeed come.

— Ngugi wa Thiong'o

One glimpse is enough. You have discovered the famous misery of the Third World. A sea of homes made from earth and sticks rising from primeval mud-puddle streets. Massive numbers of people live here: somewhere between 500,000 and a million souls. Many have lived here for decades, but half the residents are under the age of 16. All, old and young, new arrivals and long-term residents, live without running water, sewers, sanitation, or toilets.

Piles of trash line every alley and avenue, giving the neighbor-hood its trademark look: a motley patina of red dirt, green mango peels, and the festive but faded colors of thousands of discarded plastic bags. Chickens and goats wander by and scratch at the heaps for food. Upon occasion, to reduce the load, someone will rake some of the garbage into a pile, push it to the side or against a mud wall, and set it on fire. These smoldering mounds pose the biggest danger to the community: that the flames will spread to the dry wood of the huts. But what else is there to do with trash? There's no one around to pick it up.

The farther in you go, the more the community slides into the stagnant, swollen valley. On one downhill slope, sewage sluices underneath a pack of water pipes. At a rickety river crossing, a vast store of discarded plastic bags has bunched up in the flow. And near the bottom of the valley, where the murky waters of Nairobi Dam are so filled with nitrates that the reservoir has been overrun with water hyacinth, you hear a muffled grunting, and then a group of pigs comes charging down a narrow, mud-filled lane to wallow in some spreading brown swill.

Back on the main road, a man with a wheelbarrow parks in the muck. He's doing a brisk business selling small vacuum-packed cardboard pyramids of milk. Another hustles by, his cart filled with cases of Fanta. The bottles teeter and clank as he bounces his barrow across the scarred track. A fellow in a bloody apron slogs through with a side of beef on his back, headed for one of the butcher shops, where the meat will hang without refrigeration, slowly drying and attracting flies as the proprietor cuts portions for customers. With a backfire and a blast of soot, an old-fashioned gasoline engine throbs to life: it powers what's called a *posho* mill, for grinding white corn into fine flour destined to be made into *ugali*, the staple food here.

Along a main street in Kibera.

Next door, a man with an ancient iron filled with charcoal is putting a crease in a pair of gray wool pants. Across the muddy road, under a narrow awning, three men are hammering at thin steel sheets, bending and riveting, forming large carrying cases that can, in a pinch, double as tables. And in the midst of all this, on whatever piece of solid ground they can find, people have stoked wood fires. Some are frying fish or french fries; others are scorching massive bones over a high heat prior to boiling them to make gelatin or bone meal. Still other small entrepreneurs are grilling corn over charcoal (a shilling or two will get you a small piece) or selling bundles of *sukuma wiki* ("push the week," the slang name for collard greens or kale, because you can buy it for as little as 1 shilling a bunch, thus enabling you to push your family through another week). Silent street merchants sit behind their stocks of greenish-red mangos or mottled plum tomatoes that they have painstakingly set in small piles—three on the bottom, two on top of them, and one on very top —on a piece of canvas or cardboard, to keep them out of the mud. The salesperson periodically produces a scrap of fabric and lovingly polishes each fruit to make it look its best.

Nairobi is a modern city, the capital of a country that has been independent for 40 years. According to old tourist brochures, it has long boasted that it is a pleasant place: "the green city in the sun." And, indeed, if you're well-off, if you live along the quiet streets of Lavington or Muthaiga or Gigiri, if you have a job at one of the profusion of nonprofits that use the city as their base, perhaps the slogan is true.

But the mass of Nairobi's 2.5 million inhabitants—perhaps as many as 60 percent of them, or 1.5 million people—will never be part of that city. Independence has come, but conditions have not changed. They live in huge agglomerations of mud huts and scrap steel shanties. Kibera, where I lived for three months, is Africa's largest mud hut metropolis. Here, unlike Rio, squatters live in the valleys, and you go down to get into their homes. And here, again unlike Rio, people are not the proud barons of their domain. Instead, in each dark house I visited, people were desperate to convince me that they were substantial. They showed me faded, chewed-up photo albums. They showed me their high school diplomas: papers that had been fingered and folded and unfolded so many times that they were held together by threads. They showed me things that proved they were people to be reckoned with. Not idlers but wage earners. Not ignorant but educated. Not humdrum but people with a career, a business, a calling, a vocation.

Michael Owaga Obera works for the Nairobi City Council, but he lives in a place the City Council believes doesn't exist.

He came to Kibera two decades ago from the Lake Victoria region. He came to Nairobi because he is the oldest child in his family and he needed to make money to support the others. When he arrived, his uncle helped support him. And he has followed suit and sponsored several relatives who have made the trek to the city.

By Kibera standards, Michael might be considered middle class. His job as a clerk for the City Council pays more than 9,000 shillings a month (around $120). The government deducts taxes from that, so his take-home pay is perhaps 5,000 or 6,000 shillings, but that's double what many in Kibera make. Still, he struggles, because the government is always late with his pay. The city is consistently two months behind in issuing paychecks.

Michael does have some comforts, though. He has two rooms for his wife and four children. And he has a television (black and white, because a color TV would quickly be stolen) powered by a giant old wet cell battery.

Michael lives in Kibera because it is impossible for him to live elsewhere. The cheapest single rooms in the most run-down legal neighborhoods of Nairobi rent for around 2,500 shillings: half of his take-home salary. Two rooms would eat up his whole wage. A more spacious apartment—bedroom, living room, small kitchen—would cost more than his monthly pay. So he remains in his mud hut.

When he arrived, the rent was 150 shillings a month. At the time, each house had its own latrine, and the community was safe, even late at night.

By 1999, the rent on Michael's two rooms was 1,900 shillings. Then Kenya's President Daniel arap Moi ordered landlords to reduce their rents. In late 2002, he was paying 1,300 shillings, but the landlord was demanding 1,600 and had refused to accept the lower amount for three months. Michael feared he could be evicted.

Michael is frustrated with the Kenyan situation. Here is a country with wild animals, but Michael cannot afford to take his kids to the National Parks to see them. "An outing is something I heard of at school," he said with a sad smile. "But outings are not something African. What would you choose: strong tea or an outing? Better strong tea. That is why we stay in Kibera."

Kibera is, for the most part, a city of mud blockhouses. Each structure is divided into single rooms, which are approximately 10 by 10, or 100 square feet. Some blockhouses can have as many as 20 rooms. Ventilation is through the door and, sometimes, a small window. In some rooms, the door goes to an interior hallway and the window lets out on a trash-filled alley scarcely more than a foot wide.

The rooms, my friend Nicodemus joked, are self-contained, meaning that one room is all rooms: living room, dining room, kitchen, washroom, study, bedroom, and even, depending on how safe it is after dark, temporary toilet. Nicodemus' family—he, his wife, his daughter, and his infant son—all lived in that one self-contained room.

Kibera is an old-style shantytown, still made from mud. The city's newer shantytowns are made from corrugated steel sheets set into thin concrete foundations. These communities—Mukuru, Kwa Reuben, Sinai, Kwa Njenga, Gitare Marigu, and scores of others—follow the Nairobi and Ngong rivers as they run south and east from town, stretching for miles along the edge of the city's industrial area, through abandoned rock quarries, past the massive garbage dump and stretching on towards the international airport. At the dump a cadre of desperate locals descends on every new load and giant storks float overhead, occasionally swooping down to vie with the humans for particularly juicy bits of refuse.

Metal sheeting may seem more durable and protective than mud, and it certainly looks cleaner. But mud beats metal, hands down. The sun rules the world on the equator and mud, opaque and dense, blocks light and heat from penetrating to the room inside. In the evenings, mud also repels the cold air. Metal, by contrast, is a bad insulator and good conductor, so the huts made from galvanized steel sheets are stifling during the day and bone-chilling at night.

The prefabricated metal is, of course, cheaper than mud: erecting walls from sheet steel takes much less time and labor than building a sturdy mud hut.

The dark continent. I never wanted to use the cliché. After all, what does it really mean? Is Africa dark the way Europe was dark

Kibera: mud and steel and open sewage.

during the Dark Ages: dark to knowledge? Is it dark as Joseph Conrad implies in his novel *Heart of Darkness*: a place that exposes the darkest parts of human nature? Is it dark because of the skin color of the people who live there? Any way you parse it, the phrase is objectionable.

Then I started hanging out in the mud hut city. Nicodemus Mutemi, a member of the social analysis group at Christ the King Catholic Church, volunteered to be my guide. The first week we worked together, we spent 10 hours a day going from one side of the neighborhood to the other, dropping in on people he thought I should interview.

As we walked in the seething sun, scores of kids vied for my attention. "Mzungu, mzungu," they shouted. White man, white man. "How are you? How are you." Sometimes they even reached out to shake my hand, as if that touch could assure them that, yes, non-Africans actually do exist. Some would continue to chorus "How are you?" until I was out of view.

And each time we went into someone's hut, it worked the same way. They ushered us inside. We were respected guests and we were given the best chairs. They sat on hard wooden stools by the door.

Nairobi is just one degree south of the equator and the equatorial sun is harsh (the city is a mile above sea level and, despite the burning sun, the temperature seldom rises out of the 80s). That first week, Kibera was a high-contrast dialectic. I saw each person in silhouette. My eyes hadn't adjusted and the people I met were cardboard cutouts, voices in the shadows. In this prosaic way, Africa appeared to me as the dark continent.

The tomato brokers arrived long before the sun. They gathered in the predawn chill on the edge of Toi Market, visible only because of the swinging beams of their flashlights. Toi (pronounced "toy") is where many in Kibera work and shop. The wholesalers were men, the retailers women. They haggled every morning. A gang of haulers lived between the stalls at the outdoor market. They snoozed and smoked all night, until 4 A.M., when the tomatoes were trucked in. When the haggling was done, the women commanded them to haul away a crate. One man bent almost in two as two others placed a crate on his back and he slogged off to follow the buyer.

Streams of people leave Kibera before day arrives. They are quiet, serious, and they must know the pathways well, for the night is thick and there is no light, except an occasional flashlight or cigarette glow. Perhaps they are going to Toi; perhaps to the wholesale market on the edge of downtown, where the streets smell perpetually of rotting bananas; perhaps to the meat market in Dagoretti, with its waft of drying blood. By 7 A.M., when the sun blasts over the hills, they are well into their work. By midmorning they are having their tea and preparing to bring their load back to Kibera.

You can watch them arrive on the *matatus*: inexpensive jitneys that come from town. The tout—the unofficial equivalent of a conductor—climbs to the roof and throws down an enormous burlap full of cabbages. The woman who bought them is too frail to carry it. But a teenager who had been resting nearby, hanging out with the *mir'aa* dealers (*mir'aa*, or, as it is known in north Africa, *khat*, is a natural stimulant, legal in Kenya), throws down his cigarette and shoulders the burden. He is a hauler, and spends each day here waiting for people like her. She must pay him to carry her cargo into the community. It is his steady work. The haulers have semiofficial locations where they station themselves, and if they poach on another's hauling territory there will be a fight. Depending on the weight and how far they must carry it, they can make 50 shillings a load.

Sometimes, they take in 250 shillings (or $3) a day. It's hard work, but a good wage in Kibera.

The hauling is done, but the woman needs to distribute her cabbages. Some are for hotels (in the squatter areas, all restaurants are known as hotels), which must start cooking now if they are to be ready for the lunch rush.

Most hotels have a few scarred wooden tables and some wooden benches set on an uneven dirt floor. They are cramped, dirty, and overheated. This is almost unavoidable, since they do not have running water and often have no ventilation other than the door. Hotel food is most often tomato-based stews of meat or vegetables served with *ugali* or rice or *chapatis*, an Indian-style flat bread. The diet seems perfect for the climate—you burn a lot of carbohydrates on the equator. The food is generally cooked in the morning, and then kept warm in giant pots and served all day.

Running a hotel can be a good way to make money—if the location's right. But it's hard work. Sabina Ndunge, who owns Bombers Pisa Motel, not far from the bus stop called D.C. Stage on one of Kibera's main roads, opens her hotel at 5 A.M. and closes at 9:30 P.M. With those hours, it helps that she and her six children live in the room behind her hotel. She buys all her food locally, at Toi Market, which is perhaps a 10-minute walk from her hotel. She does not serve meat—not out of vegetarian principles but purely because of economics. "People like a plate to be 10 shillings [about 13 cents]," she said. "If you put meat in it, people will not buy. It will be too expensive." Stews with meat cost three or four times the vegetarian price: or closer to 50 cents. Sabina came to Kibera at the age of 20 in 1986 and has run her hotel since 1988. She wants the community to improve, and would like to see paved roads and permanent buildings and access to health care. But she does not fool herself.

She does not want upgrading if it means that costs go up. Each person—the broker, the wholesaler, the retailer, the hotel-owner—makes a minute mark-up. Sell for a few shillings more than you buy. Margins are small. That's life.

On the other side of Kibera, I visited a hotel that seemed to be from a different world. One step through the mud portal and there, inches from the slosh and sewage, was a breezy patio with white plastic chairs and tables with umbrellas. A band was playing— electric guitar, bass, drums, plus a singer. The sound was dense and textural. No solos, only quick rhythmic chord changes and repeated hypnotic lyrics. A few people were dancing.

There was a bar off to one side, a room with a pool table, and a restaurant/butcher shop where you can buy *nyama choma* (grilled meat) and various stews. A stew will cost 30 to 40 shillings (45 or 55 cents), depending on whether it has meat in it. For grilled meat you pay by weight, but 100 shillings, or $1.30, might buy a decent portion for two. A bottle of Tusker beer—served warm, British-style —will set you back 55 shillings, with a 5 shilling surcharge on weekends.

Western Motel was the nicest bar in Kibera. It was like an oasis, with room for several hundred people—and on weekend evenings it did fill up.

Western Motel was not particularly fancy—but it was fancy for Kibera. And when you're inside, it's easy to forget that you're in a mud-walled city. For you could be anywhere in Nairobi: even in middle class areas along Ngong Road or in Westlands or Buru Buru or Dagoretti. Indeed, with a few changes in decor and a real refrigerator, Western Motel could be in any other country in the world, even in the United States.

Night falls fast near the equator, and in the sudden 7 P.M. darkness merchants set out open-wick paraffin lamps to illuminate their kiosks. They flicker all along the railway line that runs through Kibera. The tracks constitute one of Kibera's busiest boulevards and are lined with hundreds of kiosks. Two commuter trains roll through every morning, heading downtown. They make two stops in Kibera, although neither has an actual station. The trains make the return run in the early evening. A mournful freight train lumbers through every few hours. There's only one track here, so there's no whizzing bullet train hubbub. Instead, people have gotten used to the risk and rumble. Along some stretches the kiosks come within a few inches of passing locomotives, and shoppers will delay moving out of the way until the train gets uncomfortably close. Even the goats seem to wait until the last second to jump away and let the trains through. The tracks are a dense pedestrian arcade during the day. Evenings are a different matter. Early on there's a rush. But by 9 P.M. most of the businesses are empty. Only a few dogged merchants are out: and they are hurrying to throw their merchandise into sacks to transport it to a secure location for the evening. By 9:30 P.M. the tracks are a ghost town. The bare branches of the kiosks illuminated by the hard glow of the moon are spearlike sentinels against the gloom. Kibera settles into the night in quiet: a hush made strange by the knowledge that several hundred thousand people live here.

Kibera disappears in the dark because night is feeding time for thugs. Almost everyone in Kibera has had a run-in with them. Some simply snatch and run, then skillfully flee down the narrow alleys and disappear into the dark. They melt into the mud-lined distance almost before you realize you have been robbed. Others wait until you've left your home so they can hammer a hole in your wall and remove everything you own. Still others—the most dangerous of the crew—carry spearlike knives called *pangas*. They will cut you to get what you have, and will cut you more if you don't have enough. Some parts of Kibera and the other mud hut areas of town are so unsafe that you cannot walk from your hut to the latrine at night for fear of being mugged. So you either hold it in until morning, or you use what Kenyans artfully but uncomfortably call "flying toilets"— you use a plastic bag and then, after sunrise, you fling it as far from your home as you can.

Water is work. Although water mains exist all around Kibera, the government has never extended water service into the mud hut city.

Train and kiosks, midday.

So entrepreneurs have paid off politicians for the right to run their own pipes. You find their kiosks throughout the community. They sell water to thirsty residents. Depending on where you live, the kiosk may be right outside your door or as much as a kilometer away. People transport water in 20-liter plastic drums called jerry cans. The cans have a small handle on the top, but that doesn't make them easy to carry. Five gallons of water is heavy no matter what method of transport you use. The price is normally 3 shillings per jerry can.

Carrying water, by and large, is women's work. Several men I spoke with suggested that this is a vestige of the division of labor in the countryside: the man often works with the farm animals while the woman hauls water to the fields Even the young are put to the task. I have seen little girls who are barely taller than the 2-foot-high jerry cans dragging them home after buying water.

Some women have affixed straps to the tops of the cans. They carry the water behind their backs, and loop the straps around their foreheads. Some carry the heavy buckets directly on top of their heads. I saw one old lady who was carrying two jerry cans. She moved one 30 feet. Then she went back and moved the other up to and 30 feet beyond the first. And then again, overtaking and joining and overtaking again. Over and over, again and again, until she got home.

And, depending on the size of your family, hauling water can also be a time-consuming occupation. Mary Muhonja and Ruben Sambuli have six children of their own and care for three who were left homeless when Mary's sister died. Their family of 11 uses eight jerry cans every day. Yet Mary, who does domestic work, and Ruben, who is a casual laborer, have been unemployed for most of the past year. So they must be very sparing with water.

When water is scarce—a common occurrence in Nairobi, where even rich neighborhoods sometimes go weeks without any water— long lines form, and the price goes up. And when lines are really long, there's a two-tiered system: people who want water without waiting can get it with express service—if they pay for it. During a routine shortage, the price of water can triple: to 10 shillings per jerry can. And in a severe shortage, the kiosk owner will often ask for 20 shillings per can. Express service can cost even more.

The kiosk owners build their systems on the cheap, and the water pipes snake along the ground. If there is a sewage trench, the tubes run right through the fetid channel. Because there is so much garbage around, the pipes often become encrusted with refuse. And, when there are small leaks, most kiosk owners simply wrap the bad section of pipe with a dirty rag and keep pumping.

A few years ago, the Water and Sanitation Program, a nonprofit affiliated with the United Nations and the World Bank, became interested in the water supply question in Kibera. The group issued a report on Kibera's water kiosks. By reading the fine print, you can determine how much Kibera people—and by extension, residents of all the mud hut communities of Nairobi—are being ripped off by the kiosk system. At 3 shillings per jerry can, Kibera residents pay 10 times more for water than the average person in a wealthy neigh- borhood with municipally supplied, metered water service. And that's when water is plentiful. When there's a shortage, metered rates don't go up, but the prices in Kibera do. So at those times peo- ple in Kibera pay 30 or 40 times the official price of water.

The group published a brochure about the study. They presented it to local and national politicians. There was only one bunch of people who never saw the study: the residents of Kibera.

Japheth Mbuvi, Operations Analyst for the program, explained why. "Our audience for this was not the people of Kibera, but the political structure," he told me. Then he added, "Anyway, maybe it's better not to publicize this: there could be riots."

I applaud Mbuvi for his frankness. He is one of the few people I have met at any of the large nonprofit agencies who was willing to be candid about his agency's shortcomings as well as its achievements.

Still, there's something sad about his concern.

Perhaps it's true that people in Kibera could riot over water. After all, Kibera has been the scene of riots in the past—most of them involving landlord tenant issues—and scores of people have been murdered in the melees. Still, Kibera's people deserve to know the facts about their lives. What's the point of studying the water kiosks of Kibera if, when the study is done, the information is not shared with the people who have most at stake?

To be fair, a few years back, the World Bank tried a different approach. It joined with the City Council to bring municipal water pipes directly into Kibera, thus cutting out the kiosks. The plan went to contract, and the contractor installed long stretches of piping. But then problems erupted. The city claimed it ran out of money. The contractor refused to complete the job. And the residents, after seeing the metal pipes lying unused for months, grew disillusioned. Those empty steel tubes became the symbol of everything wrong with outside aid. After years of looking at the dry pipes every day, a desperate few took the action that doomed the plan. They dug up some of the inactive pipes and sold them to scrap dealers. Most likely, they bought water with the money they made.

The smiling women beamed down from the walls of Shadrack's house. Dozens of them, clipped from the pages of fashion magazines and newspapers.

They were white, they were clean, they were fully made up, they were wearing fancy clothes. No blemishes, no wrinkles, no birth-marks: all individuality erased through the miracle of the modern airbrush. Their faces glowed triumphantly in Shadrack Shihundu's dark house, each an artificial sun.

People in Kibera routinely give their mud huts little homey touches. Knit coverings for tables. Oversized calendars on the wall (often two or three years out of date.) Extra furniture, such as chairs for visitors, were stowed out of the way, often tied to the ceiling or hung on the wall. People also strung sheets from the ceiling to hide their beds or the dirty dishes from last night's dinner. And most people also put newspaper on the walls. This helped prevent the mud from drying and crumbling onto their clothes and their bed, and into their food and their water.

But Shadrack's attempt was unusual: a full wall of Western women.

I asked, but he never explained his wall of beauty. Instead, he talked about what he liked about Kibera, and about the differences he thought existed between Kibera and world outside the mud hut.

"Well, I can afford life, the rent is low, and food is cheap," he said. Then he added, "The rich person will have his own toilet. The poor may share one latrine among thirty."

Kibera is full of bad housing stories. These two come from Wambua.

Wambua was Nicodemus's cousin. Or Nicodemus was Wambua's cousin. Or they were relatives in some way. Or they just liked saying they were. It was never very clear.

Wambua told me that he used to live in a hut that was right next to the latrine. One year, the hut owner decided to save money, so he didn't have the latrine emptied before the rainy season began. As the rain continued to fall, the water level in the latrine began to rise. One night, Wambua came home from work and smelled a terrible odor. When he lit his lantern, he discovered what had happened. The latrine had overflowed and run into his house.

The wall facing the latrine was like a sieve. But the wall on the downhill slope was solid. The sewage from the latrine welled up in his home. Wambua had to cut a hole in his wall to let the sewage flow into the next hut and further down the hill. He moved the next day.

But his new house—in an area that was so steep that the path to his house was three feet below his doorway—had a different issue.

Like many in Kibera, he kept his wife and children in the rural area, figuring that it was better and safer and cheaper for them to remain with his parents. Over Christmas, he went home to see his family. When he returned, he found that thugs had knocked a hole in the wall of his new home. They had stolen everything. Every piece of furniture. Every piece of clothing. The mattress and the sheets off his bed. Every pot, every pan. Everything.

He laughed. "What can I tell you," he said.

He is not a man of many words. But, as we sat in the uneven glow of his open-flame paraffin burner, he told me that he now owned just four things: a rough table, a chair, a bed, and that little lamp. To fit three people in his hut—I was there with Nicodemus—he had to borrow a chair from one of his neighbors.

In that mud-encrusted environment, where you have to purchase water at an immense markup, having clean, well-ironed clothes is a major achievement—and a major preoccupation. Many of my friends in Kibera—Joachim Maanzo in particular—were sartorially splendid (smart, Kenyans would say). Joachim's clothing glowed, and his pants—even the carpenter jeans he wore on weekends—had a perfect crease down each leg. His shoes showed not a speck of Kibera's thick soup of mud—the same mud that had already sucked the replacement heels off my nicest pair of boots. I fancied that I was dressing pretty well, given that I was living out of one overstuffed shoulder bag for three months. But no matter how I tried, I couldn't keep anything clean or crisp and could never get the mud off my shoes. Before I left Kibera, Joachim came clean about one thing: he found the way I dressed "comical." He apologized profusely for telling me this: he didn't want me to think him impolite. After discovering that I cut such an amusing figure, I asked a bunch of people in Kibera about their dominant stereotypes regarding *wazungu* (white people). I expected them to tell me that they thought white people were rich. But they had a different take. Almost without exception, they answered with one word: dirty.

There are lots of poor people in Kibera. There are some middle-class people. And there is one millionaire.

The squatter millionaire swore me to secrecy. He warned me: I could not use his name. It's not that he isn't proud of what he has accomplished. "I don't mind to say I am rich," he intoned. And it's not that he thought he could tell his story and remain anonymous. Just one mention of the businesses he owns, and everyone in Kibera will know who he is. He laughed. "You are the journalist," he said. "That is your worry."

Mostly, the squatter millionaire wanted to ensure that talking with me would not put him in sour with the politicians or the civil servants: because they could make it tough for him to make money.

He was not always a squatter millionaire. He started out at the bottom. "When I came to Kibera," he said, lighting a Horseman, one of the cheapest cigarettes you can buy, "I rented a single room, 10 by 10. The rent was 300 shillings a month. I divided the room in half, so one side was the bedroom and kitchen. On the other side, I made a small window out of which to sell. Then I started the business. My first investment capital was 600 shillings. After 1 year, I rented another room for a bedroom, and turned the original room into a store."

Two years later, he took his savings and invested in making clothes. "I rented a room across the street from my store. I started with one sewing machine, which I rented for 200 a month. But within three or four months, I bought that machine. Within one year, it was like an industry within the slum. And within two years I managed to buy 82 machines and hire 120 workers."

Recently, Nairobi has become the *mitumba* capital of East Africa: used clothing. I saw people wearing discarded American football jerseys (Bubby Brister, who once played for the Pittsburgh Steelers and the Denver Broncos, was one name I noticed) and all varieties of recovered pants and shoes. The massive Gikomba market downtown is Africa's premiere *mitumba* trading post. People journey to Nairobi from all over the continent, just to stock up on used clothing. The stuff was so cheap that the squatter millionaire could not compete, even with the low wages he was paying his workers. But the squatter millionaire is not sentimental about his businesses or his workers. He evaluated the market and made a quick decision: In 2001, he sold his sewing machines, laid off his employees, and diversified into other businesses.

First he owned *matatus* and a few larger long-distance buses. When those ventures didn't produce enough money, he sold and diversified again.

He took the money he got from his *matatus* and opened the bar called Western Motel. On the average weekend, Western Motel grosses as much as many people in Kibera earn in a year. The squatter millionaire also invested in firms that have as much dealings in the legal world as the shantytown. He owns the beverage distribution business and the flour wholesaling operation for the entire western portion of the city. In these areas of town, you cannot drink a soda or a beer that the squatter millionaire has not made money on. You cannot eat anything made from corn or wheat—including the *ugali* and *chapatis* that are the basic starch of the diet in Kenya—without contributing to his wealth. In addition, he owns several stores in Kibera and about 1,000 of the mud huts that people here call home.

The squatter millionaire is proud to note that he owns property in the richest neighborhoods in town. His portfolio includes 10 legal buildings, in neighborhoods like Karen and Dandora and Donholm and Kilimani. But he is also proud to say that despite his wealth he lives in Kibera. He prefers the shantytown, he says, because it has always been his home. Besides, he says, he is treated with respect in Kibera, even by the local thugs. He says he can travel anywhere he wants in Kibera at any hour, and no one will bother him. If he swapped his house in Kibera for a spread in Karen, he would simply become a target for thieves.

There was nothing flashy about the squatter millionaire. A small stocky man with a sly smile, he wore jeans, a comfortable shirt, and a baseball cap. The only hint that he was someone important was that he carried two mobile phones. They rang regularly while we talked.

He told me that he has thought of going into politics, that people have asked him to, because they feel only he, a squatter millionaire, can end the corruption. But he is too much of a pragmatic businessman. To run against an established politician would mean trouble. His businesses would be raided all the time. More and more payoffs would be needed. So the squatter millionaire thinks it would be better not to enter politics, because it would impede his cash flow.

In 2002, he bought himself a summer home. It's near the town of Thika. But it's not your usual small vacation house. This homestead he bought himself was the 1,000-acre estate of a former colonist, a British national who stayed on in Kenya after independence. All told, the house and grounds cost him 45 million shillings (almost $600,000). That money—more than most Kibera residents could ever imagine—came from their community.

The squatter millionaire says he loves Kibera. His voice rises as he talks about the way people in the community are consistently disrespected and ignored by government and nonprofits alike. But he is no soft touch for philanthropy. While I was in Kibera, a family that knew him had a *harambee*, or fundraiser, to help defray the cost of sending their daughter to high school. This is expensive in Kenya: as much as 20,000 shillings (about $250) per term, which is more than some families earn in a year. The squatter millionaire didn't come to the *harambee* but he did send an envelope. The family opened it expectantly. Inside was his gift: 100 shillings ($1.30).

They filed in, the women in brightly colored patterns, their hair wrapped in matching cloth, the men in the best suits or sports jackets they have, which usually means threadbare and out-of-date *mitumba*. They come by the hundreds, by the thousands. Sunday in Kibera is for *Mungu*—for God. Sometimes it seems like everyone in Kibera belongs to one church or another. In the mud walled chapels of the Pentecostal Assemblies of God, people clap and shout and speak in tongues. At the Catholic Church, Mexican priests celebrate mass in Kiswahili while a choir voices hymns with the accompaniment of a melodica and some traditional drums. The Salvation Army parades through the community to the beat of tambourines, looking for errant souls. The witch doctors shake their rattles and offer prayers for the health of the sick.

Kenya—Kibera in particular—is the most religious place I have ever been. Churches are a growth industry here. There's a good reason for this. My friend Nicodemus, himself a devout Catholic, was unusually straightforward about it. "A church is a good business," he said. "Once you get the people in, you can take a collection." It's true: the families of the pastors of Kibera's churches are some of the most well-fed, healthy-looking, well-dressed people you will find in the community. Churches do very well for their leaders.

Many women in Kibera and other shantytowns of Nairobi have developed communal self-help networks. They're called merry-go-rounds, and they work like this: A group of women all contribute to a kitty every week or every month. Once every week or two, one of the women takes home the kitty. They rotate until everyone has gotten the purse at least once. Then they start back from the beginning. Usually, merry-go-rounds are made up of groups of friends. Outsiders would be unusual in a group, so the women told me, because people now expect that anyone they don't know might be around simply to steal.

Winnie Kioko, 26, operates a business in Kibera. Once a week she journeys to Molo, in the Rift Valley to buy potatoes. She rents space in a truck and transports them back to Kibera, where she sells them to retailers. The markup on the potatoes is enough to bring her a minimum of 4,000 shillings a month. Winnie is part of a 15-person merry-go-round. Each woman contributes 1,000 shillings every two weeks. And every two weeks, someone gets the kitty.

At one point, Winnie had other expenses, and her business took a nose dive. She didn't have enough money to buy from her wholesaler. She had to drop her weekly trips for potatoes. She was only able to get started again after six months, when she again received the 15,000 shilling pay-out from the merry-go-round.

Business in Kibera depends on trust. When Winnie sells potatoes, she agrees on a price with her retailers, then turns over the potatoes and waits for her clients to sell them before she receives her money. Even illegal businesses operate this way. I spoke with a woman who distributes *ipombe*—a home-brewed liquor that she buys outside Nairobi. She buys the liquor and hauls it to Kibera, but she must wait until the bars she sells to retail it to their customers before she gets paid. Given this mode of operating, access to extra cash is important, and the merry-go-rounds help sustain many families.

Julia Wangiri, who owns two bars, one a kiosk in the center of Kibera and the other a sit-down joint at one of the major bus stops in the area, Ngummo Stage, is part of a 20-woman merry-go-round. They contribute 100 shillings every day, and the pot goes to one member at the end of the week. So, almost three times a year, each member receives 14,000 shillings.

It is significant that merry-go-rounds are not designed to promote saving. They are focused on spending. Life in Kibera is close to the bone, and, almost no one I spoke with had any savings. The point of the merry-go-round is that you sometimes need extra money. This could be for an investment in your business. Or to pay for your child to attend secondary school. Or to pay off an old debt or a medical bill. But the system is all about buying or paying or making an investment in something. It's not about thrift or savings.

One other interesting thing about merry-go-rounds: no men participate. For reasons neither the women nor the men could explain, only the women create these economic assistance networks. The men neither participate in them nor create them on their own.

Nairobi didn't exist before the British came. It was a small Masai settlement at a confluence of several small rivers. The city came into being in 1899 because the British wanted to span East Africa with a railroad. Nairobi was the staging point for the work to bring the rails down the Rift Valley, and back up around Lake Victoria and into Uganda. The city's name comes from *enkare nairobi*: "cold water" in the Masai language.

For its first few decades, Nairobi was a frontier town: a hard-boiled, hard-drinking, rough sort of place (indeed, the settlement was not officially recognized as a city until 1950). It was an odd place for a city. Terrible drainage and water shortages plague it to this day, and early administrators actually considered knocking it all down and moving the entire city to a more favorable location but the idea was simply too costly. Warts and all, Nairobi would remain Kenya's number one city (the idea of relocating the city resurfaced in 2004 after a report suggested Nairobi could face dire water shortages by 2007).

Nairobi was a strictly segregated place. Africans who came to the capital were regulated. Those who were officially approved to come to the city—most often railway workers or people in colonial service—were prohibited from bringing their families with them. They were given temporary housing in barracks containing lines of single rooms with few services and shared toilets and cooking spaces. These barracks remain common housing forms in Nairobi today, and railway workers are still living in these appalling structures that look like they have had no improvements made to them for a generation. Any African who arrived in the city without permission from the colonial authorities was on his or her own. You can still find the thatched roof neighborhoods on the edge of town where they lost themselves in the cacophony of the central city. By the 1930s, thousands of these casual laborers were living in self-built hovels just outside downtown.

The British had a schizophrenic attitude toward this phenomenon. At times the colonial administrators tolerated the unauthorized building. At other times, they brutally repressed such undertakings, fearing that they were incubators of anticolonial activism. In 1953, seeking to root out what they feared were cells of Mau Mau revolutionaries, British policemen descended on the large shantytown that had grown in the Mathare River valley and pulled all the huts down, making 7,000 people homeless. The shanty dwellers left for a time, but eventually Mathare was rebuilt and remains one of Nairobi's larger squatter settlements to this day.

Even after Kenya won its independence in 1964 the shantytowns flourished. That's because the country's new leaders did not do away with the African civil service the British created to keep the African population oppressed. This service, called the Provincial Administration, was a blend of tribal terminology and modern civil service efficiency. In it, local elders and chiefs preside over every neighborhood, and all of them are employees of the national government.

The problem is that, in addition to being a province, Nairobi is also a city. Many functions, including water, street repair, sanitation, and other essential services, are handled through the city government. That makes the local Provincial Administration a do-nothing bureaucracy. In the city, it has no true governmental role. In a sense, the chiefs and elders in most urban neighborhoods get paid to do almost nothing.

But the Provincial Administration does have control over government land, and it makes use of this power. The officers of the Provincial Administration have the power to grant temporary occupation licenses so people can build structures (temporary, of course) on government land. Since most of the city's so-called slum neighborhoods occupy publicly owned land, the Provincial Administration has power over every hut constructed.

This yields a very strange and horridly corrupt allocation. In every slum neighborhood I visited—and at one time or another I was in almost every major slum in Nairobi—people told me that the chiefs and elders take payoffs from rich people in return for granting them permission to build temporary structures. In addition, the chiefs and elders get extra money for any improvement or repair that gets done. I spoke with one Kibera chief and the presiding district officer for Kibera, and both denied that anyone in their location takes payoffs, although they did acknowledge that it might be going on somewhere else.

The system ensures that Nairobi's squatters aren't really squatters. Actually, they are tenants of rich people who have bought the right to construct temporary mud huts on land belonging to the government. And the Provincial Administration is adamant that the houses remain temporary. I asked one chief to imagine that I was a local resident who wanted to take down my mud hut and build with concrete and brick. "That is not permitted," he told me. I persisted. What if I built it anyway? "I would knock it down," he said. Thus the bureaucracy guarantees that the mud huts remain and that any homegrown effort to make houses better will draw the full wrath of the law.

Most of the hut owners live outside the shanty towns. They are rich people, important people, politicians, even. Why do these well-heeled people want to own mud huts? Because it's a fantastic investment. The up-front costs are minimal. And there's almost no maintenance expense. So you make your money back in less than nine months. After that, everything is profit, month after month, year after year. A guaranteed extra income. There's no downside to owning a mud hut.

Kibera, Nairobi's largest mud hut village, has an additional piece of colonial baggage. Initially, the land here was outside the city limits. It was considered unused bush, and in 1904, the King of England turned it over to the armed forces for use as a firing range and training ground. One of the units that trained and was housed in the area was the King's African Rifles (KAR), an army corps of Africans formed in 1891 and sent to Nairobi to guard the new railway. Most of its members were Muslims from the Sudan (although in the weird parallel reality of colonial power, when the British designated people as Sudanese it could mean they were from Egypt, Ethiopia, Uganda, Zaire, and Nigeria, as well as the Sudan).

As some of the original KAR soldiers got too old to fight, they settled on the margins near their training ground. They petitioned their superiors for permission to remain there. In 1912, British military officials granted 291 retirees from the KAR the right to live on and farm the land adjacent to the training ground. Their small holdings were called the KAR *shambas*—"farms" in Kiswahili—and, in recognition of their foreign heritage, they became known as Nubians. The KAR retirees called their community Kibera—*Kibra* means "farm" or "wilderness" in their native tongue—and they stayed behind when the King's African Rifles were redeployed elsewhere in the country in 1928.

By the 1940s, many of the original Nubians had become landlords and had leased the fields around their houses to people from other tribes who had come to Nairobi seeking to make money. A 1948 census showed that Nubians made up just 55 percent of Kibera's population, the remainder coming from almost every other tribe in the country.

Even today, 90 years on, several of Kibera's oldest villages, Lindi and Makina, in particular, are dominated by the descendants of the original riflemen. Due to their long residency, and the fact that the original settlers had military occupancy permits from the British (although those permits were revoked in the 1920s), quite a number of the Nubians are landlords. In periodic clashes over rents, the violence has often pitted the Nubian landlords against tenants, often from the Luo tribe, which hails from the area around Lake Victoria, who have flocked to Kibera in such numbers than they have become the second largest presence in the community.

Bernard Nzau is neither Nubian or Luo. He is Kamba. But Bernard has lived in Kibera since 1963, and he remembers when people took joy in the tribal differences. Nzau recalls that the only conflicts between the Nubians and others in the community existed at the monthly dance competitions, where participants faced off in the traditional *nduluka*.

It was a rural community. The Nubians kept cows, and there was a slaughterhouse nearby (the area is still called *Kijinjio*, the Swahili name for slaughterhouse). Ibrahim, the man who owned the slaughterhouse, was the richest man in the neighborhood. Kibera was so rural that people from outside the community used to come to Ibrahim's to get the freshest and tastiest meat.

Once a month, the government would set up a movie projector and residents could see a movie for free, projected onto the side of the *kijinjio*.

"Before, it was good," Bernard said, "There were places for our children to play. There were places to dispose of waste. There were places for toilets. There were places for fresh air." He shook his head. "Now Kibera is very completely bad."

They hate it and they love it. They hate the physical attributes. They want paved roads. Water in their homes. More than one room. Electricity. Sewers. More than comfort they want basic services, basic necessities, basic dignity. And they would be prepared to do the work themselves. Michael Owaga Obera brightened when I asked what would happen if he could be secure in the knowledge that he would not be evicted, if he knew that he didn't have to pay rent, but could stay and control his home. "You'll never believe it," he said. "You come back in five years and you won't believe it. I'll make sure you feel somebody is living here."

Kibera is a community. Why else, after running through the litany of problems in Kibera, would Mercy Kadenyeka, a mother of four who has lived in Kibera for a dozen years, say, "Kibera is very good. I don't feel as if there is any other place in Nairobi that I could feel so much at home. When I am here, I feel like I am in my country home. If I have a problem, my neighbors will help. People here create a society."

Or Winnie Kioko, the potato wholesaler, who told me, "People in Kibera, they like being together. Community is a part of them."

Despite the great love residents have for their community—as an oasis of friendly spirit in the city—things do not look promising for Kibera. The new government, while promising to respect people's rights, has proposed massive demolitions in all the city's shanty-towns. Kibera is no exception. The government wants to privatize Kenya Railways, and is pushing to evict people in a 200-foot-wide swath alongside the tracks. Kenya Power and Light, the government electrical monopoly, is also pushing to remove people from huts underneath high-tension wires that slash across Kibera, bringing electricity from the middle class South B neighborhood across the valley to Langata. Another federal agency is evicting people to build a road through Kibera: a shortcut from one wealthy suburb to another. There has been no discussion about these things. No planning with people for how their community should develop. No democratic process. Perhaps 20,000 families could be evicted. What's more, there's a United Nations project planned for the Kibera neighborhood called Soweto, and this has created a great amount of worry and unrest.

And it's not just Kibera. The government has been tearing down huts all over town, with little warning and no plans to help residents adjust to dislocation. Southland, where Armstrong O'Brian and his roommates have lived for a decade, has been completely destroyed, I have been told.

The government contends that these actions will make life better for the residents. But Michael Owaga Obera knows better. "If there are improvements," Michael told me, "definitely rents will go up. Such development will be for people a bit well off. Maybe I can predict that some people are going to make another slum somewhere. If people cannot afford here, they will have to go somewhere else."

The squatter millionaire, for one, has decided the writing is on the wall. In 2004, he sold Western Motel to a church, took the cash, and opened a new bar out of town. He is winding up his investments in the mud hut city and preparing to park his money elsewhere.

Once again, it seems, the people with money will prosper. The bulk of Kibera residents will suffer.

Kenya is the control. Of all the shadow cities I visited, the shanty-towns of Kenya are the only ones that are not really squatter cities. And they are the only ones that have remained stagnant, the living conditions largely unchanged for half a century. The majority of residents neither built nor controlled the community. Most of them pay rent and are tenants. And even the people who do own their own huts have no guarantee that the government will not take their homes away with no warning.

But Kibera is not a mud hut city because of its people. It remains mired in the muck because the system denies the residents control over their future. Corruption and profiteering keep it this way. It was Geoffrey Barasa Wafubwa, one of the first people I talked with in Kibera, who put it all in perspective. We spoke about a month before the landmark election in December 2002, which brought a new president, Mwai Kibaki, and a new political alliance, the National

Not people but trees . . . A Kibera traffic jam.

Rainbow Coalition, into power. People were filled with hope that a free and fair election (the first in Kenyan history) would give the government power to change all the laws. But Barasa knew that change was not as simple as the vote. Talking about rights and giving people rights are two different things, he told me. "The problem here is land," he said. "The government claims the land is forest. When they come to ask for votes from the forest, we are suddenly changed from trees to people. But, legally, we are just trees."

CHAPTER 3

Mumbai
Squatter Class Structure

Empty land sitting useless — if homeless people can live there, what's wrong?

— Rohinton Mistry

It was Alice in Wonderland in reverse: a rabbit hole in the ceiling. That's how I entered my rented room in Sanjay Gandhi Nagar: walk into my landlord's tailor shop, step around the guys stitching clothes, climb the rough, uneven ladder in the corner, and hoist myself through that 2-foot-square opening.

Home was a bare concrete cell, perhaps 10 by 14, with drab gray walls and two small windows—one that let out on a muddy sports field at the rear and another that gave out onto my landlord's balcony. My landlord, kindly, had provided a bed—a narrow pallet with a thin foam mattress—and two overstuffed chairs. A ceiling fan—the smallest and noisiest fan I had ever seen—was tied to one of the metal beams that held up the roof with twine. I positioned the bed directly under the fan, because if I didn't have air flow at night, the mosquitoes were merciless, but many times I looked at that small motor tied onto the roof beam and wondered how much shaking it could take. Yet the rope held and the fan never let go and I'm sure it's still working.

The roof was corrugated sheeting (I never did determine whether it was metal or asbestos or plastic) and it was well made: only a few droplets came down, even in the monsoon downpours.

You could call Sanjay Gandhi Nagar an upper-class squatter community. Almost all the houses in this neighborhood of 300 families in Goregaon East, about an hour from downtown Mumbai via the Western Railway, were made of concrete. Sanjay Gandhi Nagar had electricity. My room had no water or sink inside it, but the community did have water available within a few feet of almost every doorway. The water only came on between 2:00 and 5:00 in the mornings, though, so when anyone in the community needed to refill their buckets, they had to wake up in the middle of the night. I saw some of my neighbors only at 3 A.M., when we were filling our water jugs. All over Mumbai, in rich neighborhoods and poor, water comes at odd hours, but well-off places have night watchmen who have the role of turning on the electric pumps that feed rooftop tanks so they don't have these odd-timed meetings with their neighbors.

Sanjay Gandhi Nagar had two shared toilet blocks: 10 toilets each, five for women and five for men. It sounds like a lot, but during the morning rush you'd sometimes have to wait for 15 minutes or so,

My landlord's family, on the balcony
in Sanjay Gandhi Nagar.

clutching your tell-tale bucket of water (poor Indians don't use toilet
paper, and it's bring your own water for washing and flushing).
Many families in Sanjay Gandhi Nagar have built toilets right into
their homes, but they don't use them because the community has no
sewers, only small trenches covered with paving stones, and residents worry that the heavy usage will plug up the channels and flood
the streets with waste. Still, they hope some day their community will
have the kind of infrastructure that will allow them to use those
indoor toilets.

Most people bathe outside. They squat in a large bucket, dump
some water over themselves, and lather up. Then they dump more
water over themselves to wash off the suds. Men bathe in their
underwear; women bathe wearing saris.

I paid 1,000 rupees a month for my room: about $22. This was apparently a fair price, but it also put my room beyond the means of many squatters in Mumbai.

The story of Sanjay Gandhi Nagar is a story of despair, desperation, and triumph.

The neighborhood got its start a world away from its present location. It started on the edge of downtown. In 1976, a construction company building some new high-rises leased land between the downtown neighborhoods of Colaba and Nariman Point so that its workers could have a place to bunk. This is a common practice in India: construction workers living on-site, in improvised hovels that they build themselves. When the job finished and the lease expired, some of the people simply refused to move. Slowly, others joined them on their small plot, and soon theirs was a colony of 300 families.

My landlord, Janakram F. Wadekar (known to one and all simply as Wadekar), was not one of the original invaders. He had emigrated to Mumbai from elsewhere in Maharastra, the Indian state of which Mumbai is the capital, and bought into Sanjay Gandhi Nagar in 1981. He paid 6,000 rupees (around $670, at the time) for the chance to have a home, although it was only a temporary shack in an illegal neighborhood.

The community was growing. People were putting down roots, improving their modest bamboo huts with wood and metal, and beginning the slow process of saving to make even more improvements to their homes. The men of Sanjay Gandhi Nagar were an amalgam of the original construction laborers plus hotel workers (their plot was just a few blocks from the city's venerable five-star institution, the Taj Mahal hotel), taxi drivers, factory workers, and street vendors. Many of the women worked as servants for old-wealth families that lived in mansions on the tree-lined side streets of Colaba.

But to the rich people surrounding them, their homes were an eyesore, a blight, a cancer in the community. And every so often, a local homeowners association would clamor for their removal.

Then, in 1985, disaster struck. Fire hit Sanjay Gandhi Nagar the night before one of the Hindu religious festivals. Two-thirds of the neighborhood burned to the ground and a 2-year-old child perished in the flames. They found his charred skeleton in the ashes. "I still remember it as if it were today," said Bhaskaran Kunjan Sambavar, the burly head of the local residents association who is known simply as Bhaskar. "How the child looked was unforgettable." Although suspicious fires were a common mechanism used to drive squatters from their homes, Sanjay Gandhi Nagar's leaders insist that this fire was accidental. But they see it as a horrible portent of what was to come.

First, they say, a local politician collected a huge sum to provide for the community after the conflagration, and then pocketed it for his own political use. Then, just as they began to save and rebuild, the residents of Sanjay Gandhi Nagar received the notices they all dreaded: their community was considered an encroachment and was subject to demolition. On March 12, 1986, with no replacement housing on the horizon, the police moved in. Using lathis (thin wooden staffs) on the residents and hammers and crowbars on the buildings, the police crushed the rebuilt neighborhood.

With their homes smashed and their belongings trampled into the mud, the residents convened to face the future. Ultimately, 90 of the 300 families from Sanjay Gandhi Nagar took a fateful step. They could not reoccupy the property because the police had posted guards there. So they moved onto the sidewalk adjacent to the lot that had been their home. They held the sidewalk for nine months. During their stay on the street, the 12-year-old son of one of their most dedicated members died after being hit by a speeding car. Still the residents persisted.

Their plight drew the attention of the news media. A group of leftist intellectuals and public figures came together to support them. These nonsquatters formed a new organization, *Nivara Hakk Suraksha Samiti*: the Shelter Rights Protection Organization. Although *Nivara* was newly formed, it had some clout, in part because two prominent Bollywood stars, actress Shabana Azmi and director Anand Patwardhan, were among its founders.

P.K. Das, one of *Nivara's* current leaders, is a successful architect in Mumbai. A small, intense man with an immaculately trimmed beard, he told me that Nivara is interested in building power for squatters not bargaining for city services. "We have believed in waging struggles," he said. "This has meant acting physically—recapturing land and obstructing demolition. Rights have to be won, not negotiated. Rights have to be snatched." And that sometimes means putting your body on the line, Das told me. At a rally not long ago, police attempting to break up the demonstration roughed up another Nivara leader, breaking his arm.

Together with the Nivara celebrities, several Sanjay Gandhi Nagar residents decided to go on a hunger strike to up the pressure on the government to return them to their homes. They didn't have to starve themselves for long. It took only three days to work out a solution with the politicians: The 300 families who had called Colaba their home were offered a 3-acre tract in Goregaon East, 25 kilometers from their current homes. The new land was unused, owned by a foundation called the F.E. Dinshaw Trust. The residents were offered a 10-year lease at a nominal rent of 500 rupees per month.

The squatters grumbled. They worried. They complained about being so far from their workplaces. Then, as if to force a decision, the government moved in and demolished the huts they had built on the street. The following day, December 4, 1986, Sanjay Gandhi Nagar officially relocated.

When residents arrived in Goregaon East, they discovered that their new Sanjay Gandhi Nagar was little more than a hole in the ground. The area was undeveloped—an Indian version of America's frontier—and some *goondah*, or thug, who happened to be the local political leader had sold dirt from the site to local builders. When the squatters came to claim their turf, they found their new home was a pile of rubble surrounding a 40-foot-deep crater.

"We bought some bamboo sticks and plastic and made ourselves as comfortable as we could," Wadekar recalled. The first order of business was to get rid of the hole, "We filled it in with garbage. Garbage from every corner was dumped here. We had two bulldozers here working every day for four months. Every day, 200 to 300 lorries dropped their garbage here."

The rubble was another problem. It lay on top of solid rock, which had to be smashed up and either spread on the ground or carted away. Wadekar told me he had spent 1,200 rupees breaking up the stone on the portion of the lot his house sits on. He lost a piece of one of his fingers to the stone.

Those were difficult times for Sanjay Gandhi Nagar. "It was horrible," Wadekar remembered. "We had to put up with everything—the bad smells, the mosquitoes, the flies. Everything."

What's more, they had no water (there was a well not far away, but it was too shallow to be used except in an emergency), no electricity, no sewers, no toilets (like Sartaj Jaipuri, they used the jungle).

But they had something more important: confidence. They scraped, they borrowed, and they improved. The first problems was what to do about the hole. After filling the hole with garbage, they discovered they had to top it off with soil, to seal the garbage beneath an impenetrable barrier so that the whole community wouldn't smell like rot and attract mosquitoes and flies. That cost 200,000 rupees (around $16,000). Somehow, they found the money. Then they divided the land into 14 by 17 foot plots, and they allocated one to each family. The toilets, which came next, cost another 125,000 rupees (they put down 50,000 and borrowed the remainder from their *Nivara Hakk* allies, repaying it slowly). They had to pay the municipality to bring in water. Over the years they have paid for three different water lines to be run into the community, with dozens of taps rising out of them. The total cost of the work was about 260,000 rupees.

By 1989, the residents managed to get the electric company to install 15 electric meters, and all 315 households drew their power from those 15 lines.

Two years later, halfway through their lease, the trust that owned the land realized that it could never evict the residents of Sanjay Gandhi Nagar. So it agreed to sell the land to the squatters for 50,000 rupees. The squatters jumped at the chance, and bought the plot as a cooperative society. Then they created some rules. Among them: that none of the original residents could sell their houses for 10 years. And then if they wanted to sell, the society would have the right to buy the building first. Only if the society didn't want to buy it could they sell it to an outsider.

Today, Sanjay Gandhi Nagar has water taps outside almost every one of the 300 houses in the community. One-third of the houses even have pipes bringing water directly inside (my landlord had water on the ground floor, but not upstairs). As a cooperative, Sanjay Gandhi Nagar shares water bills, paying a total of 28,000 rupees every three months, or about 30 rupees per month per house (about 75 cents a month).

In 1998, the electric company installed individual meters for every house in the community, and almost all of those homes are now solid, two-story, poured concrete buildings.

The land in Colaba, from which they were evicted, is still unused. Rajman Soni, who was born in one of the original Colaba shacks and now lives with his mother and father in the two-story steel-reinforced concrete home they built in the new Sanjay Gandhi Nagar, showed me the old location. It's a narrow weed-filled lot penned in between two ugly office buildings. To me it seemed that the land still misses the people who used to call it home.

Early in my stay in Mumbai, I spoke with Adolf Tragler, who runs a small nonprofit called the Slum Rehabilitation Society (SRS). Tragler is a former priest, originally from Austria but now an Indian citizen, who hung up his cassock but remains committed to the social ideal of decent housing for all. He founded the SRS to tap into government programs and construct new buildings that will remove squatters from their self-built and, what he considers, substandard housing.

Tragler viewed the history of Sanjay Gandhi Nagar, the neighborhood where I would come to live, as a tragic tale. "This was not rehabilitation," he told me, shaking his head. "This was just dumping them there. After this, my impression [of Nivara Hakk] sank." He told me that in the fight over Sanjay Gandhi Nagar, the leadership of

Nivara Hakk "did nothing except to get their names into the newspapers."

I wasn't yet living in the community when I spoke with him, so I wasn't able to counter his perception. But I don't see it that way. While it may be true that the upper-crust leaders are publicity hounds, it's also true that Wadekar and Bhaskar and the others in Sanjay Gandhi Nagar are not stuck in rehabilitated single rooms. Through their own hard work and resourcefulness, they have built a stable and desirable community. If the municipality would simply extend the sewer system to their neighborhood, Sanjay Gandhi Nagar would be every bit as good as any of the buildings Tragler has built. In fact, it would be better, for the squatters would have more control of their homes, streets, and destinies.

Mumbai is thick with squatters. It is a city of an estimated 10 or 12 million people and 6 million of them are squatters. There are so many squatters that there are distinct social tiers among them.

Wadekar and the others in Sanjay Gandhi Nagar are at the top of the heap. They have achieved permanence, with many of the comforts of the legal world around them.

But there are all sorts of others.

There are the people like Laxmi Chinoo, squatters who have nothing and, if they weren't ensconced under a roadway overpass, would be living on the street. There are people called pavement dwellers, who dominate the streets throughout many older neighborhoods. In Byculla, and out P. D'Mello Road and Tulsi Pipe Road, people have invaded the sidewalks and built two-story wooden huts. These are some of the most amazing dwellings you have ever seen: they are open to the incredible dust and haze of the city, yet are often

Unclogging the sewers in
Sanjay Gandhi Nagar.

amazingly clean inside. People have created elaborate custom-built hutches to hold their meager possessions. Essentially they create tiny built-in wooden shelving systems to organize every possession. Each plate has a separate slot. Each fork. Each pot. Each frying pan. When you are essentially living on the street, exposed to the grime and dirt and bacteria of the city, you have to find an orderly way of upholding basic rules of hygiene. These hutches keep a person's belongings off the street and out of the way of bacteria.

At the same time, one of the most common sights, particularly if you pass by just before school hours, is young girls sitting on a chair out in the street while their mother or a sibling picks the lice out of their hair. When water is scarce, as it sometimes is for squatters, keeping your head free of lice is a never-ending task.

Then there are the people like Gita Jiwa and Sureka Gundi, who have erected small tents on tiny dirt parcels between roadways or on median strips or small traffic triangles at intersections.

There are the thousands of families who invaded the Borivali National Park, literally hacking their plots out of the jungle and now facing a court-ordered eviction.

There are teeming wooden villages like Behrampada, built over a fetid swamp, a warren of narrow alleys where the upper floors of buildings jut out at eye height. Here, you must often duck to avoid smacking your forehead into the thick packs of cables that bring electricity from house to house. Residents admit it's a fire hazard— one spark could set the whole neighborhood ablaze—but it was the

Pavement dwellers in Byculla.

The squatter community in Borivali National Park. The vacant area in the foreground was once covered with homes, but 30,000 families have been evicted.

only way to bring services into the community. Here, also, are scores of small-scale garment jobbers, and the whir of hundreds of pedal-operated sewing machines is almost constant.

There are more spacious squatter villages, like Geeta Nagar, towards the far tip of Colaba, just outside the Indian Navy compound. Here the residents have survived for so long that they have upgraded their shanties into nice concrete homes that are washed by the ceaseless spray of the Arabian Sea. Or Squatter Colony, in Malad East, a Muslim enclave since 1962.

And there's Dharavi, 1 million people strong, a squatter community so massive and developed that it looks like a real city neighborhood. Here, thousands of people live in self-built but sturdy houses that have been cantilevered over the narrow alleys so the balconies from each side practically kiss and only a slit of light hits the ground at high noon. Dharavi is a magnet for business as well and, according to some accounts, its stores and factories do $1 million in business every day. At the same time, some parts of Dharavi are extremely primitive and have horrible sanitation. This plus the population density means the community is also a breeding ground for disease.

Strangely, many of these squatters actually pay rent to the city. Sartaj Jaipuri told me that Squatter Colony started with a ground rent of 3 rupees a month. Today, residents pay 100 rupees a month. Given that there are 1000 homes in Squatter Colony, the City of Mumbai receives $1.2 million rupees a year, or a bit more than $25,000, from these illegal residents.

Given a chance to stay put, squatters improve their homes in a novel way, one that is most likely more in keeping with the medieval method than what is the norm in the developed world. In the West, developers are efficient because they can borrow a lot of money up front and pay it back over time. Squatters are the reverse. They build as money becomes available. So each wall is turned from mud to concrete separately, over time. No interest costs. No overhead. No problems with storage and site security. No accounting headaches. On a small scale—and small, sometimes, can be beautiful—they are quite efficient.

Shaik Banu Bitton came to Borivali National Park when it was still a jungle. "There were reptiles and snakes and we were truly living under the trees," she recalled. For seven years, she lived under a simple plastic tarp set on bamboo sticks. "After seven years, I at last constructed my house," she told me. "Each time I had the money I did one thing and then another. First I did the front wall. I did each wall when I had enough money. I bought bricks, bought water, bought sand. The construction was done by a guy I know. I paid him

80 rupees a day. One time brick, one time concrete, one time the roof."

In this way, over years, and only when she had the money, she reinvented her house. Today, it is a permanent dwelling, completely constructed of brick and concrete.

Mumbai is one of the few cities in the world with a definite and, indeed, progressive policy towards squatters. Any squatter family that owns its structure and can prove that it has been there ever since January 1, 1995, will be given a new home at no cost if their community is targeted for a government-aided project. Developers also can qualify for a valuable zoning bonus if they build replacement housing for squatters. And they can either sell the additional floor area to other builders looking for a density boost or they can apply it to their own higher-income buildings.

There are, as always, a number of catches that make the policy much less in practice than it seems on paper.

- It ties building for squatters to a tight real estate market. The lower the vacancy rate and higher the prices on newly built homes, the greater the value of the zoning bonus. In fact, the people who wrote the squatter policy admit that it is predicated on a boom real estate market, and that few developers are currently making use of the plan. "Markets were very strong at the time and the sale price of real estate was at its highest," said Niranjan Hiranandani, head of the Maharastra Chamber of Housing Industry, a property owner's lobbying organization. "Between 1996 and 1999, prices fell by 50 percent. So you can say the policy is not working."

- It limits the size of the home you can build for a squatter family to 225 square feet, regardless of family size. This means that each family that participates will get a single room. It will have a toilet inside, and a kitchen alcove with running water. But it will be a single-room apartment. Sartaj Jaipuri noted that he already has 300 square feet in his self-built home, and that others in Squatter Colony have 500 square feet. And Squatter Colony already has water and toilets in each home. So the government is offering squatters less than what they already have. "What's the point," he asked. Similarly, Naren Makwana, a city employee who lives in a squatter area of Kurla with his wife and child and parents, is the kind of hard-working, smart person who knows a good deal when he comes across one. "I would take a new home if it was beneficial," he told me. And would 225 square feet be beneficial? "Ah, no, sir. I have a big family." For another example, take Wadekar, my landlord in Sanjay Gandhi Nagar. If he had participated in a government-regulated Slum Rehabilitation Scheme, he, his wife Manda, and their five children Aasha, Vijay, Rajkanya, Nisha, and Manisha would be living in a single room that measures 225 square feet. It would be in a solid concrete building with a toilet inside the apartment. And they would pay no rent. But there would be seven people in one room and no hope for expansion, because that's how the law is written. This did not happen in his case. Instead, he and his neighbors were ejected from their homes, relocated after a lengthy struggle, and then faced the daunting task of rebuilding their bamboo and plastic huts in a new neighborhood, and, essentially, starting over. Wadekar lived through hard times and tragedies, but he also saved and invested and built and created. It took 15 years, but today the

Wadekar family has a three-room house that they built themselves. Wadekar has a tailor shop next door with a loft room
above it: the room I rented.

- The promise of free housing is seductive, but not always the
best approach. If they feel secure in their homes, squatters will
invest and improve their neighborhoods. But if they simply
have 225 square feet in a high-rise buildings that they don't
control, they lose that incentive. Their communities cease to
develop.

- The policy does nothing for tenants, who are generally the
poorest squatters and who will simply be evicted if their community elects to participate in one of these plans. Laxmi
Chinoo, who lives alongside the train tracks in a metaphysical
enclosure marked in the dirt, is one of these tenants. Her community, which surrounded the railway line, was relocated. This
was a good thing, in that the trains were a danger to the people
there. But Laxmi and many others received no benefit because
they were tenants, and that is why Laxmi is stuck at the side of
the tracks.

Hiranandani believes that Mumbai could build new housing for all
its squatters if it approached the existence of their communities the
way Singapore did, and forced investment in affordable housing.
"Singapore tackled slums by requiring that the funds of the provident society [a sort of pension fund where workers invest their sav-
ings] be invested in housing." Though Singapore is a state-controlled
economy, India too has a mandatory public provident fund. "You
need what I would call a benevolent dictatorship to do that kind
of thing," Hiranandani admitted. Still, he continued, "We are one of
the richest states in India. The Mumbai region provides 40 percent of

the revenues collected by the government of India and 65 percent of the revenues collected by Maharastra state. We are a rich city. We could do this if we wanted."

If the government didn't want to put forth that kind of money, Hiranandani offers another idea—perhaps a more feasible one—which he calls the cafeteria approach to squatters. Different squatter areas could get different types of government assistance. People living in communities that are totally unsafe—that get flooded out or are in the middle of sewage outflows—would need completely new housing on a new site. But other neighborhoods—such as Squatter Colony or Gita Nagar, which are both reasonably decent and safe, would be able to apply for infrastructure investments and loans for other improvements. And some areas, where it's appropriate, could simply be given title deeds and permission to build.

Hiranandani has built some of the highest-profile luxury housing in the city—a new mega-development alongside Lake Pawai is actually called Hiranandani Gardens—yet in conversation he sounds almost like a socialist. Perhaps he's simply very savvy with the press. For whatever reason, he has not used the power of his real estate lobbying group to press for either the full-scale government solution or the more modest cafeteria approach.

Politicians, it seems, prefer not to deal with squatters at all, except at election time. I got a taste of this when Abdul Kalam came to Goregaon. I heard about it days in advance: Avul Pakir Jainulabdeen Abdul Kalam was a rocket scientist who built India's missile program and is now President of India (this is largely a symbolic position, since the real power lies with the Prime Minister), and he was coming to Goregaon East. Everyone in Sanjay Gandhi Nagar was excited.

The evening preceding the day before Abdul Kalam arrived, the police ticketed all the vendors and store-owners who had shoved their wares onto the shoulders of the nearby main road. By nightfall, the vendors had disappeared, and the stores had pulled their merchandise off the street.

The day before Abdul Kalam arrived, road work suddenly began. Gen. A.K. Vaidya Marg, which runs between the Western Express Highway and Film City Road, had been a rutted mess for years. Suddenly, it was a high priority. A crew came in and paved the street, laying gravel and asphalt on top of the rutted old concrete. At one spot, where drainage was particularly bad and the monsoon rains routinely created a huge puddle, the crew, working painstakingly by hand, laid yellow and gray bricks.

Early in the morning on the day that Abdul Kalam arrived, workers erected a blue plastic barrier in front of a field that was occupied by a particularly squalid squatter encampment. This community— dozens of haphazard tents on a soggy lot—was a place where I had seen women doing their laundry in the sewers. The workers used the bright blue construction fencing to wall off this community, so Abdul Kalam would not see it as he drove by.

Half an hour before Abdul Kalam arrived, the police stopped all traffic on the busy street. And then, in a flash, his motorcade drove by. The cars didn't stop. They didn't even slow down. Abdul Kalam was on his way to an event at the Indira Gandhi Institute of Development and Research, a government-sponsored high tech facility further down the road.

That evening, after Abdul Kalam was gone, the street vendors began to reappear and the stores slowly pushed their wares onto the sidewalks. By morning, the tent dwellers had ripped down the blue plastic barricade. And the following day, everything looked the way it had before Abdul Kalam arrived. The new roadwork began to wash away in the rain.

All this solely so Abdul Kalam, the President of India, would not get any vision of real life in the biggest city of his country.

Dharavi is Mumbai's largest squatter community: home to between five hundred thousand and 1 million people (estimates vary depending on who's doing the counting). It is huge, sprawling, and dense, and it is hard even for a Dharavi resident to know all its alleys. Dharavi is an imposing place, and some squatters from other areas fear it. Whenever I told my neighbors in Sanjay Gandhi Nagar that I was going to Dharavi, they always had one response: "Be careful."

Dharavi wasn't always an illegal colony. Before the British arrived in Bombay, it was one of six *koliwadas,* or fishing villages, that perched on a series of small islands projecting into the Arabian Sea. The islands were the city's great attraction: the sheltered currents of the harbor they created made it great for fishing and merchant shipping. Indeed, some say the city's original name, Bombay (it was officially changed to Mumbai in 1996), derives from this maritime heritage, from a British corruption of the Portuguese *bom baia*: "good harbor."

Dharavi was unique among the islands in that it fronted on a creek rather than the sea. It was the only maritime community in the city where you didn't need a boat to be a fisherman. You could simply wade into the crystalline waters of Mahim Creek and spear or net as many fish as you might need.

But the gaps between the islands disappeared as Bombay developed. Contractors building Bombay's seaside neighborhoods found it cheaper and easier to drop debris in Dharavi than in the city's official dumpsite, which was farther out of town.

Today, Mahim Creek is still vigorous, but you wouldn't want to fish there. Many nearby neighborhoods use the creek as a giant toilet. Sewage from homes and businesses pours untreated into its waters. The once-gorgeous fishing hole still has a vigorous flow, but the water is turgid and brown, with a strong foul odor that rides the wind into nearby areas. Simply put, the creek stinks.

Perhaps because of the stench, perhaps because it fronts the creek rather than the Arabian Sea, or perhaps simply because marshy conditions and poor drainage made it difficult to build there, Dharavi remained a dark spot on the city's map for decades. At first it was simply an outlying area at the edge of the developed city. Then, as Mumbai grew, and the high-density city spread north, the developers simply leapfrogged Dharavi and built further out. The work of developing Dharavi was left to poor people and new immigrants from the countryside. They flattened the hillocks of trash and built on the new land.

To this day, Dharavi remains a zone of cheap housing for recent arrivals to the city and a magnet for small businesses: the undesirable ones, such as slaughterhouses, tanneries, and factories that brew illicit liquor. Each day, an estimated 300 people flee their homes in the hinterland and move to Mumbai. They all come looking for jobs, and Dharavi accommodates many of them. And the government made use of Dharavi, too, periodically relocating whole communities that had occupied valuable real estate downtown to its narrow lanes.

When S.A. Sunder arrived in Bombay from Tamil Nadu 30 years ago, he headed straight for Dharavi. There, he found what he calls a bachelor room: a shared dormitory contained in a rickety wooden structure. "Ten or 15 men stayed in one room. At that time it cost 10 or 15 rupees per person per month," he said. Such facilities exist today, but the cost has jumped dramatically. A bed in a shared room would cost around 600 rupees a month. Not having a kitchen in his dormitory, Sunder ate at one of the neighborhood's small mess halls: illegal businesses set up to feed the workingmen. He got three meals a day for 70 or 80 rupees a month. Today such meals would likely cost 10 times as much.

Waqar Khan, originally from Uttar Pradesh, has been in Dharavi since he was 13. Now close to 40, he has worked his way up from selling bananas on the street to owning his own business, Royal Campus Shirts, which manufactures and wholesales men's shirts. He lives above his showroom on one of the alleys of Dharavi's Social Nagar. When he acquired the site, it was a simple shed. He has improved it to the point where it boasts a modern-looking store and an upstairs residence: all illegal, of course, but that's the norm here in Dharavi. Sitting with his young son in his shop, he recounted a bit of his journey.

"When I came here, we got a little plot almost for free," he says. "You wouldn't have been able to come here to have this interview, because there were potholes and dirt and no drainage."

Behind him in his store, the walls are decorated with dozens of his gaily patterned products, all stitched by jobbers in Dharavi and sold under official-sounding brand names: Executive, Seasons, Office Man.

Yes, Khan said, Dharavi has grown over the years, and it has improved. But the bulk of the work was done by the residents. "There has been progress in the slum only because of the people who live here," he told me. The city, by contrast, has done little for Dharavi, although the population has increased dramatically. "Water connections were provided 25 years ago, but have not been upgraded. Yet there are so many more people here."

Dharavi today is a combination shantytown and high-rise squatter neighborhood. In some areas, three- and four-story buildings front on both sides of extremely narrow alleys. Here, hidden in the maze, are factories and showrooms, small businesses and workshops, wholesalers and retailers. Although there is no garbage pickup and there are no sewers, there are scores of food businesses, some of which produce sweets or spices sold at some of the city's upscale stores and hotels.

Sunder, who today is a local leader and social worker for the Bharatiya Janata Party, a conservative Hindu Nationalist party that ruled the country until early 2004, estimates that there are 10,000 small scale house industries, often working as jobbers for larger Dharavi wholesalers. He guesses that Dharavi is home to 5,000 small printing businesses, and that there are more than 1,000 businesses related to the clothing industry with more than 50 sewing machines, and perhaps 3,000 businesses with fewer than 50 machines. Although it's impossible to know exactly, since all of these businesses are technically illegal, and therefore don't report income or pay taxes, the total turnover of all these firms probably amounts to $1 million a day.

But, of course, even as Dharavi has developed, Mumbai has developed, too. The city remains one of the most expensive in the world. Rents in the city, and costs of land per square foot, are as high, if not higher, than in London, Paris, and New York. That's because the city is squeezed onto a peninsula, and there's not much more available land. So Dharavi, once the edge of the known world, now surrounded by the sprawling city, has become valuable turf.

Enter Mukesh. Although he grew up in Bombay, Mukesh Mehta is a New York-style developer. That's because he moved to the United States a number of years ago and made his money financing and building fancy houses in suburban Long Island, just outside New York City. He returned to India in 2001, but he remains an American-style operator. He plays all the angles.

Mukesh had a plan for fixing Dharavi. At first, it was a simple plan. Make nice homes. Improve the slum. Gain the zoning bonus. And make a little money.

Mukesh sees the squatters as horrifically ill-housed. And he derides people who romanticize the notion of the squatters building for themselves.

"Self-building is idealistic," he said, "but it keeps people at a lower level. It is a way for nongovernmental organizations to continue to have power over the slums. I am not satisfied with this. I am saying: please rise and go to a higher level. I believe you help slum dwellers by giving them something better."

Originally, Mukesh decided that Dharavi should be a mixed-income area. He would tap the local slum rehabilitation policy, which guarantees him a massive increase in density if he builds free replacement housing for the poor, and use that increased density to build adjacent housing for the middle class.

"You have an opportunity here to rebuild the city," he said. "So why not rebuild it right?"

He sees Dharavi from a developer's point of view and lists its advantages. As usual in real estate deals, it's location, location, location.

- Dharavi has perhaps the best access to mass transit of any city neighborhood, being surrounded by four train stations.
- It is adjacent to the inner city ends of two major highways.
- The city is developing a luxurious office park called the Bandra–Kurla Complex just across Mahim Creek, which includes a dia-

mond trading center, major office buildings for multinationals, and luxury housing.

Mukesh took one look at Dharavi and realized that, even with the land costs and the cost of relocating current residents, he could still bring in new apartments much more cheaply (perhaps 75 percent cheaper) than any developers working in nearby middle-class areas. That bargain price, he believes, will bring the middle class to Dharavi.

Thus his plan was born.

Mukesh wanted to use the government program for slum rehabilitation to raise the standard of housing in Dharavi, and make a bit of money besides. The government plan would give Mukesh a zoning bonus if he builds free housing for the squatters. Each squatter household gets a single-room apartment of 225 square feet, regardless of family size or age. For each unit he builds, the developer gets the right to develop another 225 square feet of market rate housing, or to sell that right to other developers. Mukesh wants to use that extra density to create a new, mixed-income Dharavi. He developed three principles for the job.

"First, the slum-dwellers must get out of their intolerable conditions," he said. "Second, whatever the scheme is, it must make money. And third, you cannot redevelop Dharavi piecemeal, because then the provision of better houses and actual services becomes fragmented, and change in the community is not possible."

To that end, he divided Dharavi into 12 sections—"the dirty dozen," he calls them—which he hoped to farm out to different developers to create different plans. Mukesh said he and his son Shaan would shepherd one of the sectors through the redevelopment process.

When I rode with him through Dharavi, he was constantly taking calls from people whose approval he needed for his plan. "I met with the CM [Maharastra state's Chief Minister] this morning," he told one caller. "He says we should wrap this up in eight days." He put his hand over the phone and turned to me. "It's total bullshit, of course," he whispered, rolling his eyes. "But this is what you have to do here to get things done."

But, as Mukesh moved through India's political circles, seeking support and financing, the plan kept getting more and more elaborate. By the time I left India, his simple plan to improve the life of slum-dwellers had become a luxury theme park. The poor, it seemed, the people he had set out to help, might get new housing, but most would have to move out of the community they had created and called home for decades.

When I last spoke with him, in late August 2003, Mukesh had just been to Delhi. "To brief the prime minister's people," he told me. The politicians, he said, were looking for something more grand. They were thinking of a new tourist attraction: a Bollywood Hall of Fame to honor the stars of India's film industry. And, he was also proposing a series of monuments to honor the builders who made Mumbai great: British and Indian investors who saw the possibilities of creating a great city on the string of soggy islands that front the Arabian Sea.

The mixed-income dream that seemed to central of Mukesh's vision when I first met him was quickly fading. Now, he suggested, he would use what is called salt pan land (coastal flood plain areas that have traditionally been off-limits to developers but that the government intends to free up for building) to relocate the poor. His idea now is that residents can stay in Dharavi if they want to pay 20,000 or 40,000 rupees (the equivalent of $500 to $1,000: a vast sum for most squatters). Or they could save the money and move for free to new housing on the remote salt pan lands.

"Even if only 30 percent of the people move, I can do this," he said. In early 2004, Mukesh got the go-ahead from the national government, which promised to put $100 million behind the plan. At the same time, the total cost of his Dharavi effort had ballooned to an estimated $1.5 billion. Later in the year, though, Indian voters dumped the conservative ruling party and thrust the more progressive Congress Party into power. It's not yet clear how this will impact Mukesh's scheme.

In any case, observers like Niranjan Hiranandani are not sure it can succeed. They point out that Mukesh still has not convinced any other developers to join him in working on the "dirty dozen." And without that, his plan to renovate Dharavi in a big bang could be in jeopardy. "I don't think he has the internal capacity to do it," Hiranandani told me. Recent articles, however, have suggested that Hiranandani would be willing to bid on the deal if it seems to be politically wired.

What's more, Mukesh may underestimate the power of small businesses, which need the unregulated, illegal space to maintain their modest profit margins. Mukesh says he will provide replacement space: additional buildings that will contain small factory or loft spaces. He insists that most Dharavi businesses don't need the slum to operate.

But Sunder, who supports Mukesh's plan, is more realistic about the fate of Dharavi's 10,000 small businesses.

"When the slum gets redeveloped, small-scale businesses will decrease," he said. "The small-scale businesses will transfer from this area. Things will be more expensive. Mostly, the small-scale businesses here don't have licenses, never have to pay taxes. To locate in a redeveloped building, they will have to pay taxes. They will have to follow all the duties and regulations of the government. Many will have to go to other slum areas."

Sunder doesn't think the businesses will actively oppose the luxury rehabilitation scheme, in part because many of the business owners are actually quite wealthy and would stand to benefit if they bought into the plan.

And, as developer Hiranandani notes, the rest of the local opposition could simply be swatted away. "You're bound to get some people who will come in the way," Hiranandani says. "But that's part of the game."

Back on the streets, however, few in Dharavi had focused on the plan. It is a ferociously busy place, and most residents are hard-working people, which means that their days are made up of working, eating, and sleeping. They don't have time to sit around and consider the ramifications of this or that political action. They must work. If their jobs move, they will move, too. They will follow the work wherever they need to go.

As in Kenya, Mumbai's slums are also in part a product of British influence. Mixing of Asians and Europeans was frowned upon during the 300 years of British control of the country. Low-income people who flocked to the city to work in factories were housed in what are called *chawls*: apartment blocks where each family had one small room that functioned as kitchen, bedroom, and living area. Major firms would build *chawls* near their factory compounds.

But as migration to the city continued (the urban economy is much more vital than the rural), even the overstuffed *chawls* were not an option for new arrivals. And when the factories closed, as many of Mumbai's textile plants have over the past two decades, they often evicted their former employees. People set up their homes wherever they could, even on the sidewalks. Today in older areas like Byculla, and along the working waterfront in Sewri, you will find people who have lived for a generation in tiny wooden structures just 14 feet tall, built right on the sidewalks.

Squatters also took over many low-lying and undesirable areas. Even in luxurious Bandra, squatters have long occupied the marginal areas along the banks of Mahim Creek and on a marshy plain of sewage run-off that today is called Behrampada.

I never understood how tough and dehumanizing life can be for some of these squatters until I took the bus early one day, around 6 A.M. As we traveled down the access road alongside the Western Express Highway, I saw a dozen men lined up, squatting by a drainage ditch. They were spread out at various points along the ditch. I wondered what they were doing. Then I noticed the buckets.

I realized then that in a country of a billion people, in a city of 12 million, toilets are a major issue, perhaps even the most important issue. And not just because of the indignity of defecating in public. Living without toilets can be dangerous. People actually die because of the lack of toilets. Small boys who venture into fields to use them as toilets are sometimes swept away by the strong and sudden monsoon runoff. Death is a sad reality of life for those without proper plumbing.

Mumbai's middle class and wealthy—the true policymakers in the city—have always had a schizophrenic relationship with the squatters. Publicly, they deplore the unhygienic conditions and the sprawl. Their conversation is full of references to the horrible crime and the amount of parental neglect in the squatter settlements. But many of them hire squatters as maids or cooks or drivers or watchmen, or even to care for their kids. They pay pitiful wages, thus perpetuating the need for the squatter settlements. Laxmi Chinnoo, who lives in the railway cut sheltered by a road overpass, in one of those metaphysical line in the dirt homes, actually works for two families. One pays her 500 rupees a month, the other 300, giving her a total of less than $20 a month. With that she must feed her family and pay for her daughters to attend school. My single room in Sanjay Gandhi Nagar cost more than Laxmi earned.

As long as wages remain so low, squatters will remain. And, as more plans like Mukesh's go through, the new arrivals and the businesses that attract them will simply be forced farther out of town.

One of the sad realities of life in Mumbai's squatter communities, and, indeed, anywhere in the city, is the increasing tension between Hindus and Muslims. Ever since massive religious riots broke out in 1992, neighborhoods have become increasingly segregated.

In Malad, for instance, Sartaj Jaipuri told me that before 1992 people from his area used to be friendly with their neighbors up the hill in the mostly Hindu squatter community called Govind Nagar. But during the riots, he said, Hindus with rifles stood in Govind Nagar and shot down the hill at the defenseless Muslims in Squatter Colony. "Before 1992, Squatter Colony and Govind Nagar were united," he said. "Now we don't go up there and they don't come down. There is no more understanding or even relations between the communities."

While I was in Sanjay Gandhi Nagar, the only Muslim family moved out. They sublet their home and shifted to a mostly Muslim neighborhood a few minutes away because, they told me, they felt more comfortable there.

Out of the earshot of Muslims, many Hindus told me I had to understand the innate violence and fundamentalist tendencies of Muslims. For their part, when Hindus weren't around, many of my Muslim friends urged me to research what they claimed was a common Hindu rite: killing the wife when her husband passes away. (This practice, called *suttee*, existed in ancient times but has been against the law since 1829, and many Hindus dispute that it was ever a required religious rite.)

The divide is political as well. The most powerful politico in Mumbai is Balasaheb Thackeray, leader of the Shiv Sena, a Maharastrian nationalist party that preaches a kind of Hindu-first doctrine. Although I didn't get to see Thackeray, a friend set up an appointment with Madhukar Sirpotdar, one of the founding members of the Sena, at his office in Bandra East, just down the road from the notorious overcrowded wooden shanties of the Muslim-dominated squatter community of Behrampada.

"This city has become overcrowded," he complained. "People from Pakistan and from Bangladesh have poured into our country."

I wasn't attuned to the language of Indian politics, so I thought he was talking about refugees. It wasn't until the following day that I realized that he was talking about neighborhoods full of people like Sartaj Jaipuri: Indian citizens who are Muslim and have been living in the city for decades.

Although the Sena has supported providing new housing for many squatters, Sirpotdar said that that was a pragmatic solution to a problem that should have been dealt with long ago. "All the slums should have been demolished and the entire slum population should have been asked to go," he told me. "There is no place for them to stay here in the city. Unless the city implements this mercilessly this problem will never be gotten rid of. We don't say don't come to Mumbai. You are welcome here. But if you are going to construct free housing on land owned by the government, you are not welcome. You cannot go all over the United States and acquire land forcibly and construct illegal housing, can you? We say: Go purchase land and construct your house and enjoy your life."

Mumbai is the home of a man who has dedicated his life to building a movement of squatters. Jockin Arputham—known simply as Jockin—applies the tools of capitalism to a critique of capitalism. He sees savings as the salvation of the urban poor. He preaches the gospel of communal self-reliance, molded through mass mobilization, and tempered by thrift. You might label his ideology Mahatma Gandhi meets Saul Alinsky by way of Andrew Carnegie.

He works out of an office in what used to be a garage for the Byculla Municipal Infirmary, not far from the Mumbai Central train station. Byculla is both a wealthy community and a squatter community. Here, some families live in impressive apartment towers behind equally impressive walls, while an equal number live on the sidewalks, in worn out wooden sheds with no water, no toilets, and, in some cases, no electricity.

When I got there, at 5:30 P.M., there were already a few people waiting. By 8 P.M., when the Jockin arrived, there was a crowd in the alley.

A delicate man with thinning hair, a sparse gray mustache, and the suggestion of a Buddha belly beneath his button-down shirt, he sat barefoot on the floor behind a low table. The supplicants gathered around his desk. There were contractors who were building toilets in communities that have been without them for decades and wanted to be paid. There were desperate people who wanted to stave off eviction, hoping that a word from him would work wonders. There were those who didn't want to relocate, even though they were being promised new housing courtesy of the government. There was a foreign video crew, ready for an interview. There were members of an organization of women involved in a savings group who wanted to plan strategy.

All of them waited for a chance to sidle up to the desk for a consultation.

You might say he is the world's only squatter philosopher. Jockin is the head of the National Slum Dwellers Federation and Slum Dwellers International. Through both groups, he preaches a kind of feel-good organizing based on daily savings and holding inspirational meetings—toilet festivals and model housing exhibitions—designed to bring people together in a nonthreatening way to work on fundamental issues.

Savings is the key to his work. Each squatter community that joins the federation creates a savings association, and each family can join by contributing as little as a rupee (about 2 cents) a day. The pooled money will be returned to the community in the form of small business loans, or loans to pay for crises such as medical treatment. The loans generally carry an interest rate of 2 percent a month, or 24 percent a year, making them much cheaper than funds from an underground lender, who will often charge 60 percent a year or more. The statistics are impressive. In Byculla alone, one of 13 offices in the city, 20,000 families have been participating. If you combine savings and small loans, they have created an economic engine of 800,000 rupees (more than $17,000).

"Savings brings confidence to the people," Jockin said when it was my turn to slide toward his desk. "Through savings, we don't have to demand that the politicians improve living conditions or economic conditions or homes. We can do what we want to and achieve what we want to. Because of savings, you empower yourself."

In a sense, Jockin is developing a parallel government, one that, perhaps, when money and capacity meet, will be able to provide services that the government currently refuses to provide to squatter areas.

And there's a second benefit to organizing through savings: Before endorsing the savings strategy, when simply using pressure tactics, Jockin's organizing primarily involved men. Now that savings are the key organizing tool, women are integrally involved in the work. In India, as in Africa, they are the ones who worry about money, perhaps because they have the primary responsibility for feeding their families.

"We are seeking development at the bottom, not intellectual development," he said. "For this, you need three ingredients. Number one: information. Number two: finance. Number three: communication. Women provide all three." Then he listed the reasons why. "If you ask the women whose husband is having an affair, whose husband is drinking, they will vomit up information. They know everything about their communities. Second, there's a saying in Hindi that the well-dressed man will not have a penny in the pocket. The woman has finances. She has to look after the house, the kitchen, the kids. You shake a woman, the money will fall down. Now, communication. Who has the communication? The woman. Given a 24 hour time period, she will speak for 25 hours. When you have these three things, it's development. And we have these three in the women."

Using the savings strategy, Jockin said, his organization has reached around 2 million of the city's 6 million squatters. People like Raimath Shaik, who has been living on the sidewalks of Byculla for 35 years and who became a leader through the savings circle on her block. I accompanied Raimath as she made the rounds on Meghraj Sethi Marg. It was monsoon season and everything was damp. Some of the homes were sitting in large puddles on the road. Still, the houses were neat, each with small custom-made shelving units to hold the family's meager possessions off the ground. Raimath stopped to chat at every door, and, as her neighbors handed over a few crumpled rupees, she marked each deposit in a ledger.

"Twenty years ago we were uneducated," Raimath told me as we moved from family to family. "We didn't know anything about banks. We didn't know how to save. When we had money we spent it. Now we know what a bank is and we choose to save. Slowly, slowly we make improvements."

In 1985, Jockin hooked up with a nonprofit agency called the Society for the Promotion of Area Resource Centers (SPARC), which was working with pavement dwellers. With SPARC's fundraising expertise and his talent for organizing, Jockin has been able to establish savings groups in 23 other Indian cities, and has expanded his noncombative style of organizing to 11 other countries. SPARC regularly flies some of its savings circle leaders around the world to spread the gospel of savings. Raimath, for instance, who still lives in her hut on the pavement, told me that she has traveled to South Africa, Uganda, Kenya, and the United States, to promote the value of savings.

Jockin's feel-good methods have won him kudos in international circles. In 2000, he won the Ramon Magsaysay award for International Understanding (the award, honoring a former Philippine president, is given annually to "outstanding individuals and organizations working in Asia who manifest greatness of spirit in service to the peoples of Asia"), and his work is popular with the United Nations Human Settlements Programme.

But he wasn't always an advocate of such toned-down tactics. After emigrating from South India to Bombay in 1964, Jockin built his organization by being a firebrand. In the 1960s, Jockin mobilized children in his community to collect garbage and dump it in front of a nearby city office to dramatize unsanitary conditions. In 1974, to get the city to clean a public toilet near their community, he and his neighbors locked a municipal official in a latrine for 8 hours.

"When we started, it was only to demand services," he recalled. "It was all tactics and agitation. How to use your strategy in order to get the message across. You had to push the responsibility onto the administration. It was kind of a militant movement. We knew how to put on a demonstration. We knew how to stop things. We knew how to block the road. We knew how to close someone's office. This was our principal method. It was the only method we had."

But, Jockin argues, the hard-nosed tactics ultimately were unproductive. "After 10 or 15 years, you realize that you become more powerful and you get into the limelight," he said. "You become a recognized figure. It's good for you, but what does your community get out of this. Seventy percent of the time: nothing. No development, no improvements."

So, after he allied with SPARC, he dropped his confrontational tactics.

Jockin insists that the change set the stage for achievement. "We can make policy now," he said. "Today there is a clear right and a law that all pavement dwellers [people like Raimath, who built homes on the sidewalk] have a right to a house. Not just land, but a house. Today, government has a dialogue with the community. Today, we deliver services on our own." And, he added, he is working with the government of Uganda to create a humane housing policy for squatters in that African country.

Still, I had questions.

I wanted to ask Jockin whether he thought there was a difference between giving people experiences that are empowering and building towards true empowerment. After all, I'm sure that Raimath and the others who have traveled the globe feel better about themselves and have become wiser and more confident after their journeys. But I wondered whether the journeys alone were giving them the confidence to take on the fundamental questions that restrain squatters rights in India.

Also, I wondered about power inside the federation. Jockin has been the leader for three decades. And still he has no other squatter with whom to share the load. He is the policymaker, and the people who line up to see him in the Byculla office sometimes act with exaggerated respect, as if they are waiting to see an eminence, not a squatter like themselves. Indeed, the only experience I had in Mumbai that could match the way people treated Jockin was when I went to visit powerful politicians.

I put the question about the top-down style of organizing to Celine D'Cruz, one of the leaders of SPARC, who was about to join Jockin on a quick trip to South Africa to check on his group's operations there. I pointed out the similarity between the way people treat Jockin and the way people treat politicians.

"What you're saying has an element of truth to it," she acknowledged. "The point is to open up the space with the city to talk. And it is true that a few of us have mastered the art of translating poor communities to the outside world." But, she was quick to add, it was not something Jockin sought, rather it was thrust upon him as his influence grew.

It's likely that Jockin's early street-fighter style intimidated many people. His current nonconfrontational method no doubt soothes those fears, and it clearly has gotten results (although the fact that squatters have become a massive voting block may also explain why politicians are paying attention). And it's clearly why the United Nations and other world nonprofits are comfortable with his work: it involves no threat to local or national governments. Instead of promoting political action, Jockin preaches the gospel of savings and ignores the corrupt political structure. In Kenya, this approach winds up being a kind of joke. A Kenyan friend allied with Jockin's program confided that it was incredibly difficult to convince his neighbors to join any savings program. People in his neighborhood distrust savings, he said, because they fear that someone will run away with the money. And when all actions regarding their communities involve payoffs, they are suspicious of a program that seems to buy into the system.

The last time I saw Jockin, I started to lay out my questions. If his federation really reaches 2 million squatters in Mumbai, I suggested, then squatters should have the power to run their communities.

Jockin had been idly examining a blueprint on his desk. Now he glared at me over his lightly tinted bifocals. "Are you making a statement or asking a question?" he said.

I backed off. "Asking," I said.

He replied with a lecture: "This is the only state [in India] with a slum rehabilitation policy. This is the only state where pavement dwellers have rights. And why do you think this has happened? It is a direct result of our work. We very strongly believe that the problems of the urban poor can be solved by the urban poor, not by anybody else. People always see the change agents as the intellectuals. I don't agree with that. The urban poor will be the change agents of the city."

I agreed with him, but wanted to engage in a more detailed discussion. Jockin has won some important victories. But true stability and control—the kind of political and social stability that squatters in Rio and Istanbul have won—still seems elusive. Given that Jockin has been organizing for almost 40 years, I wondered if he would agree with my assessment, and what he believed was the impediment to full-scale rights.

But perhaps I wasn't sufficiently deferential, because Jockin was clearly miffed by my attitude. "Oh, you want to do a real interview," he said, and quickly ended our conversation. Pointing to the people waiting outside his office, he said, "Let us take a break now so I can do my volunteer work."

Then he turned back to the crowd, to the people he is most comfortable with, the people waiting patiently, the people who need, who will always need, his help.

Although Jockin's group has the highest profile, his is not the only organization in the city to preach the value of savings. In fact, women in squatter colonies all over Mumbai have savings programs. A number of them are organized through the Navjeet Community Center at Holy Name Hospital in Bandra. Here, nuns and lay workers act as community organizers, convening the women and working with them to create meaningful changes in their communities.

In Behrampada, a warren of tight alleys above what use to be a sewage outflow just east of the Bandra railway station, Navjeet has helped organize several women's groups—called *mandals*—in the mostly Muslim community. In addition to savings, the women have created a kind of alternative dispute resolution system. They meet once or twice a week to "take cases," as they call it. In most instances, a family must pay 250 rupees to register a case with the group. The women hear evidence—everything is painstakingly recorded in longhand in thick old-fashioned ledger books—render decisions, and, if need be, visit the interested parties to attempt to enforce their rulings.

At one such meeting, 20 women from a group were stuffed into a tiny room on the second floor of a small building next to an abandoned railroad spur east of Bandra station. They sat silently in a circle around a thin woman with deepset eyes, who was wrapped head to foot in a gold print sari and matching shawl. The woman said her husband had thrown her and her four children out of the house a year ago, and calls the neighbors to beat her if she tries to return. She was seeking a divorce plus the return of the house (which was a gift from her relatives) and the dowry her family paid: 15,000 rupees plus a ceiling fan and a kitchen mixer. The woman's father, the only other man present besides me and my translator, squatted just outside the circle of women.

"Women's rights exist in Muslim personal law, but men don't want to follow them," explained Khatoon Gafoor Shaik, who heads the group. "The men want the right to marry four women at a time, but they don't want to give women their rights."

After hearing the young woman's tale, the group decided to visit her husband the following day to explain the charge she has made and to get his side of events.

Hoorbano Ziaee, a particularly vocal member of the *mandal*, explained that the group exists because all the members have experienced similar problems. Most of their marriages, she noted, were arranged by their parents. Hoorbano was married for four years before being thrown out of the house by her mother-in-law. That was two years ago, when her child was just six months old. Although clearly angry, she is working with the *mandal* to achieve a negotiated settlement. "I'm ready to stay, if he accepts me," she said. But, she admitted, it's really for her child's sake that she's seeking a rap-prochement. "I'm ready to stay because of my kid. Without my kid, I would say: 'Enough. Forget about you.'"

The church-based organizers have been trying to get the women to consider taking a stand to end the ancient tradition of dowries. But many of the women say one of the reasons they join the savings scheme is to be able to take out a loan to pay the dowry when their daughters reach marrying age. Even Hoorbano, who is quite outspo-ken, was mum about the dowry system. She understood the problem, she said, but did not see any other way to organize marriages.

Behrampada itself is an interesting area. It grew in extreme poverty, on what was a drainage pool. Razi Allaudin Sheik, who has lived in the community for 40 years, remembers when it was still a fetid pool surrounded by 800 homes. "There was no need to have a toilet," she said. "You just threw everything outside your door. Underneath were rats and dogs and flies. And on top of them we lived." Strangely, despite the sorry conditions in which the commu-nity grew, Behrampada residents have always paid ground rent to the city. The payment started at 5 rupees a month and is up to 20 today. Behrampada has improved, and most homes now have water and electricity. But the construction has not changed much from those early times. After four decades of monsoons, Razi Allaudin Sheik's house is a bit waterlogged. She used to rent out her second floor, at 1,500 rupees a month. But the wood has become weak now, so she and her husband had to empty the unit. Her new plan is to take 10,000 rupees as a deposit and use the money to fix the structural deficiencies.

Financial need. Waterlogged wood. Monsoon mud. A constant battle with bugs and disease. Despite all this, Mumbai's squatters endure—and even flourish.

One evening during the final month I was in Mumbai, I was invited to appear on New Delhi Television, a 24-hour cable news channel. I would be interviewed live on the 11 o'clock news. When our segment began, the anchorman asked whether squatter communities—slums in Indian parlance—had become a city within the city. I agreed that they were so prevalent within Mumbai that they did seem to constitute a sort of separate city. But as soon as the interview ended, I kicked myself. I had missed my best response. In a city that is more than 50 percent squatters, it is not the squatters who are the city within the city. Rather, the middle class and wealthy neighborhoods constitute the small, separatist enclave. The well-off are the city within the city. The squatters are the majority, so they are the city. When they fully understand that, politics and policies will change for the better.

CHAPTER 4

Istanbul

The Promise of Squatter Self-Government

You don't need to choose freedom — you are free. This freedom, it's a sorry thing under the stars.

— Nazim Hikmet

It was not yet a town when they seized the property. It was just a field full of weeds and snakes, land you wouldn't notice, treasury land, owned by the federal government, way out on the Asian side of Istanbul, almost as far as you can get from the historic city of the Sultans and still be within the city limits. This was where they decided to make their stand. They waited until nightfall, then seized the land and built their homes.

The authorities caught them and tore the buildings down.

So they waited, bought new materials, and took again the land.

Once more the police descended.

They had no homes. They were living in makeshift tents, in mud. They were desperate. But they learned. The third time, they made friends with someone who knew some city officials (perhaps some money even changed hands) and, finally, their homes lasted through the night. By morning, they had become official gecekondu residents (the word is a combination of *gece*, "night" in Turkish, plus *kondurmak*, meaning "to happen" or "appear").

Ulter Kaya, who told me this story, crouched in the meager shade of a parched tree outside the house that she and her husband built in 1987, and served glasses of homemade *ayran*, a salty yogurt-like drink. Her brother-in-law, Hussein Baykara, who was part of the initial invasion, joined the conversation. "We would just finish it and they would knock it down. Always we had just put on the doors or the roof. It was frustrating."

They survived that first night only to find that every day was a struggle. They had no water, no electricity, no sewers. It would have been easy to have no hope. But this was where they put down roots. This was where they raised their families. This was where they finally made the city their own.

They hauled water from a well. They stole electricity from the poles that ran to the factories farther out of town. They grew their own food. They bought milk from one woman who lived nearby and owned a cow.

They lived illegally on this obscure pasture in the big city for five years. Then a politician arrived with a promise: he said he would provide each of the two dozen families in their enclave with *tapu*: a title deed.

Had the municipality that initially knocked down their homes changed its mind?

Not exactly.

Fikret Şahin (the Ş in Turkish is pronounced "Sh") was the politician who promised them *tapu*. A wiry man with limp, graying hair whose soft voice belies his toughness, he had been living in the area called Sarıgazi since 1977 and was a teacher and administrator at the local school. When he arrived from the town of Tunceli, Sarıgazi (pronounced Sar-uh-gah-zee) was hardly a hamlet: just a collection of a few dozen houses in the fields around a dusty intersection. But as he educated the local kids and watched the community grow, he had an idea.

His move into politics was smart. He had a natural constituency: the hundreds of Sarıgazi kids he had educated, who had stayed in the community after becoming adults. But Sahin also had a vision.

Under Turkish law, communities with at least 2,000 residents can organize and apply to the federal government for approval to organize as a quasi-independent municipality. Communities can register as an *ilçe* (district) or *belediye* (municipality.) The technical requirements are different, but the result is the same: control over some aspects of land-use planning and the ability to collect revenues and start government services. In a giant city like Istanbul, every resident is actually a citizen of two elected governments: the *büyük şehir*, or "big city," and the *belediye*. Every resident has two mayors: one from the big city and one from the small.

Fikret Şahin's plan was to found a new municipality. He pushed for support and, in 1992, won approval from the federal government to establish Sarıgazi as a *belediye*. He was the town's first and, until 2004, when he lost an election for the first time, its only mayor.

Once Sarıgazi won its quasi-independence, Şahin tried to wriggle out of his campaign promise. "If I were mayor when they invaded," he told me, "I wouldn't have let them build. I was planning to replace these little huts with five-story buildings."

But the squatters spurned the offer. They had voted for Sahin because he had promised them title deeds, and they were determined to get their piece of turf. What's more, they didn't like the idea of living in an apartment block. "We wanted our field," Ulter Kaya explained.

Şahin ultimately relented, and today Ulter Kaya and her neighbors own their self-built homes and the land they are on. The price for a 225 square meter lot was about 115 million Turkish lira, $72 at today's exchange rate, but equal to around $2,600 in the early 1990s. "At the time it was a small fortune," Ulter Kaya said. Given that the average Turk today may earn around $100 a month, it was almost impossible for Ulter Kaya or her neighbors to find this kind of money. So the mayor came up with another plan to help his constituents. He borrowed funds from his political party (the Social Democratic Party) and used the money to purchase the land from the federal government. The squatters must repay the town, and the town in turn reimburses the party. So everyone was happy. The people were happy to get title deeds, the town was happy because it had a more stable population, and the party was happy because it had a dedicated voting block in Sarıgazi.

The mayor still has mixed feelings about his role in legalizing the squatters. He doesn't want his action to spur more invaders to come to Sarıgazi looking for land. Indeed, to guard against further gecekondu outbreaks in his area, Şahin has designated all the remaining large vacant parcels in the community for parks or schools. "That way people are more apt to leave them alone and not settle there," he said.

To find the old-fashioned gecekondu communities, you must leave the central city and head for the fringes. And even there, you have to walk quite a distance from the main roads to find them. You'll see them behind a bigger development, perhaps, or hidden in a gully near a bend in a side street. You'll know you've found them when you see houses that seem to hug the ground, trying to be as unobtrusive as possible. Sometimes they even disappear below grade, and you will simply see the peak of a roof peeking over the horizon.

These homes are built to take advantage of the Turkish law I described earlier in this book: if you are already moved into your house and the structure is sound, you cannot be evicted without due process of law (i.e., being taken to court). To make the most of the law, the original invaders built quickly: they constructed one-story houses using the most easily available materials around: quick-drying plaster and concrete. Often the roofs are little more than corrugated plastic sheets placed over a wood frame: not much, structurally, but enough to repel snow and rain. To keep the houses snug and to prevent leaks, the roof sheets hang out 2 or 3 feet beyond the walls, giving the houses a drooping, gingerbread appearance. Over time, some people have put insulation over the plastic roof sheets and covered that with ceramic or terra-cotta tile.

They seem like summer cottages, these rustic dwellings. They are built in that style, each alone centered on its property, with just enough room on either side for little garden plots. Even when the old buildings are torn down and people erect bigger ones, the style is the same: detached houses with space in the front for parking.

At one community I visited, in Emek Mahallesi ("Labor Neighborhood") the families were outside, the kids playing soccer on the dusty gravel road, the elders sitting on plastic chairs or packing crates or simply on improvised benches made of boards set on rocks. They smoked, swapped stories, shared tea. The old-fashioned buildings had pitched roofs. But a few residents had framed out houses with low flat concrete roofs, which made them hold the heat. It's cooler in the sun, they said, because our houses get very hot in the summer. So we sat outside.

Selvi Kaynak plucked a few apples from the tree in front of her door.

The older folks turned down the apples: they said their teeth were too weak from years of sugary tea. Selvi's 4-year-old son Mert declined, too. He was holding out for cookies. But the rest of us partook. The apples were small and green and crunchy and tart. Truly the fruit of knowledge.

The apple tree, Selvi said, grew on its own: someone must have tossed a core on the ground and it sprouted. But the rest of the garden she had planted herself: beans, tomatoes, corn, squash. Her house had tremendous privacy, for she had left a border of scrubby trees between her and her neighbors. The sun was soft in her yard, the rays filtered through the leaves. She had a few plastic barrels of water placed in the direct sunlight, so her family would have warm water for bathing that evening.

As darkness fell, Selvi and Mert heard rustling in the garden. Mert ran to inspect. A porcupine, he shouted. Two of them, in fact. They were tucked into tiny balls, their small snouts and round red eyes peeking out over quivering quills.

"The meat is very good," Selvi said. "It's *halal* [the Muslim equivalent of kosher] and also very medicinal. Good for problems with the joints. Good for rheumatism."

They let the porcupines alone.

It was an idyllic moment, if you didn't take in the surroundings. Eighteen-wheelers rumbled past one side of the house. On the other, a noisy factory forklift moved back and forth and workers hammered endlessly, breaking up wooden pallets.

As we munched the apples, Selvi told the history of her home.

The plot is 130 square meters. She bought the land a dozen years ago from a man who lived nearby for 3 million Turkish lira (about $80 at the time). Selvi understood that this purchase didn't mean she actually bought the land. She knew the piece of paper he gave her was worthless. She knew that he didn't really own the property, and therefore neither did she. But he was part of a land mafia and had taken control of the parcel. He would have ratted her out to the authorities without the payment. So she paid. About a dozen other families did the same thing. Her brother built the house—a single-story plaster and wood dwelling—then turned it over to her.

In those early years, Selvi and her neighbors had to take a wheelbarrow and some plastic drums to a Nestlé plant a bit more than a kilometer away to get water. The neighbors strung their own wires, looped from house to house, and stole electricity from poles on a nearby street that led to other factories. And they dug a pit between Selvi and her neighbor, where they placed a large plastic tank that functioned as their sewage system. When it got full, they pooled their money and hired a company to come and empty it.

After two years, the municipality began trucking in fresh water every week, and they would fill large plastic drums that would last them a week. Two years after that, Şahin's administration got the big city to bring water and sewage lines to the community. Electricity is now legal, too, although one of Selvi's elderly neighbors couldn't afford the bill and is again living without lights. Like Ulter Kaya, Selvi and her neighbors have purchased their title deeds, also courtesy of Fikret Şahin. Selvi paid 2 billion lira (about $1,250.) But her factory job brings in just 150 million lira a month (a little less than $100), which must support herself, her mother, and her son. So she had to get help to acquire the *tapu*. Initially, the mayor refused to accept the idea of giving Selvi and her neighbors loans, because he knew they would take a long time to pay them back. But ultimately he had no choice, because the people did not have the money to pay all at once. So Şahin gave her a billion from the municipal loan program and she got another billion from a friendly uncle. She pays 30 million lira to her uncle every month, although he is pressuring her to increase her payments dramatically because he is planning a pilgrimage to Mecca and needs the money. She has yet to pay anything on the loan from Mayor Şahin.

Selvi showed me how her finances work. After paying the loans plus food, utilities, household expenses, bus fare, and cigarettes (a very important expense to most Turks), if she resists all other temptations she can save about 10 million lira a month (about $6.25). Some of her neighbors make extra money by having their kids do some work at home. They have arranged with local factories for the kids to piece together small metal clips: the kind you might find on backpacks or dog leashes. They get 300,000 Turkish lira for every kilo of clips they finish. But Mert is too young and undisciplined to be doing this, and, besides, Selvi said, a child shouldn't be forced to work.

The economic scorecard also shows two things Selvi doesn't say. First, without squatting she would either be homeless or hungry.

Rents in Sarıgazi and other outlying neighborhoods are around 100 million lira a month. That would be two-thirds of Selvi's income, and at that cost she would not have enough money to feed her family.

And second, she'd be better off if she had remained a squatter and had not been forced to buy her *tapu*. Without that expense, she'd have 30 million lira more every month for food and expenses. And she wouldn't have her uncle breathing down her neck and Mayor Şahin complaining that she hadn't paid him back. Without the expense for the title deed, Selvi would have the ability to save more than $6.25 a month, which would enable her to improve her house and plan for the future.

There are no longer many squatter neighborhoods in Istanbul that look like Ulter Kaya's or Selvi Kaynak's. Theirs are throwbacks, reminders of how things used to be.

Today's squatter communities are, at least from an architectural point of view, almost indistinguishable from the legal neighborhoods of the city.

Sultanbeyli is a perfect example. This is a squatter community that seems determined to defy all the stereotypes. It is a sprawling city of apartment houses. Its downtown area is full of big buildings and stores. It even has a seven-story squatter city hall, with an elevator and a fountain in the lobby.

The town touts its growth: 150 major avenues, 1,200 streets, 30,000 houses, 15 neighborhoods, 300,000 people, 91 mosques, 22 schools, 48,000 students. The local government had prevailed upon the *büyükşehir* government to help it out. ISKI, the city's water authority, has invested more than 143 trillion Turkish lira (almost $90 million) to pipe in water to every home. In 2002, two-thirds of the city's neighborhoods had water available to every house. Streets in the remaining five neighborhoods were already being ripped open so the massive water mains could be installed. (to hook up to the water, each house owner needs to pay a one-time fee of $160 and accept a meter). Sultanbeyli is even installing gas pipes, which is quite unusual, because in most neighborhoods of Istanbul, even many legal ones, people run their stoves on bottled gas. In fact, one of the trademark sounds of the city is the familiar recorded jingle of the Aygaz truck (reminiscent of the tunes played by soft ice cream vendors in the United States) as it makes the rounds to deliver the bulbous containers to people's doors.

"In the 1970s, Sultanbeyli was just a village," said Mustafa Karataş, the city's communications chief. "People used to do farming here. People had cows and sold milk. They worked the forest and sold lumber."

When Mayor Yahya Karakaya came to Sultanbeyli, in 1969, it was a tiny town. As a child he remembers that there was one bus

Fatih Boulevard, downtown Sultanbeyli.

that left early every morning to bring workers to the port at Kadikoy. If you missed that one bus you had to walk, or hitch a ride with a farmer, which would take hours. Today, his city runs its own buses to Kadiköy, and the *büyük şehir* also has several bus routes that terminate at the far reaches of Sultanbeyli. These buses are packed almost all the time. The mayor smiled. "I grew up and Sultanbeyli grew up," he said.

Sultanbeyli boomed in the mid 1980s, when the Turkish economy stagnated and many rural residents were forced to leave their ancestral villages and trek to the city to seek work. At the same time, a highway that runs through the middle of Sultanbeyli finally opened. The opening of the highway made Sultanbeyli suddenly desirable turf: between 1986 and 1989, people erected 20,000 houses within the city limits. The local government collected a fee from each family that built a house.

Over the years, central Sultanbeyli became a true downtown. Here, along Fatih Boulevard, is a line of impressive buildings housing impressive businesses: banks, travel agents, money exchange shops (with particularly good rates on euros and bad rates on dollars), jewelers, car dealers, Internet cafés, department stores, restaurants, and a post office. There are even real estate offices that specialize in selling these titleless properties.

I had been warned about Sultanbeyli before arriving in Istanbul. People told me to watch out, that it is strange, separatist, dangerous. They told me that it is *kuyu Musselman* ("deep or dark Muslim"), a reference to the black shrouds many observant women wear. One report denounced the squatter city for having more mosques than schools. This may be true but, in my experience, it is also normal: Most outlying communities are like this because each wave of new arrivals wants its own mosque in order to complete a sense of arrival and identity.

It certainly is true that Sultanbeyli has many devout Muslims. Walking downtown on Fatih Boulevard, you can see scores of women wearing the *çarsaf* (the black robe that is traditional for a true believer) and *peçe*—the head scarf that is wrapped to cover everything but the eyes. And it is true that the political leadership of Sultanbeyli has always come from the bewildering array of fundamentalist parties that seem to change their names every time one of them is outlawed: first Refah, then Fazilet, and now Saadet.

But that is not all there is to Sultanbeyli.

Savaş Karamanoğlu (the ğ is silent, thus: "Kah-rah-mon-oh-lou"), a college student who grew up in Sultanbeyli and still lives there with his parents, says that the image of Sultanbeyli as a fundamentalist stronghold ignores the reality. "Sultanbeyli is a mirror for Turkey," Savaş told me, because people from every region have migrated there. Savaş told me he would rather live in a fancy neighborhood like Kadiköy because it's more fun and closer to his girlfriend. Nonetheless, he thinks the fundamentalists are honest and have made great improvements in life and infrastructure in Sultanbeyli. This, not zealotry, he argued, is the reason the religious parties continue to win elections. Anyway, he pointed out, Mayor Karakaya, while still representing a fundamentalist party, unseated a man who wanted the city to adhere to a much stricter Islamic code, but seemed personally corrupt. People, even the very devout, grew tired of the former mayor's corrupt land dealings and did not hesitate to remove him from office.

I spent quite a bit of time hiking the hilly neighborhoods of Sultanbeyli and never encountered any of the hesitation or hostility that outsiders predicted. In fact, people were amazingly open. For

A new squatter mosque in Akşemsettin with its
sheet metal minaret.

instance, I was walking up Selcukhan Street to the crest of the hill
that marks the beginning of the new Battalgazi neighborhood when
some residents waved me over. Cemal, who used to run a small garment manufacturing business but now works as a cook at City Hall,
stepped into the shade of his vacant storefront and pulled out a
small round watermelon. He sent his young son to grab a knife from
the kitchen, and then sliced the ripe melon for me and another visi-
tor. As he handed me a slice, he thanked me for coming to
Sultanbeyli. "Many people write things about us without ever having been here," he said. "You have to meet people to know people."

Zamanhan Ablak came to Sultanbeyli in 1995, buying 300
square meters of land and building a home in the Akşemsettin
neighborhood. He and his neighbors didn't wait for the *belediye* to
get around to helping them. They chipped in their own money to
pay for their services. Each household contributed money towards

sewers (200 million Turkish lira), schools (310 million), and a local mosque (65 million).

Yet, he complained, Akşemsettin residents now are forced to pay taxes to the municipality. "For what, I ask," he said. "And if we don't pay we get a big fine." What's more, before he was allowed to build his house, he had to pay 6,000 deutsche marks (about $4,500, paid in German currency because many Turks were returning from stints as guest workers in Germany and the mark held its value while the Turkish lira was losing value rapidly) to get a *ruhsat* (a document that gives municipal planning department permission). But he didn't call it a *ruhsat*. He called it a *rusvet*: a bribe. "It's the same thing," he explained. "Ruhsat, rusvet, what's the difference?" Zamanhan is also upset that it costs 260 million lira to hook his house to the new water main. So far, he had refused to pay the fee. So, although the home he built has full bathrooms and showers inside, his building still does not have water. He shook his head. "I love you Akşemsettin. I no love you Sultanbeyli."

Zamanhan was a hothead and a polemicist. He grew up in a small town in the mountainous region of Turkey that borders Iraq. He told me this town no longer existed. It had been destroyed by the Turkish army in one of their periodic crackdowns on the radical movement known as the PKK: the Kurdish Separatist Party. Now his family lives in another nearby town called Yuksekova. Zamanhan told me that when he was young Turkish soldiers made him and other Kurdish kids lie down in a local river so that the soldiers could cross on their backs and not get their boots wet.

He wanted me to come with him some time, to visit his beloved Kurdistan. The Kurdish region was said to be dangerous, so I asked some other Turkish friends whether they thought I ought to go.

"Kurdistan?" they asked. "Where's that? Are you talking about the southeastern region of Turkey?"

What's in a name? Everything, apparently. To Zamanhan and his fellow separatists, Kurdistan is their nation. To the rest of the Turks, Kurdistan is the destruction of their nation.

When Zamanhan wanted to talk Kurdish politics, he whispered. Sometimes he would teach me Kurdish words. Innocuous phrases, innocent words. *Tu çanni? Navete çiye? Tue koda hari? Sipas.* How are you? What is your name? Where are you going? Thank you. But they were also liberating words, because the Kurdish language had been outlawed by the Turkish government. You could go to jail for saying one simple word. Now Turkey wants to join the European Union, and so it has liberalized a bit and no longer imprisons people just for whispering in Kurdish. But still the Kurds are furtive. They worry they can still get in trouble, particularly if, like Zamanhan, they are leftists.

Zamanhan spoke a bit of English because he had attended what Turkey calls tourism high school. I spoke half-wit Turkish. For the most part, the way we communicated was by pointing at words in my *minisözlügü*: my "little dictionary."

His name was Zamanhan Ablak. It's a strange and poetic name. *Zamanhan* is a beautiful term that, loosely translated, means "time and place." *Ablak* is a nasty word that means "chubby, ugly face." Zamanhan would never tell me whether it was his real name or an assumed one.

Zamanhan worked as a waiter in his cousin's kebab restaurant. But that wasn't his identity. What he was, mostly, was a committed but failed revolutionary. He had trained as a revolutionary, learning how to shoot a gun, how to engage in guerrilla warfare, how to be a terrorist. A dozen years ago, he had been in a shoot-out with police, had been wounded, taking two bullets—one in the leg, one in the side—and had spent four years in jail.

Still, Zamanhan liked one thing more than radical politics: freedom. So, he assured me, he was done with violence. He supported the PKK and its struggle to create an independent Kurdish nation. But he was not willing to engage in revolutionary action. He did not want to go back to jail. Four years had taught him that much.

When he got out of jail, Zamanhan came to Istanbul to start over, because there was nothing left for him at home. He came to the most conservative place in the whole city: Sultanbeyli. Zamanhan's neighborhood, Akşemsettin, is a relatively new part of Sultanbeyli and it is like a Kurdish homeland. Ninety percent of Akşemsettin is Kurdish. There, the more secular Kurds have managed to coexist with the conservative forces of the city. In Akşemsettin, there are fewer mosques (although there are mosques) and the community even boasts a few stores that sell liquor (alcohol is prohibited in most other areas of Sultanbeyli.) Zamanhan went there because some relatives were there already and also because, as a squatter area, it was easy to get a piece of land. Perhaps he also went there because Sultanbeyli is a good place for a radical to disappear.

Zamanhan took special pleasure in baiting Turks. Turkey was consumed by World Cup football fever when I was there. For two weeks, the national soccer team was the only story on the front pages of the newspapers. One of the Turkish team's players had a mohawk haircut, and by the end of Turkey's World Cup run, several of the kids who lived near me in Sarıgazi were sporting the same cuts.

Turkey was doing well. It had a quarter-final match with the unlikely, fairytale team of the match: Senegal. Game day was like a holiday. Trucks festooned with Turkish flags rode around neighbohoods all over the city. The news was full of the pictures: scores of people jumping up and down, waving flags and chanting: *Turkiye! Turkiye! Turkiye!*

Zamanhan responded by buying a Senegalese flag. Whenever a carload of football fanatics drove by the restaurant where he worked shouting their patriotic slogans, he would charge out into the street with his Senegalese banner and shout back at them.

Zamanhan was one of the few people I met in Turkey's squatter areas who enjoyed reading and was familiar with works beyond popular literature. He read socially concerned novels and had pored through many iconic Communist texts. One day, when we were discussing how contemporary entertainers seldom risked making

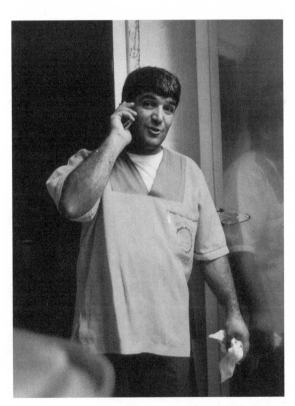

Zamanhan Ablak: "I very working."

major political statements, he told me he knew of at least one important American singer who had not been afraid to be political: Paul
Robeson.

Zamanhan didn't like killing, but he thought the Kurdish effort
(in which radicals not only battle the Turks but also kill fellow Kurds
who are seen as collaborators) was not only justified but also necessary. "There is good violence and bad violence," he said. "APO violence" (this referred to Kurdish radical leader Abdullah Ocalan, who
is serving a life sentence in Turkish prison) "is good violence."

In between his waiting on tables—"I very working," Zamanhan
told me, apologetically—we had many arguments about political
ideology. Passing the dictionary back and forth, we debated radical
theories. One day, not long before I had to leave Turkey, Zamanhan
summed up his position. He ticked off his comments on his fingers.
"Marx idealist. Lenin fascist. But Engels." He stopped to kiss his fingers. "I love you, Engels."

Although a suburb of Istanbul, Sultanbeyli is actually outside the
legal city limits. It is an independent city, becoming a *belediye* in
1989 and an *ilçe* in 1992. But Sultanbeyli does not desire to be independent any longer. In 1995, it applied to become part of the *büyük
şehir* of Istanbul. This shows that Sultanbeyli is interested in joining
the wider world. The big city government agreed. But the deal was
rejected by the federal ministry of Internal Affairs. "For political
reasons," charged Sultanbeyli press representative Mustafa
Karataş. He said the national government—at the time run by the
secular rightwinger Tansu Çiller—didn't want to do any favors for
the fundamentalist parties that govern Istanbul. Things may
change now that R. Tayyip Erdoğan, who was mayor of the *büyük
şehir* of Istanbul when the merger with Sultanbeyli was negotiated

and at the time was a member of one of Turkey's fundamentalist parties, has become Turkey's prime minister.

Karataş conceded that joining the big city would infringe on the power of Mayor Karakaya and the Sultanbeyli administration. Yet, he said, "We would still like to do it. It has both advantages and disadvantages. They have very rigid rules regarding construction and they would take about 30 percent of our tax levy. But in exchange for that, they would make all repairs to the infrastructure. So in that sense life will be better."

The next step for Sultanbeyli, both Karataş and his boss, Mayor Karakaya, declared, is to provide *tapuler* ("title deeds") to its residents. Perhaps 70 percent of the land in Sultanbeyli is held under what is called *hisseli tapu*, or "shared title." *Hisseli tapu*, Mustafa Karataş explained, is a very complex phenomenon. "There might be thousands of shares," he told me. "It's not even certain how many square meters is one share. And even if you had one share, you could have built on five." Many share owners do not live in Sultanbeyli, and most probably do not even know their names are written on the deeds. The city is currently working in two directions. First, it is mapping all the lots within its boundaries so that it has a record of all the buildings and property lines in town. The survey alone, the mayor told me, will cost a trillion Turkish lira (about $625,000) and this will have to be funded by the taxpayers. Then the city must research who has paid what for the right to the land. Ultimately it will try to buy out the *hisseli* owners and resell the land to the current occupants.

Karataş believes that having true private ownership in Sultanbeyli will be unbelievably positive. "The people will have many opportunities. Like if you want to get a credit card, you will be able to show you have an asset. People will be able to leave their house to their kids and return home to their village. And it will never be lost. No one will be able to dispute your title, because the municipality will have a record of it."

Of course, all these things are possible without title deeds, if people develop legal instruments like the ones Jorge showed me in Brazil. Indeed, they already have similar items. Most property transactions are already registered with the local *muhtar* (elected official of each neighborhood within a *belediye* who is part executive officer and part justice of the peace). And banks, which are already located in Sultanbeyli, can be convinced to give credit cards on the basis of that legal possession.

What's more, it's likely that converting to *ifrazli tapu* would set off a frenzy of speculation in Sultanbeyli. People will have to pay to get their *tapus* (Karataş admitted that the price could be between 1.5 and 2 billion Turkish lira—about $1,200—for the average house, payable in installments) and that will put them in debt, which is the same problem Selvi Kaynak faces in nearby Sarıgazi. If this happens, people might ultimately have to sell their homes to pay off their debt. Illegal ownership, while perhaps legally precarious, is safer for poor people because they don't have to go into debt to create their houses. They build what they can afford, and when they can afford it. Zamanhan, who stays without city water because he cannot afford the fee to get a water hookup, would not be likely to fork out a major amount to purchase his *tapu*.

Nonetheless, Karataş and Karakaya insisted that the municipality would work out good payment terms and people would willingly line up to buy.

And what if the *hisseli* owners refused to sell? Mayor Karakaya had a good answer for this. As a politician, he understands that the city has a good bargaining position. "The owners don't have much choice, do they?" he said. "After all, who else will buy it?" Of course, if the news gets out that Sultanbeyli is planning to become a privately owned area, a speculator who decided to buy up some of these shared interests could force the municipality to pay more and thus make a good profit.

The gecekondu neighborhoods owe their existence, in part, to Turkey's history as the center of the Ottoman Empire. The Ottomans, the superpower of their day (and a long day it was, lasting from the 13th century to the early 20th century), had a very different notion of land ownership than Europe does today. Essentially, all land was property of the Sultan. A favored few received imperial grants of land. But that designation wasn't ownership as we know it. The Sultan granted only the right to collect rents from the land. In return, the Sultan expected landholders to supply soldiers for the military. The holder of the this kind of title could sell the designation or pass it on to his heirs, but the right to the land was always revocable on the Sultan's whim. Tenancy, by contrast, had more protections, and a small farmer could pass his lease on to his children without fear of it being expropriated by the Sultan.

Ottoman land law protected the use of land, not control over the commodity value of land. As late as 1858, the empire's law gave citizens the right to seize vacant parcels owned by the government, as long as the appropriators were willing to use the property—to give it some function. The laws regarding land were designed to keep farmers farming, soldiers fighting, and the empire growing.

By the second half of the 19th century, however, military reversals and palace intrigues had reduced the power of the Sultans. The rulers could not keep the fractious empire together. To shore things up, the Sultans started adopting laws similar to those in northern Europe: giving outright property ownership to ensure the loyalty of their beneficiaries.

Fast forward to the modern era.

After Mustafa Kemal Ataturk led the country to independence in 1923, the government adopted Roman laws, which endorsed private ownership (at almost the same time, Turkey adopted the Latin alphabet). But tradition dies hard, and the Roman concept was simply laid on top of customary Ottoman traditions. Now, the two sets of conflicting laws coexist uneasily.

The overnight builders began in earnest in the 1940s. They exploited a quirk of Turkish law that requires due process of law if you are in your dwelling and it is deemed habitable. If the authorities caught you while you were building, they could destroy your construction immediately. But if you could get it built without their knowing, then eviction was a judicial matter. So the original self-builders built quickly: framing their buildings and installing doors, windows, and the roof in one night. That way, when the authorities found them in the morning, they could not be summarily thrown out.

In 1949, the federal government made its first attempt to regulate such gecekondu by passing a law requiring municipalities to destroy the illegal dwellings. But this was politically unpalatable, so four years later the government modified the law, allowing existing gecekondu to be improved and only mandating demolition of new developments. In 1966, the government rewrote that law again, granting amnesty to all gecekondu houses constructed over the 13 years since the previous law had been enacted, and adding new programs to promote development of alternatives to gecekondu housing.

The government handed authority to enforce this law to the municipalities. Given that squatters are voters, this made it very unlikely that politicians would rein in the overnight builders. Statistics in Istanbul show the growth. In 1958, city authorities counted 40,000 gecekondu houses in Istanbul, with a population of 280,000 people. By 1963, that had tripled to 120,000 houses with a population of about 660,000 people, or close to 35 percent of the city.

By 1984, the government essentially gave up the fight against squatters. It passed a new law that again gave amnesty to all existing gecekondu communities and authorized the areas to be redeveloped with higher-density housing. Even without true planning permission, squatters quickly realized that they could take advantage of the new law. They began ripping down their old-fashioned single-story homes and building three- and four-story ones, of reinforced concrete and brick. Around this time, a government census showed that the number of gecekondu buildings in Istanbul had jumped to 208,000. In 1990, the government issued a new gecekondu amnesty, accepting all the illegal neighborhoods that had already been built. Suddenly, most of the gecekondu were legal —even if they didn't have title deeds.

Today, many of these *gecekondu* areas are indistinguishable from legal neighborhoods. Through a combination of political protection and dogged building and rebuilding, these neighborhoods have become developed. They are thriving commercial and residential districts. They are desirable places to live.

The biggest problem facing the squatters these days is sprawl. Sultanbeyli, Yenidoğan, and Paşaköy are three squatter areas that border Omerli forest, which contains the city's biggest reservoir. For a time it seemed as if the squatters would chop their way all the way to the water supply, or that run-off from squatter developments would contaminate the reservoir anyway.

The *büyükşehir* embarked on a major plan to protect the reservoir. In response, the squatter municipalities have all taken steps to end sprawl. Sultanbeyli has decreed that there should be no new construction in the forest and, by and large, people have honored this. In a few isolated locations where there were forest fires, people have grabbed the burned out land, but otherwise the forest remains. In some places, small walls have been constructed along the outskirts of the built-up area, and there are strict penalties if people attempt to leapfrog the walls and grab land.

Back in Sarıgazi, Hussein Baykara proudly explained that he finally was able to do something he never thought he'd do: "I knocked my building down myself," he said with a smile. That was in 1999. "Now I have a bigger house, with a basement and two flats."

Ulter Kaya will soon follow suit. She told me that her husband is about to retire from his job in nearby Dudullu, where he is a gardener for the municipality. This is a great irony, because Dudullu is part of the Umraniye municipality, which was the governmental entity that demolished her home twice back in the 1980s. When her husband retires, she said, he will receive a pension, and then they will hire workers to knock down their old-style gecekondu and build a new home like her brother-in-law's.

"We are poor people here," she said. "We have always been poor. When we own a place we are so happy. Owning land in Istanbul is a very valuable thing for us. We would never sell it."

She is from Erzurum. Her husband is from Ordu. By tradition, these places ought to be closest to their hearts, what is called in

Turkish their *memleket*. But she has a different viewpoint. "Wherever you have income, wherever your stomach is full, that is your *memleket*. So this"—she spread her hands to indicate her tiny dwelling and all the tiny dwellings around it—"this is my *memleket*."

As for Selvi Kaynak, things were not as rosy as she presented them. Yes, she and her neighbors have purchased their title deeds, but it turned out that Mayor Şahin had pulled a fast one. He had not actually sold them the land on which they live. Apparently, he felt that their homes were not in a desirable location (he didn't like houses being so close to trucks and factories) and so he had sold them deeds to land nearby. At some point, they will have to move. Selvi knows that moving will mean building all over again, which will likely cost another billion Turkish lira—money she clearly does-n't have. And she also frets about losing her idyllic spot. "I think of this all the time," she told me. "These trees are as important as my house to me."

As we drove away from Selvi's house, the sun slanted towards the horizon, and Mayor Şahin turned philosophical. At the time, his was the only leftist regime in the region. He claimed that the funda-mentalist *belediyes* that surrounded Sarıgazi received major infu-sions of capital from the *büyük şehir*, while he could never get the government to put any money into his city. But Sarıgazi does profit from these regimes indirectly. As the one municipality that wel-comes beer halls and nightclubs, men from those more conservative districts often come to Sarıgazi to spend their money. The mayor reported that there were starting to be too many nightclubs and he had decided to turn down some liquor licenses because there were too many bars in the center of town.

Then his thoughts came back to a simpler thing: to Selvi Kaynak and the apple tree in front of her home. For an instant, he seemed to

Old-fashioned gecekondu Sarıgazi.

rue his drive to move the squatters to more modern structures. "Small houses with beautiful gardens," the mayor mused, almost whispering, as if it were a thought that was forbidden. "Wouldn't it be better if we all lived that way?"

Of course, it was a romantic thought, said as the sun was setting over the Sea of Marmara. But there's a truth to it. The squatter way of building, the squatter way of life, has lots of advantages for poor people. If Selvi Kaynak and her neighbors were truly able to stay in their homes, and didn't face the high prices of construction and land purchase, they could develop them at their own pace. Life would be easier.

Nonetheless, the popular imagination doesn't see it that way. Increasingly, people see gecekondu areas as dirty and unfit for habitation. And, most recently, a new charge was added to the indictment against squatters: danger.

In 1999, two serious earthquakes rocked the Istanbul region. More than 18,000 people died and more than 50,000 were injured. As authorities tried to determine why buildings collapsed, the government was quick to blame the gecekondu, asserting that the squatters had used improper construction methods.

About a year after the quakes, an article appeared in the American press profiling a group of architects who were there to consult on construction techniques. According to the article, the architects toured an Istanbul gecekondu community called Kuçuk Armutlu, which had been severely hit by the earthquake. They complained that the squatters were not building properly. They said the old-fashioned buildings were fine, but that the newer squatter structures could never withstand another earthquake. There was one problem with this, I discovered when I was in Istanbul: It wasn't true.

I made a special effort to get to Kuçuk Armutlu. It's a small squatter area on the European side of the city, situated on a hill that overlooks the Bosphorus. It's a hard area to enter unless you know someone who lives there, because it has become a center of radical activity and, at times, is under 24-hour lockdown. When I visited, the barricades were down, but there was a big police presence on the main road into the community.

I asked Aladin, who has lived there since he was 7 years old and had volunteered to take me around, whether there was much destruction during the earthquake.

He gave me a strange look. "I was here," he said. "I remember it well. There was a big rumble and the air got very heavy for a few minutes. We all ran outside. And then it was very beautiful and very still."

I asked again about damage to the houses.

Maybe one or two developed small cracks, he answered. But nothing serious. Then he pointed up the street. Look around. There are no tall buildings here.

I followed his gesture. In truth, most of the houses in Kuçuk Armutlu are one or two stories. None of the ones I saw—and we walked around the entire small community—had been pulverized during the earthquakes. None of them looked the least bit damaged.

In fact, people who had who worked in the areas with the worst devastation told me that the buildings that represent the real problems in future earthquakes are not the true gecekondu, but the false. It seems that private developers have determined that they can use gecekondu techniques to save them a bundle. So they build using the overnight technique. They erect buildings—sometimes 10 or 12 stories high—without building permits and without proper engineering studies. These structures are often made with substandard concrete and without enough rebar. Those were the buildings that collapsed during the quakes, not the squatter-built houses.

Aladin was looking to hire out as a waiter on a cruise ship, to pull in big money, so we went down to Taksim Square, in the center of town, to visit the manager of the employment agency where he had signed up. Aladin told him what I was writing and the manager said, "Ah yes, gecekondu, Turkey's biggest problem. That and the traffic. People think, like my father, that they can just come here and find land and build anywhere. This is Turkey's problem. The government has no control."

Aladin nodded in agreement.

Both grew up gecekondu communities. Aladin still lives in one. But neither of them was willing to defend their homes. So I did. Yes, I said, but if there is no housing, where are people supposed to live.

Doğru. True. They nodded.

Gecekondu is wrong and right. Even the squatters themselves can't make up their minds. Clearly, building a gecekondu house is the only way someone who journeys to the city in search of work can survive. Yet—by contrast with everything American, everything European, everything rational and rich, everything people are told they should want—gecekondu is wrong.

Back in Sultanbeyli, the frenzy of urbanization can't mask a village atmosphere. On the edge of Orhangazi, one of the newer Sultanbeyli neighborhoods, chickens, goats, and cows pick their way around the huge water pipes that are being installed and graze next to the gangly poured concrete and rebar skeletons of buildings on the rise. Around one corner, I passed a man and two boys who were chasing chickens. I stopped and watched them snag the birds and then hold them on the ground in the shade of one of these new concrete buildings on the rise as an older man produced a sharp knife and, with a flourish, slashed the birds' throats. A group of teenage girls, their interest piqued by the carnage, gathered around. One of them poked at the severed heads with a stick. This is not something you would see in Sariyer or Kadiköy or any of the more developed areas of Istanbul.

At the same time, people build with an increasing sense of style. Some of Sultanbeyli's homes are undeniably spartan: simple single-story buildings, hardly more than poured concrete frames with windows. Others are comparative palaces, with mosaic decorations, fluted columns and balustrades, and all sorts of expensive design items indoors as well.

Turgut and Inci Akcağoz and their two children live in one of the more proletarian homes: a snug but unadorned building in the Fatih section of Sultanbeyli. Originally from Samson, on the Black

Sea, Turgut emigrated to the big city in search of work. A waiter and
kebabci (maker and slicer of kebab sandwiches), he originally rented
an apartment in the legal city before he decided that there was
opportunity in building his own house in Sultanbeyli. His single-
story, three-room ranch-style home has few decorative features. It is
comfortable and homey without ostentation: just a poured concrete
box with a roof laid on the top.

Turgut works for Hamdi and Hasan Koç. He prepares and slices
the chicken kebab that they serve at their fast food restaurant in
Sarıgazi. Originally from Bingol, the Koç brothers came to Istanbul
and invested in restaurants. They now have nine *pastanesis* (pastry
and tea shops) throughout the squatter areas on the Asian side of
the city. I met them at their shop in Sarıgazi and saw their operations
in Sultanbeyli (where Hamdi also runs a jewelry shop), Samandira
(where they also have a busy kebab restaurant), Taşdelen, Dudullu,
and Umraniye. The business is lucrative, and Hasan once told me
that in Sarıgazi alone he took in more than 1 billion lira every day,
which means his store alone has a turnover of more than $200,000
a year. Put the nine stores together and do the math: It's a million
dollar business.

In contrast to Turgut's modest house, Inci's brother, who works
as a *pazarci*, or seller at various local bazaars, built a true extrava-
ganza in a nearby squatter area called Alemdağ. Working in partnership with a friend, he erected a five-story apartment house that
features a central spiral staircase. Each of the spacious apartments
has a large balcony. These squatters live the good life, and Inci's
brother's house was bursting with furnishings: hutches filled with
glassware, large dining tables, display cases with knickknacks. The
kitchen had a refrigerator and dishwasher, and the pantry had a
brand new washing machine.

Fifteen of us sat out on the top-floor balcony as our host—a burly, bearded, high-spirited man—grilled chicken wings and told jokes. The assembled family laughed when I told them that rents in New York average more than $1,000 a month. Inci's brother peered over the edge of the balcony and pointed at a vacant lot across the street. "You come and build there," he told me. "The land will cost you nothing and you can put the money you save into the home you build."

He spread his hands across the horizon, taking in not only the view of the orderly rows of self-built buildings that made up his neighborhood but all of us on the balcony. The crescent moon was behind him, and a few stars, as if stolen from the Turkish flag and pasted high above the squatter community. He laughed a great laugh, his whole body moved by his mirth, and gave me a final piece of advice. "If you do this," he said, "you will be free."

Time Past

CHAPTER 5

The 21st Century Medieval City

"Several families inhabit one house. A weaver's family may be crowded into a single room, where they huddle around a fireplace."

"Nine out of ten of the shanties have only one room, which does not average over twelve feet square, and this serves all the purposes of the family."

These descriptions, stripped of any cultural markers, could fit any of today's squatter communities. But they are not about present-day life. They are from the faraway past.

The first is a description of the typical poor person's house in Troyes, France, in the year 1250, taken from the book *Life in a*

Medieval City, by Joseph and Frances Gies. The second is a description of the standard dwelling in Jackson's Hollow, a Brooklyn squatter area, from *The New York Times* in 1858.

It's true: very little has changed since the Middle Ages. The *barracas* of Rocinha, the mud huts of Kibera, the wooden shanties of Behrampada, or the original *gecekondu* houses in Sarigazi are not far removed from the dwellings that were common centuries ago in Europe and North America.

The businesses, too, are quite similar. This is a description of the main shopping strip in Troyes, in 1250, courtesy of the Gieses: "Each shop on the city street is essentially a stall, with a pair of horizontal shutters that open upward and downward, top and bottom. The upper shutter, opening upward, is supported by two posts that convert it into an awning; the lower shutter drops to rest on two short legs and acts as a display counter. At night the shutters are closed and bolted from within."

Home improvement, Kibera, 2002.

This typical kiosk from medieval Troyes was a more stylish and sophisticated design than the traditional stall in Kibera or in the *passarella* in Rocinha. There, free-standing businesses don't have locking windows or fold-down display shelves. Instead, the kiosks are raw, little more than a table and some sticks on which to hang display items. Business owners often haul off their inventory every night so it is not carted off by the police or by thieves.

Finally, here is how medieval Troyes dealt with fire: "Buckets of sand and tubs of water quench many fires in the early stages, but once furnishings, floors, and partitions take flame little can be done except to pray, and form a bucket brigade—measures about equally effective." In the squatter areas of Nairobi and Mumbai, residents still fight fires this way.

There's no way around the conclusion: the 21st century squatter cities are positively medieval. And there's no way around another conclusion as well: the history of cities teaches that squatters have always been around, that squatting was always the way the poor built homes, that it is a form of urban development.

All cities start in mud.

Before these journeys through the world's squatter communities, I thought that shantytowns were solely a Third World phenomenon. But as I began to learn more about the subject, I found that I was wrong. There's nothing Third World about squatter settlements. They existed in the First World, too, and not so long ago. The concrete, steel, and glass cities that we take for granted today were once shantytowns, and the mass of their residents lived in dirty shacks along slimy, impossibly crowded alleys, or hard against fetid river banks.

This squatter history is found in foul-smelling corners, in little-noticed alleys, in finger-stained documents, and fumbling fragmentary mentions. Squatters didn't pay taxes, didn't go to court, and didn't much want to get mixed up in the business of governments and nations and countries. They tended not to be literate, so they seldom documented their affairs. And their homes were made of materials easily removed or mulched. So they are mostly absent from the written and archaeological record.

Here are some scenes of squatter life in western cities that go all the way back to the ancients and forward to the cusp of the 20th century.

THE ANCIENT WORLD

We know that the Agis, king of the Greek city-state of Sparta, and Tiberius Gracchus, the Roman Tribune, were put to death by other ruling families who opposed any system of land redistribution to help the poor (Agis was beheaded, Tiberius was blugeoned to death). We know that they were concerned about the urban masses, and that their proposals for rural land reform were designed, in part, to slow the pace of people fleeing the country for the city. We know quite a bit about these rulers and their motivations. But we know very little of the people they were trying to help.

The cities of the ancient were putrid places. People migrated to the cities—as they do today—because the cities were hubs of manufacturing and trade. No matter how bad things are, you can almost always find a way to get by in the city. It is true now; it was true then. These new arrivals had no place to live, so they made homes for themselves: sometimes colonies of freestanding bowers on the outskirts of cities, sometimes single lean-tos in unused spaces along the sidewalks or under archways or even on rooftops.

M. I. Finley, a historian of the ancient world, has noted that eight centuries before the birth of Christ, when Greece was at the height of its world power, "'squatting' on vacant or derelict public or temple property" was a common response to the land pressures that wracked the city-states. Sadly, he adds, the history of these poor people in ancient Greece has never been told.

We know from Roman authors such as Tacitus and Juvenal that the *cenaculae* and *insulae* and *tabernae* (tenements, boarding houses, and bars of their empire's central city) were putrid, sodden and sagging. Rome doubled in size between 130 and 30 BCE to become a behemoth of 800,000 people. This eruption of residents was stuffed into the most unlikely dwellings. But many couldn't even afford the horrific privately built housing. So they simply built for themselves. "There was nothing romantic about the really destitute who lived under Tacitus' nose in these conditions in Rome," historian C.R. Whittaker has written. "If they were lucky they could build *tuguria*, lean-to sheds which made a sort of 'Bidonville' or shanty town, perhaps on the edge of the city, but sometimes above workshops or up against public buildings. The authorities regarded them as a fire risk and might tear them down, but they were allowed to remain if not obstructive and were even charged rent." Other historians record incidents in which migrants took over streets to build their homes. "Overnight, someone might close off what had been a public passage and build a house on it. From time to time the aediles—magistrates in charge of the city—would order interloping buildings to be cleared; but others would spring up in their place." Rome's ferocious soldiers were apparently unwilling to patrol the maze of alleys and byways that made up these illegal neighborhoods. These were real-life labyrinths, and getting lost there could cost you your life.

EUROPEAN CITIES

Other European cities had large numbers of squatters too. During the Middle Ages, Paris was swelling with new arrivals and had similar concentrations of overcrowded rotting huts. According to historian Bronislaw Geremek, "The very poor also lived in huts and shanties on the town moat, near the marsh, in the fields, and on the outskirts of town, in the shanty-towns of the middle ages . . . These slums certainly constituted a large part of the urban landscape in poor districts." Geremek suggests that the Court of Miracles, the rough district made famous by Victor Hugo in *The Hunchback of Notre Dame,* was initially a squatter settlement. The area, which he describes as "a labyrinth of evil-smelling rutted lanes led to a collection of mud huts teeming with beggar families . . . a slum, or shanty-town," existed until the 18th century. But to root the squatters from that central area, the government had to resort to a full-scale siege.

Fernand Braudel, in his study of the growth of capitalism through the Middle Ages, recorded some impressive statistics. In July 1587, when the population of Paris was around 260,000, 17,000 homeless were living in shacks around the walls of the city. Two hundred years later, when the population of the city had doubled, the number of persons without fixed abode—people who reportedly lived in shacks and, if they were lucky, were employed as day laborers—had mushroomed to 91,000. "Despite economic expansion, and because of demographic expansion which worked in the opposite direction, the numbers of the destitute swelled," Braudel concluded.

Like my friends Nicodemus in Nairobi, Maria and Zezinho in Rio, Wadekar in Mumbai, and Zamanhan in Istanbul, the poor were coming to the city. And like them, they could not find places to live.

So they massed in illegal communities, either renting from others or building for themselves.

Medieval England also teemed with squatters. They lived in small cottages on the town commons, or moved from town to town in search of work, living in hastily erected houses on what was considered waste land. Indeed, squatting was so prevalent that invaders even took over land held by the Crown. Almost every royal forest had its contingent of illegal residents. In 1578, a royal survey showed 178 encroachments on the Forest of Inglewood. Forty years later, that number had quadrupled to 757. In the Forest of Dean, royal surveyors reported 79 cabins containing 340 people in 1615. By 1646, there were 300 cabins; by 1653, 100 more, and in 1736, a royal census recorded 589 cottages and 1,798 small enclosures in the forest. Other forests, too, had squatters. Kingswood Forest had 46 cottages in 1629, and 152 in 1652. And in 1789 squatters in New Forest had taken over 902 acres.

Forest workers argued that "for the preservation of the forest some vigorous measures must be speedily taken." But they also pressed for lenient treatment of the squatters. "So long as the Cottagers remain in the forest without committing depredations, their cottages do little harm," one wrote.

But while royalty may have been lenient, private landlords were not. This was the era of enclosure, during which wealthy individuals gradually fenced off historically common areas and evicted the residents. With parliamentary approval, landlords enclosed whole towns, making hundreds of people homeless and landless with a single stroke of a pen.

Squatting remained common in England for the next few centuries. In Wales in the early 1800s, squatters considered themselves authorized to invade land under the principal of *ty unnos*, a point of customary law that held, much like gecekondu, that a family could establish a right to whatever it could build or enclose in the course of one night. In out-of-the-way areas, squatting was quite common. For instance, an 1851 survey of Scotland's Isle of Skye showed that more than 40 percent of the residents on the isolated island were squatters.

And squatting was not just a rural affair. In the 1500s, the outskirts of London (areas that are quite central today) were being built up by squatters. By the middle of the century, squatters had erected shacks in the shadow of the Tower of London. There were even squatter landlords, and, in 1587, the Gentleman Porter of the Tower (the royally appointed curator of the Tower land) went to court to recover £54, 10 shillings that some of the squatters were collecting in rent from others.

John Stow, in his *Survey of London*, from 1598, notes that beyond Whitechapel Church a common field had been "so encroached upon by building of filthy cottages, and with other purpressors, inclosures, and laystalls (notwithstanding all proclamations and acts of parliament made to the contrary), that in some places it scarce remaineth a sufficient highway for the meeting of carriages and droves of cattle; much less is there any fair, pleasant, or wholesome way for people to walk on foot." He also records that unauthorized builders had taken land not far from the Tower of London, where they had made "encroachments for building of small tenements and taking in of garden-plots, timber-yards, or what they list."

A few years later, when the leaders of Wapping's local council had fled to avoid an outbreak of the plague, squatters took advantage of the absence of authority to build scores of homes. A governmental survey from 1638 recorded that 188 unauthorized buildings had sprung up on marshes, garbage dumps, and other unused properties in the area.

After the Great Fire of London, which burned for 4 days from September 2 through September 6, 1666, and reduced a huge swath of the central city to ash and rubble, squatting rose again. Even before the King began thinking of how to rebuild the city, squatters started the effort, taking positions on the margins of the charred area: in Leadenhall Street, Castle Yard, Broad Street, Pye Alley, Fenchurch Street, and Cripplegate. Squatters were so persistent that the government issued a series of decrees giving the London authorities emergency powers to rip down all illegal constructions without having to get specific approval.

Two centuries later, squatters were still hanging on in far-flung districts of London. John Hollingshead, in his book *Ragged London in 1861*, visited The Potteries, a 9-acre marsh behind what were then the villages of Bayswater and Notting Hill. On that "dreary swamp of black manure-drainage, broken bottles, old bricks, and mud," Hollingshead found 300 shanties. "The huts have grown a little worse for wear, as all things do," he wrote, "and they hold together by some principle not yet discovered or laid down by theoretical builders." Though unauthorized, he reported, "the old inhabitants defend their right to the place, not only with legal parchments, but with energetic tongues."

Still, he concluded, "if settlers are wedded to a place like this, where, according to a sanitary report for 1856, the average age at death is under 12 years, and where there is nothing to look at but clay, pools of stagnant water, and the most wretched hovels, there is no help for them."

Agar Town was another London district that featured squatters. Here, 6,000 or 7,000 people lived in conditions that would fit the darkest Dickens novel. Here's a description taken from a London guidebook of 1851: "In some rooms there are no doors, in others no windows; in others the garden walls, moist, soft, like wet ginger-bread, have fallen down from very rottenness."

Agar Town existed because a landlord had rented the plot from the Ecclesiastical Commission and, when the commissioners refused to renew his lease on favorable terms, he simply let local workers build shanties on the land. "The huts in Agar Town were built of old rubbish, on a 21 years' lease. Some of the builders still live in them, happy and contented, dreading the time—about 1866 —when their term will expire. They are always ready to rally round the place, and call it a "pretty little town."

Squatters occupied much of the rest of the St. Giles district, too. Here's another description from the London guide:

> The stagnant gutters in the middle of the lanes, the accumu-lated piles of garbage, the pools accumulated in the hollows, the disjointed pavement, the filth choking up the dark pas-sages which open like rat-holes upon the highway—all these, with their indescribable sights and smells, leave scarce so dispiriting an impression on the passenger as the condition of the houses. Walls of the colour of bleached soot—doors falling from their hinges—door posts worm-eaten and greasily polished from being long the supports of the shoul-ders of ragged loungers—windows where shivered panes of dirty glass alternate with wisps of straw, old hats, and lumps of bed ticken or brown paper—bespeak the last and frailest shelter that can be interposed between man and the elements.

The reporter gave the colony some grudging respect: "The inhab-itants have one advantage not often enjoyed by persons in low districts, their air is remarkably pure. Though some of the roads and most passages between the huts are still rivers of mud and receive the slops thrown into them from each ill-regulated household; and though the dwellings are low, the spaces between them are very open, and St. Giles evidently gathers health by being a little way out of town."

A few years later, in 1864, *The London Times* seized on a new reason to denounce the squatters. These weren't hard-working people braving miserable conditions, *The Times* wrote, but in fact were dangerous speculators:

> The open lands close to London are contracting every day. The prize is too great. A squatter builds his worthless hut, and it is nobody's interest to go to the expense of pulling it down once a week. Perhaps he pays an acknowledgment to the lord. In 20 years, the commoner's right is gone, and the lord and encroacher can together make a title. The site is then sold and a villa rises on the spot. The smart villas between Wimbledon and Kingston, with their outlook over Richmond Park, have all risen in this way. To leave these open lands untouched is to lose them.

Over time, monied interests asserted themselves and London was carved into private parcels. But well into the 20th century, out-of-the-way plots in and around London seldom remained vacant for long. They were quickly seized by squatters. The banks of the Thames River, for instance, were occupied by squatters in the early 1900s. "Between Staines and Penton Hall Hotel the Surrey bank gives hospitality to a ragged array of those wooden shanties which are dignified by the name of bungalows and which, with their fluttering flags and enameled trellises, impart a tawdry flippancy to the banks of the river," one report recalled. And the bungalows were still there in 1930, when the British government surveyed the Thames shoreline: "Generally speaking it may be said that wherever land on the banks is unprotected by public or crown ownership or by wise private or public control the bungalow springs to life," the surveyor concluded.

Squatting reared up again throughout Europe during the difficult economic times after World War II. But as governments desperate for development ceded more public land to the private sector and expanded the zoning envelope to allow for bigger buildings, it became harder to find room for any self-built bungalows. There was another burst of squatting during the 1980s (most notably in London and Amsterdam) as groups took over buildings that had been abandoned by their landlords. But by and large property in Europe's cities had been fully privatized and squatting had become the domain of young single people and radicals rather than the families of old.

SHANGHAI

To travelers in the first half of the 20th century, Shanghai was an exotic and glamorous urban melange often dubbed "the Paris of the East." But beyond the central district, it was a squatter town.

Yaoshuilong, or Lotion Lane, was one of the Shanghai's principal squatter encampments. It was established, as the name implies, by workers at a lotion factory, and, from its birth in 1920, it quickly grew as other factories located nearby. By 1930, Lotion Lane had 10,000 residents; by the 1940s it boasted 16,000 inhabitants. Fangualong, or Melon Alley, was another squatter settlement, alongside the city's train tracks, with perhaps 20,000 residents.

Many immigrants came to the city in traditional covered boats. They would ground the boats and then strip them to form shelters on the muddy banks. Although these were probably the most precarious form of squatter housing, they had a poetic name: *gundilong* ("rolling earth dragons"). After years of working and saving, the *gundilong* dwellers would probably be ecstatic to move to a straw hut. Others with less money simply banged bamboo poles deep into the muck at the bottom of the river and built their houses as high above the water line as possible. A study from the late 1940s revealed that almost 1 million of Shanghai's residents were living in straw shacks: about one in five people in the city was a squatter.

These were difficult dwellings and life was tough. Children routinely died of exposure and disease. But to immigrant families, being in the city was worth it. As historian Hanchao Lu has written, "To go to Shanghai was something quite like immigrants entering the United States to pursue their "American dream." Although hundreds of thousands of the "Shanghai dreamers" ended up by squatting in shack slums and living in shelters that can barely be called homes, the allure of the city never faded."

The Communist government that came to power in 1949 removed most of these squatter communities and, by strictly restricting migration to the cities, prevented the formation of new shantytowns. But today, as China engages in the Communist version of economic laissez faire, people are again leaving their farms to come to the cities in search of work. Reports are that Shanghai may again have a million immigrants, and that they are establishing their own self-built communities just beyond the city limits.

THE UNITED STATES

From the beginning, the United States, too, has been a land of illegal occupiers. Long before the revolution—before George Washington and the legions of lesser-known men and women who fought for self-government were even born—squatting was a way of life on the North American continent. Jamestown, one of the early European outposts on the North American continent, legalized its squatters. The Pilgrims were squatters for the first year after they landed at Plymouth Rock. Revolutionary War hero Ethan Allen was a squatter. So was famed frontiersman Daniel Boone. As the country grew, it was largely settled by squatters (or "squatlers," as a Philadelphia newspaper termed these land invaders in 1790). Squatter agitation in Maine was one of the primary reasons it won its independence from Massachusetts in 1820. And the great push west, of course, was fueled by squatters.

The squatters were aided by two federal actions. The Preemption Act, passed in 1841, made squatters' rights the law of the land. All squatters who settled on government land were to be considered legal settlers and could buy their holdings for $1.25 an acre. In its first four decades of operation, the government used the Preemption Act to hand 170 million acres to squatters. The Homestead Act, which was on the books from 1862 until 1976, guaranteed a free 160-acre tract to every settler on government land, whether they applied for the right before occupying or squatted first and became legal second. In 1968, a government commission concluded that more than 270 million acres were handed out under the Act, much of it to squatters.

But there is another squatter history in the United States, one that has been mostly expunged because it lacks the resonance of the pioneers' push westward. It's an urban history, a tale of city squatters who occupied valuable real estate for decades, but, like the buffalo and the passenger pigeon on the plains, were exterminated.

MINNEAPOLIS/ST. PAUL

In 1837, Indians ceded land on the east side of the Mississippi River near Fort Snelling to the U.S. government. The news arrived at the military outpost in the summer of 1838 and it led to Minnesota's first land rush. One settler, Franklin Steele, marched overnight to the riverbank and by morning had erected a cabin and staked a claim. He held his acreage for almost a decade as a squatter, until the government allowed him a preemption right and he purchased the property. He was the first true resident of the city of St. Paul.

Col. John H. Stevens was the first to occupy the western bank of the river—the area that would in time become the city of Minneapolis—by building a one-story wooden structure. He had no title, but did get unofficial permission from the Army that he could remain on the condition that he ferry troops and supplies across the Mississippi. Over the next several years, a few dozen intrepid squatters joined him.

"Besides those who obtained permits from the army officials were other settlers who had no shadow of authority, and the claim shanties of these 'squatters' were frequently destroyed by the officers and their builders ejected from the reservation," a local historian reported, adding that "the administration of this authority was radical and claimed to be tyrannical and charges of bribery were frequently made."

Like their rural brethren, these city squatters formed a claims club (an association of like-minded land invaders) and vowed to defend their turf. There was huge competition for land and claim jumping—attempting to seize the land another squatter had already declared as his own—was common. As soon as a squatter left his plot, one local history recounted, "jumpers, like sleuth-hounds scenting their prey . . . discovered his absence and took instant advantage of it. During the night, lumber was hauled upon the land, a shanty built, furnished with a bed, chair and stove, and after an occupancy of a few hours, the enterprising jumper filed his claim of preemption." Often squatters paid hundreds of dollars to get the jumpers to depart. In 1855, Congress allowed the Minneapolis squatters to prove up, or preempt, their land.

Less than 40 years later, squatters would face a very different reality. By 1889, the Twin Cities were well established, real estate interests were heavily entrenched in government, and the localities had little use for their squatters. The government of St. Paul worked with private owners to drive out more than 2,000 immigrants who for several decades had been squatting along the so-called upper flats on the east bank of the Mississippi.

SACRAMENTO AND SAN FRANCISCO

Gold was the madness but squatting was the method. After the discovery of the precious metal at Sutter's Mill in 1848, thousands journeyed across the continent to stake their claims. But land grants in the region were complicated. John Augustus Sutter claimed the entire gold mining area, including the city of Sacramento, asserting that he had bought it from the Mexican government. But Sutter refused to show his title to anyone.

Rather than buy at Sutter's exorbitant prices, settlers simply squatted on any vacant parcels they could find. One of the immigrants to nascent Sacramento was a young newspaperman named James McClatchy. McClatchy wrote for the local paper, *The Placer Times*, for a time, but then struck out on his own, starting the prosquatter *Settlers' and Miners' Tribune*.

The settlers were a hotheaded bunch. They claimed that Sutter had lied about his land grant (later evidence would show that their suspicions were correct, but by that time it was a moot point: the courts had accepted Sutter's claims as valid) and vowed to protect their holdings, by violence if necessary. The squatters created a parallel administration, a government of, by, and for the squatters to record their illegal land deeds. Each property registration form was emblazoned with their motto: "The public domain is free to all."

At the same time, owners were agitating against them. In 1849, Sutter's son took out an ad in *The Placer Times*, warning the squatters to stay off his land: "All persons are hereby cautioned not to settle, without my permission, on any land of mine in the territory."

Things came to a head in the summer of 1850. Squatters had established so many claims along the river that a prosperous local merchant and major property speculator named Samuel Brannan, who, along with his colleagues, controlled 500 lots in central Sacramento (roughly 80 percent of the city) claimed there was no space for the boats that brought merchandise to the city to tie up and unload. Brannan and his merchant comrades established a "Law and Order Association," or what one local reporter called, more accurately, a band of "destroying angels." They stormed the waterfront, ripping down scores of offending squatter homes.

Brannan and his ilk may have had good economic reason for their effort: speculation was running rampant and lots were obscenely valuable. A property that originally sold for $250 could command as much as 32 times that amount within a few months. The squatters stood in the way of other people's fortunes.

At the same time, the speculative economy was precarious. In early August 1850, one of Brannan's colleagues, Barton Lee, declared bankruptcy. Lee was Sacramento's largest landholder and wealthiest banker. His fall would take down a bunch of other major interests, and would threaten the economic stability of the gold-boom city. Landlords, understandably, were worried.

The squatters, meanwhile, were facing their own struggles. They knew they would not get a fair hearing in the district courts, since most local judges were appointed by the landowning politicos or were landowners themselves, but thought they could get a chance at justice if they could appeal all local rulings to federal court.

On August 8, 1850, a controversial judicial decree roiled the town. Judge Edward J. Willis, himself a wealthy Sacramento landholder, ruled that a squatter named John T. Madden should be ejected and specifically barred Madden's lawyers from filing an appeal.

The squatters were outraged. Madden refused to leave his property and began hoarding weapons. Both squatters and landlords held raucous meetings every night. After a few days, the authorities muscled Madden out of his home and reduced the house to rubble. Fearing violence, the local sheriff rounded up some particularly vocal squatters, most notably McClatchy and his newspaper partner Richard Moran, who had both been supporting the squatter cause in print, and held them in a ship that was used as the local jail.

That night, the squatters held a noisy rally. Although *The Placer Times* reported that the gathering was rather good-natured ("The proceedings were characterized by great excitement, with a mixture of mirth, which made the meeting decidedly rich and racy") the squatters were quite bold. The assembly adopted a petition declaring that "if there is no appeal from Judge Willis," the squatters "deliberately resolved to appeal to arms and protect their sacred rights, if need be, with their lives . . . The lives of those who take the field against them will share the fate of war."

On August 14, that shared fate arrived. And here is where the story differs depending on who's telling it.

To law-and-order types, a band of several thousand squatters raged across town, organized under the slogan "War to the knife and the knife to the hilt." When they hit the intersection of 4th and J streets, they ran into a small posse led by Mayor Harden Bigelow. Someone shouted "Shoot the mayor," and the squatters opened fire. With that, the battle was joined.

The squatter version is a bit different: a rag-tag platoon of perhaps 15 or 20 cadres marched through the city, followed by a crowd of perhaps 1,000 sympathizers and onlookers. They met the mayor's men at 4th and J. The authorities shot first and the squatters returned fire.

Whatever the truth, when the dust cleared a squatter leader (James Maloney, treasurer of the settler's association) and a high-ranking city official (J.W. Woodland, the city's tax assessor) were both dead. The mayor was gravely wounded—he ultimately had to have an arm amputated—and Charles Robinson, a doctor from Massachusetts who was one of the main squatter activists, took a bullet to the stomach.

The crowd scattered after the gunfire, and the violence was over for the night. But early the next morning Sheriff Joseph McKinney decided to finish the fight. He attacked a settler stronghold just outside of town. The squatters, barricaded in a tavern known as the Five Mile House, returned fire. According to one source, the sheriff, hit by a shotgun blast, raised his hands, exclaimed, "I'm dead, I'm dead, I'm dead," walked 8 or 10 paces, and fell to the ground, true to his word. The final toll for the 2-day battle: eight dead, six injured.

Robinson, who remained in custody while he recovered from his injury, ran for state legislature from the jailhouse—and won. The taste for politics never left him: he soon migrated back to Massachusetts and then west again to a new frontier, joining the squatter movement in Kansas and speaking out against slavery. Robinson worked both sides of the land issue, squatting and speculating, and he became a very powerful and successful man. So much so that in 1859 he was elected Kansas's first governor.

McClatchy, who was never charged with a crime, was released from jail after the riot and resumed his reporting career. His squatter journal didn't survive, but in 1857, he started a new paper, the *Sacramento Bee*. The *Bee* remains Sacramento's paper to this day and, 154 years after McClatchy's arrest for squatter agitation, the firm that bears his name—the McClatchy Company—owns 12 daily papers across the country. McClatchy's descendants, who still control the newspaper firm, are worth more than $650 million. Not a bad return on an investment with squatter roots.

San Francisco, too, was a city of squatters. Until the Gold Rush, San Francisco hardly qualified as a city. It was smaller than Sacramento: just a sleepy Mexican *pueblo*, population 459, with a beautiful and placid harbor, more of a fishing village than a major port. But, as the jumping-off point for the so-called Forty-Niners seeking their fortunes in the gold fields, San Francisco swelled with desperate men and women who had no place to live. They raised tents and built cabins on military reservations. One squatter fenced in Union Square, claiming it as his own. Others seized parts of the beach and dunes. At 1st and Howard streets, squatters dragged an old clipper ship inland, removed the timbers, and built a protective barricade they dubbed Fort Larkin. Squatters even marked off lots in the harbor, sinking sticks into the muck, and declaring that they owned the underwater real estate. Frank Soulé, an eyewitness, described the frenzy:

> Where there was a vacant piece of ground one day, the next saw it covered with half a dozen tents or shanties . . . Hundreds of rude houses and tents were daily in the course of erection; they nestled between the sand hills, covered their tops, and climbed the heights to the north and west of town . . . Rents were correspondingly enormous. Three thousand dollars *a month*, in advance, was charged for a single story, of limited dimensions, and rudely constructed of rough boards.

In such a crazed situation, cash was always tight, and money lending was a big business. Interest rates in Gold Rush San Francisco ran as high as 60 percent a year (interestingly, this is the same rate charged by unscrupulous lenders in current day Nairobi and Mumbai).

Unlike Sacramento, no single street battle defined the squatter movement in San Francisco. Instead, illegal settlers engaged in repeated shoot-outs with landlords and court officers. Contemporary dispatches from San Francisco tally the human cost of the real estate woes.

> *July 20, 1853*: "The under-sheriff, John A. Freaner, was shot on Mission street by one Redmond McCarthy, a "squatter," when the former, in the performance of his duty, was endeavoring to execute a writ of ejectment against the latter." Other reports indicated that Freaner was lightly wounded in the hip, while two bullets had penetrated McCarthy's lungs, a grave injury.

June 4, 1854: "A serious squatter riot occurred on the lot owned by Capt. Folsom corner Mission and Third streets. After a severe conflict in which death shots fell thick and fast, victory was declared for Capt. Folsom." A later newspaper report added, "The parties ejected subsequently got possession of the lot, and erected a sort of fort, within which they assembled to the number of fifteen, arming themselves with guns, pistols &c., and in this way keeping possession of the lot."

July 10, 1854: "In one of the squatter riots, revolvers, double barrel guns and axes were freely used, and Geo. D. Smith, of Rochester, N.Y., shot through the head and killed."

January 11, 1855: "An important case which had been on trial for 9 days before the Fourth District Court, involving the question whether neglect to improve a lot caused a forfeiture of the grant, as against a subsequent grantee who had improved and remained in possession, was decided in the affirmative." This, of course, sparked new violence.

In May 1855, the city's Joint Committee on Land Claims issued a most unusual report. It acknowledged that 95 percent of the property holders in the city would not be able to produce a bona fide legal title to their land. The committee concluded that the only solution was to "secure the actual possessors against all future disturbance. In this way every honest end will be gained without expense."

Ultimately, San Francisco's land titles were so convoluted that the city had to compromise with squatters. In June 1855, the city passed the Van Ness Ordinance, named after Alderman James Van Ness, who brokered the deal. This, plus several legislative decrees thereafter, set the boundaries of the central city and legalized many squatters. In return, squatters agreed to give up their claims to a huge tract of dunes: today's Golden Gate Park.

Three days after it passed, jubilant supporters lit bonfires on the hills around the city to honor the transaction.

To be fair, the Van Ness Ordinance favored certain powerful squatters while hurting others. As an anonymous squatter complained to *The California Chronicle* in early 1855, the ordinance was "a most curious sort of document, ingeniously prepared, and was designed as to specially benefit a certain few only, at the sacrifice of the interests and equitable rights of other parties."

Many of the squatters probably were, as Frank Soulé alleged in his 1855 *Annals of San Francisco*,

> "secretly instigated in their reckless proceedings by people of wealth and influence, who engaged to see their pupils out of any legal difficulty into which they might fall. Such wealthy speculators shared, of course, in the spoils of the proceedings. To this day, many of the most valuable districts in and around San Francisco are held by 'squatter's titles,' which had been won perhaps at the cost of bloodshed."

Of course, the new law didn't stop the land wars. But this much changed: they were now handled through court battles instead of gun battles. This was proved a few years later. The Van Ness Ordinance established a 5-year statute of limitations on actions to eject illegal occupants of the newly privatized land. Sure enough, in the spring and summer of 1860, former squatters who had gained titles under the Van Ness Ordinance used San Francisco's courts just like their old enemies did. They filed court actions to eject as many as 1,000 families whose only sin was that they were squatting on the land that now belonged to people who used to be squatters.

CHICAGO

On July 10, 1886, George Wellington Streeter piloted a small steamboat called the Reutan across Lake Michigan. He was testing the bark before bringing it out the Illinois and Mississippi rivers to the Gulf of Mexico and on south to Honduras. But he never got farther than Chicago. His riverboat, buffeted by a big storm, became wedged on a sunken peninsula of sand and garbage that lay just below the water's surface 451 feet 6 inches from shore.

When the storm subsided, Cap Streeter (he was always called Captain, although whether due to his tour of duty in the Civil War or his short-lived steamboat journey has never been established) decided not to fight fate. Instead of struggling to free the steamer and continuing the pilgrimage to Central America, he and his wife remained in their beached boat. "I concluded that I would build up a rock wall on the seaside of the boat," he told a sympathetic scribe. To do so, he invited contractors, who were busily building up the area in anticipation of the Columbian Exhibition coming to Chicago in 1893, to dump hundreds of loads of rock and refuse around his abode. "Some of them even paid for the privilege," he noted. Eventually, sand, silt, and the illegally dumped debris created a connection to the mainland. Just a few years later, Streeter's garbage plantation had grown to 180 acres, and the old sandbar on which his boat had snagged was perhaps half a mile inland.

His neighbors, rich industrialists, all coveted his newly made land. One of them called him a squatter. But the Captain resisted the appellation. He professed to be a veritable Columbus: the discoverer of a new land. He planted a flag and claimed the acreage he called the District of Lake Michigan for himself and his family. He filed for federal recognition of his property under the Homestead Act.

Streeter irked city authorities. He sold alcohol without a license and without paying taxes. He argued that the city and state could not regulate his business, because his land was not subject to their jurisdiction. And to back up his claim and taunt the powers that be, he opened his tavern on Sundays. In response, the cops raided his establishment and carted off more than 8,100 bottles of beer.

Rival owners hired goons, but they couldn't push Streeter off his illegal isthmus. The wily Civil War veteran sold lots on his holding, thus recruiting his own force to repulse the speculative invaders and at the same time earning a tidy sum (perhaps as much as $100,000) on his land deals. Streeter even sold parcels to a city alderman, thus ensuring he had some leverage at City Hall.

It took an invasion by the Chicago police to push Streeter's forces off the land. On May 26, 1900, 500 police officers surrounded the parcel. After a dawn-to-dusk standoff, the handful of faithful defenders of the district surrendered. "Chicago was threatened with a revolution within her borders," *The New York Tribune* reported in a front-page dispatch. In fact, however, the squatters surrendered peacefully to a single police officer who sat down and reasoned with them. The only person seriously injured in the day-long standoff was Reuben Manley, a 14-year-old bystander, who was hit in the leg by a stray bullet.

Streeter was not in his kingdom during the siege. But he was later arrested by authorities and charged with conspiracy to commit murder. *The Chicago Tribune* howled for blood, arguing that Streeter and his followers "should not be allowed to escape with mere jail sentences." Nonetheless, a jury acquitted the group, but not before the Captain lectured the court on its authority: "Judge, you ain't got any more right to try this case—you ain't got any more jurisdiction than if we was citizens of Serry Leone."

Streeter returned to the site with his allies and erected tents on the disputed property. The authorities continued to harass him, and a grand jury issued a report citing Streeter for fraud in representing that he owned the 180-acre site. When nothing could drive the Streeterites out, nearby owners brought in a group of ruffians to put pressure on him. One of them was killed in a skirmish in 1902, and Streeter and several colleagues were charged with the murder. The Captain was convicted of manslaughter and spent two years in jail before successfully appealing the verdict. When he walked out of the penitentiary, his world had changed. His wife had died in his absence and the police had knocked down whatever had been built on his realm. Nevertheless, he and his allies returned to the illegal isthmus, where they again erected a tent city. Over the next decade, they even managed to build some brick structures on their freehold. Streeter's house was one of them, but after authorities pulled it to the ground and torched his belongings, he was forced to take to the lake once again for a home.

The Captain died in 1921, at the age of 84. Although his heirs continued to litigate for the property, his island paradise was ultimately incorporated into the city, and is now some of the ritziest land in Chicago, along Lakeshore Drive. His four-decade fight for the land that he claimed to have discovered, was, as *The Chicago Tribune* proclaimed in his obituary, "Chicago's Iliad." Today, his name lives on only in the name of the downtown locale he believed was his: Streeterville.

Streeter may have failed, but some long-term squatters were able to hold on. When Drusilla Carr and her husband squatted on the shores of Lake Michigan in the state of Indiana in the 1870s, the area was still a wilderness. Half a century later, her property was in the center of the city of Gary. And, although city fathers and steel mill owners wanted her out, she won several court judgments backing her claim to 200 acres of lakefront land.

Almost every schoolkid in the country knows Woody Guthrie's song "This Land is Your Land." It's one of our unofficial anthems, a paean to the great vistas and the liberty to travel freely through them. Guthrie's poetic lyrics extolling the nation's diamond deserts and waving wheat fields, and its golden valleys stretching from California to the New York island represent America as a new promised land.

But the last two stanzas, which I don't remember learning, make clear that the tumbleweed troubadour had a more controversial idea when he wrote the song:

> As I was walkin' I saw a sign there
> And that sign said "No trespassin'"
> But on the other side, it didn't say nothin'
> Now that side was made for you and me!
>
> In the squares of the city, in the shadow of the steeple
> Near the relief office, I see my people.
> And some are grumblin' and some are wonderin'
> If this land's still made for you and me.

Guthrie understood that land was the country's common heritage. When he sang that "this land was made for you and me," he wasn't simply honoring the beauty of the landscape—the kind of benign ecofantasy I remember learning. Guthrie's song was a cry against land monopolization.

A little more than 50 years ago, a historian studying the growth of California wrote that "every American is a squatter at heart." Today, the sentiment sounds ludicrous. We no longer remember that we have a squatter inheritance. In just five decades we have lost all connection to our squatter roots. The nation is weaker as a result.

Read on for the true history of squatters in the most developed city of the western world.

CHAPTER 6

Squatters in New York

"It's all the home we've got, and we don't want to lose it."
— A "Goat Town" squatter about to be evicted,
Brooklyn Daily Eagle, Sunday, February 26, 1911

Louis Heineman and William Beard. They fought for more than a generation. The loser got a street named after him. The winner didn't rate a memorial. He lived a full life and then, like his brethren across the five boroughs that make up New York City, disappeared from history.

Beard was a builder, a savvy speculator who joined with New York's players in money and politics (one of his partners was a former mayor) and saw riches in the swampy shoreline of South Brooklyn. Heineman was a laborer, an immigrant from Switzerland

who made his life along that same Brooklyn waterfront. They fought ·
the quintessential New York fight: a real estate war, in this case over
a seemingly insignificant sandbar. But it was not a landlord–tenant
dispute. Rather, it was a clash over competing concepts of ownership.

Heineman vs. Beard. Home vs. investment. Poverty vs. power.
Squatter vs. speculator.

Michael Cooney and Patrick Kinglety. They fought a similar battle. Cooney was a laborer who, in 1880, happened upon a piece of
fetid swampland in Brooklyn and set about making it suitable for living. He and his wife Catherine filled the land with dirt and stone and
erected a wooden house on the rubble. They spent their life savings
improving their home, but they didn't fret: it was city land and they
were sure they would be able to stay.

Six years later, Kinglety decided to buy some cheap property sight
unseen. He went to a city tax sale and purchased a lot on the corner
of Clinton and Garnet streets in Brooklyn. A few days later, Kinglety
went to look at his new domain, and found the Cooneys in peaceful
possession of the land he thought he owned.

Kinglety went to court to enforce his title, and, armed with a judgment, the sheriff's men pushed the Cooneys out. But as soon as the
lawmen left, the Cooneys moved back in. In March 1887, five
deputy sheriffs again ejected them. This time Catherine Cooney
pressed assault charges against the five.

On June 6, 1888, the sheriff invaded again. This time, Mrs.
Cooney met the officers with a knife in each hand and Mr. Cooney
appeared carrying a lead pipe swathed in a stocking. The officers
pulled their guns and the Cooneys backed down, but not before
Catherine Cooney threw an iron (one of the heavy, charcoal-heated

varieties) at one of the lawmen and someone smacked one of the deputies on the hand with a hammer. By nightfall, the Cooneys and their possessions were in the street. But when Kinglety's agents went to take possession on June 7, the resourceful couple had moved back in.

When the case was publicized in the newspaper, the Cooneys gained some sympathy. "Who can read this description of legalized robbery without having passionate feelings of indignation aroused?" a supporter wrote to *The Brooklyn Eagle*. "Michael doubtless believed no one could own such a bit of unused land and proceeded to enter on its use; but no sooner has he accomplished something of benefit to the city and settled down to enjoy the fruits of his labor than he has it snatched away . . . Are not cases of this kind, varying in detail, occurring every week? Those 20,000 evictions—beg pardon, ejectments—in New York City alone in 1886 were different, so far as surface manifestations are concerned, but the foundations on which they are rooted is the same, viz., the robbery of men of their natural, unalienable rights."

But sympathy and support are two different things. The battle at Clinton and Garnet Streets continued, but not for long. The law was on the side of the landlord, and despite their dogged antics, the Cooneys soon lost their home.

His admirers called him King Corcoran, his detractors Paddy or Rats. He was never convicted of any crime, but he had a reputation as a terrible criminal, famous even during an era when New York was thick with rackets and cons.

James J. Corcoran grew up in Balbriggan, Ireland, and emigrated to the new world when he was in his 20s. He arrived in New

Orleans, but moved to New York just before the Civil War. Finding no place to live, Corcoran created his own kingdom, atop a bluff along Manhattan's First Avenue that was originally known as Prospect Hill and, later, Dutch Hill. He wasn't the first squatter to seize the cliff, but he became the most powerful. And over the years the old names would die out and the cliff would become famous—or, to be more precise, infamous—as Corcoran's Roost.

Corcoran had two basic laws: if people showed proper hatred of the police and agreed to stand by him as the supreme leader, he would let them join his shanty paradise. In addition to his supportive subjects, cows, goats, and dogs had the run of the roost as well.

Corcoran worked as a truckman, or moving man, as did many of his shanty neighbors, but his roost was reviled by many locals as being a den of thieves. The daily papers, particularly *The New York Times* and *New York Tribune*, which catered to an elite audience, covered the doings of the denizens there with fearful interest. "Robberies are of daily occurrence and assaults on peaceable citizens and wandering peddlers are so frequent as hardly to excite passing notice," The *Tribune* thundered. "Women are assaulted. Vessels lying at the docks are plundered, and the Sabbath is desecrated by the hideous revelries of the ruffians."

Despite their criminal reputation, or perhaps because of it, Corcoran's band of squatters became a valued political force on the East Side. They stuffed the ballot boxes for the local alderman, Pat Kinney, who owned a tavern just across from the roost. Through that connection, some of the squatters got jobs with the city. One, John Dineen, was a clerk for the Corporation Counsel, the city's law office.

With good political connections and a talent for opposing the police force with equal force, the citizens of the roost fended off the bulldozers for better than a quarter of a century, but Corcoran finally vacated his shanty in 1882. The Roost, that hilltop hamlet where even the police feared to tread, was quickly graded and covered with tenements. Corcoran bought himself one nearby, at 317 E. 40th Street.

Time treated Rats Corcoran kindly and when he died, in 1900, both *The Times* and the *Tribune* honored him as a New York original rather than a scoundrel. *The Times* reported he left an estate of about $25,000, including several horses.

Around the same time that the former slaves in Brazil founded the first *favela* and the Nubians in Kenya were settling the land they called Kibera, landowners in New York City, aided by the government and the courts, were driving squatters from their homes throughout the five boroughs.

New York today is a real estate city. It is carved into precise parcels, mapped, described, and set down in surveyors' terms and on deeds and mortgages. New York is designed for the speculator, drawn so that every morsel of land is well defined, and any landlord's investment is secure.

But it was a different world in the mid-1800s, when Louis Heineman claimed his small piece of surf at Red Hook Point. He beached a barge on the tidal sands not far from the site where, less than 100 years before, America's revolutionaries had manned Fort Defiance in an attempt to prevent the British from entering New York harbor.

Brooklyn was an independent city (population 200,000) and its far-flung areas were as wild as the West. At Heineman's barge, you could shoot migrating water fowl or drop a line into the water: either way you'd surely come up with your dinner.

A vestige of the first favela.

At first, Heineman operated a bar (the Beach Tavern) and sold food and drink to the hardy hunters who wandered by. But, given the barrenness of the area, it could not have been a busy place. Together with his wife Eliza, who came from Germany, he raised a hardy bunch of children. And later he dropped the restaurant trade, and established himself as a house-mover—for in those days it was often cheaper to move buildings than to build them new.

Heineman held onto his beachfront berth through a variety of means: sometimes physically ("I remember once setting the dogs at him, and I often threatened to shoot him when he used to be bothering me about the place," Heineman said in a curious appreciation of his landowning foe, Billy Beard, in *The Brooklyn Eagle* in 1891), sometimes in court. Heineman actually filed a fake deed in 1870, selling the land to his son Benjamin for $2,000. He paid taxes on the property. Beard could not force him out, so he bought him out, paying Heineman $1,000 and giving him two lots across the street— one as his property, the other as a cheap rental—in exchange for the waterfront land. Heineman then applied for and won the borough's approval to put his skills to work and drag the house he had built on the waterfront across Columbia Street to his new, privately owned lot.

"I did not get as much for the old place as I had a right to, and I could have got $4,000 more for it if I wanted to, but I would not do it," Heineman told *The Eagle*. "There was a secret between me and Billy Beard, but I have never told it to anyone and never will."

The paper speculated that Heineman knew about a deficiency in Beard's title to the land, and circumstantial evidence suggests that *The Eagle* may have been right. Beard's records of his property transactions, now in the collection of the New York Historical Society, show that he and his partner, Jeremiah Robinson, were very concerned with proving that they held title to a strange strip of land called the beetch. This was apparently a freshwater vein that ran down Red Hook peninsula. The beetch was an old Red Hook fishing hole (one 18th century owner sold the beetch, but reserved "a right for himself and his heirs to come and Katch a mess of fish" whenever they wanted). It is described in these ancient deeds only through physical markers: a boulder with the initials NV (for Nicholas Vechte, one of the early owners) carved in it, a black cherry tree 37 yards away, the low-water line, and the point where the marsh gave way to the beach. Beard's attorneys note that "Messrs. Beard and Robinson own the "Beetch" or Nicholas Vechte title to the waterfront which we consider to be the true title." According to newspaper accounts, some local wags swore that Beard had several rocks removed or repositioned to stymie anyone who disputed his title. Of course, who better to shift the heavy slabs than Red Hook's famed house-mover?

Heineman was one of the early squatters, but he was not alone for long. In time, there were so many squatters across the mud flats of South Brooklyn that *The Eagle*, in 1851, compared them to the gold rush settlers who squatted in San Francisco and Sacramento. Their houses, the paper said, had been "built on what has been called the California plan." And the newspaper looked favorably on the illegal action: "They expect, if matters turn out satisfactorily, to be enabled to retain the ground themselves, which is certainly a laudable ambition, and we hope will not be disappointed."

Every nook of the neighborhood had a different name. There was Slab City, so called because its occupants stole boards from a local sawmill to make their homes; Tinkersville, home to many metal-smiths; Phoenix Park, because it rose on the borough's ash heaps; Texas, because local wags considered it so far from downtown Brooklyn that if you were going to go there you might as well be traveling to Texas; and Cuba, whose residents admitted they had no idea why it got the name. And all around Brooklyn, on low-lying areas or craggy hills, other squatter zones cropped up: Darby's Patch, Slickville, Jackson's Hollow, Crow Hill, Gowanus Beach, Smoky Hollow.

At its height, Slab City had 10,000 residents—and its so-called mayor (elected by acclamation, or perhaps simply by his own proclamation), Hon. William Farrell, was a stalwart of Brooklyn's Democratic political machine. Indeed, no local politician could afford bad relations with the shantytowns because they were a powerful voting bloc. In 1884, Brooklyn Mayor Seth Low, known as an honest, good-government politician, made a historic state visit to Slab City, and authorized $23,000 to bring health improvements to the district. In return, of course, he expected the residents' votes. Such was the power of the squatters.

Squatter homes were quite imaginative. John Connell, designated by Mayor Farrell as Slab City's road commissioner, thatched his roof with flattened tomato cans. One of Heineman's neighbors, a man named Norton, built himself a floating house that *The Eagle* christened "a sort of ark—which can be fastened to the side of the street, and which can be floated away at pleasure." In Tinkersville, Daniel Burns chose to defeat the sea rather than harness it. He built a walkway above the tidal flatlands and erected his shack on the wood pilings. Slowly, he filled in the gap between the water and the house, fighting the tides and the winds. Eventually, he created his own piece of property: a hillock that jutted out into the water. And when speculators torched his home, Burns and his family perched in the one room not gutted by the fire and rebuilt, erecting a larger, more substantial house to surround the smaller one within. Burns did this because he knew that if he were to move, even temporarily, he would lose his claim to the land. Unfortunately, his son Henry, who took over the house when Daniel and his wife Isabella died, was not so savvy. When the Cuttings, a major landowning family, tried to evict him, he argued that his mother had a title deed that had been destroyed in the fire. A local court decided his claim was plausible and dismissed the eviction case. But the Cuttings appealed, and, in a 1901 opinion, an appellate judge derided two family members who testified that the deed had existed (the judge suggested that what they thought was a deed, with a price of $1,400, was actually a rent receipt; that the landlord might have misled the ill-educated squatters was not, apparently, a possibility), and ruled that Burns could not claim adverse possession:

> To hold that one who is in occupancy under the circumstances of this case, weighted, as he is, with the presumption that his occupation is in subordination [to the landlord's title deed], can establish adverse possession by mere lapse of years, would be to go too far, in the absence of all proof of actual, open, notorious, continued or exclusive acts, or of any claims continually asserted and maintained that such possession was hostile to the title of the plaintiff.

The case was thrown back to the lower court and Burns lost the land his father had created and the house in which his family had lived for better than 40 years.

The law remains skewed against squatters to this day. In 2001, a panel of New York judges ejected Mark Whitcombe and his family from a house he had taken over almost two decades before. The case involved a single-family home on Ditmars Street in City Island, a small waterfront community in the East Bronx. Whitcombe moved into the vacant frame building in 1982. He stayed there, fixing the house, tending it as if he were the owner, but never paid taxes and never attempted to establish title. Over the years, the property was sold several times, and finally a title-holder took Whitcombe to court to evict him. Whitcombe countersued claiming adverse possession, but five Judges from New York's Appellate Division ruled

that Whitcombe could not substantiate the claim. In a ruling similar to the one that booted Henry Burns a century before, the judges
noted that New York law requires squatters to seize a property in a
manner that is "hostile and under a claim of right, actual, open and
notorious." They ruled that Whitcombe "entered with no greater
intention than that of enjoying, in effect, free tenancy" and therefore couldn't make an adverse possession claim.

In a sense, squatters like Burns and Whitcombe were lucky. At
least they got their day in court. The squatter citizens of Slickville
didn't have time for legal bickering. The tides were so tough in their
locale that residents were constantly on the edge of desperation.
Many built their homes like pushcarts, so that when waves came
crashing in, residents simply went outside and rolled the entire
domicile to the safety of the high-water line.

Most squatters dwelt in fetid marshy areas. As the city of
Brooklyn developed the area, the streets were bermed up—in many
places 20 or 30 feet higher than the adjoining lots. It must have
been a surreal sight: these collections of shanties whose roofs didn't
even rise to the level of the road.

Despite their sunken appearance, the squatter communities were
lively and commercially active. There were squatter groggeries and
groceries. Squatters ran the rag trade and boiled bones. Squatter
children collected swill from some local distilleries to feed to the
hogs. They scoured the streets for old cans, which they would heat
over an open fire to remove the solder: both the solder and the scrap
metal could be sold for reuse. There were even squatter rooming
houses. In the nicer establishments in Slab City, a bed in a shared
room could cost 25 cents a night. People in the shantytowns raised
cows, goats, and pigs, and milk from Slab City's herd was sold every
day on the streets of nearby fancy neighborhoods. In Brooklyn

Heights, one local writer recalled, smart salesmen marketed Slab City milk as being fresh from upstate cows.

And the squatters weren't all eking out a living from primitive recycling or herding animals to pasture. They were entering public service as well. The most famous Red Hook squatter, from the 1870s through 1890s, was Inspector Edward Reilly, a decorated Army veteran (he was wounded during the Civil War at Antietam) and longtime member of the Brooklyn police force. He grew up in the shanties, on Clinton Street, nor far from where Michael and Catherine Cooney set their home, although with a police salary and Civil War pension he later moved out and acquired some properties around the borough. When he died in 1895, prominent politicians and police officials attended his funeral.

Two other long-term squatter villages were prominent in Brooklyn: Crow Hill and Jackson's Hollow.

Crow Hill was the squatter area cultivated by African-Americans. Its history was given by a sympathetic journalist for *The Eagle*. Before the Civil War, he wrote, New York was a segregated and horribly prejudiced place. "In those stirring times the Metropolis was not a healthy place of abode for colored men. They were hunted like wild animals from hole to corner, and eventually large numbers of them in very fear of their lives fled across the river and did not stop until they reached Crow Hill."

There were two principal reasons why Crow Hill was relatively safe. First, Brooklyn already had a legal African-American colony at Weeksville, where the farm employees of the wealthy Suydam family had made their homes. Crow Hill was just a bit beyond Weeksville, and so few people noticed when squatters began building shacks there. Second, in the 1850s there was much less pressure for land, and Crow Hill was far enough from the center of Brooklyn that it had yet to become subject to speculation. Still, to protect themselves, the early residents of Crow Hill barricaded their homes behind an earthwork embankment they called Fort Sumter.

Many Crow Hill residents worked at the Fulton and Washington Markets in Manhattan—doing hard manual labor hauling crates of fish and produce—and they would trudge miles each way to get to and from work because the stagecoach that plied Atlantic Avenue was designated for whites only.

Crow Hill had its businesses too, and several pleasure palaces. Castle Thunder, in an old farmhouse at the corner of Bergen Street and Rochester Avenue, was one of the most popular taverns. Another was a true squatter phenomenon: a man named Bob Williams fenced in some land and established a shaded picnic ground that he called a hotel and that was busy on summer weekends. Crow Hill really grabbed the headlines in December 1882, after a sensational love triangle murder. Alexander Jefferson, a Crow Hill resident, confessed to killing two women in their shanty because he suspected that one of them was dating his brother. After a lengthy trial, he was sentenced to death. But the hanging—held in public—was botched, and Jefferson thrashed for 4 minutes and tore the black hood from his face before he died. In another gruesome detail, his skeleton was donated to the collection of a museum of anatomy on Manhattan's lower Broadway.

By the early 1900s, part of Crow Hill was wiped out to make way for a golf course. Private owners took care of the rest, evicting the remaining squatters.

Jackson's Hollow was a chunk of property beyond Fort Greene Park and running all the way to the water, which was tied up in a contentious inheritance case. The property had been part of a farm owned by Samuel Jackson, who emigrated from England and settled in Brooklyn in 1642. His grandchildren and great-grandchildren squabbled over the land, and the case played out like a local version of Dickens's Jarndyce vs. Jarndyce, lasting about half a century. While the heirs battled it out in court, Irish immigrants took over a swampy portion of the land, bordered by Myrtle Avenue, Greene Avenue, Grand Avenue, and Classon Avenue. They were never quite squatters (most paid $10 or $15 in ground rent annually), but they operated completely outside local laws. In 1858, more than 1,000 people were living in the Hollow. The neighborhood had a reputation as a breeding ground for ruffians: a hard-drinking, hard-fighting place. The local papers were full of allegations of illegal boxing matches being organized in Jackson's Hollow. In 1876, when Edward Scott, a police officer, died after being hit by a brick thrown by one of the inhabitants after an altercation, Jackson's Hollow won the reputation as a neighborhood of pure evil. The feud over the Jackson estate was settled in 1888, and the squatters, although some had been in residence for 50 years, were soon ejected.

Manhattan, too, was a squatter city. Today the Upper East and Upper West Sides are among the city's wealthiest neighborhoods, but they were quite different a century ago. Picture more than 20,000 squatters living in self-built communities on the knolls and cliffs that made up most of Manhattan Island before it was graded and tamed for easy real estate development. "All over the round land, dropping riverward to the west, we see, side by side with desolate old mansions, that were fashionable water-side villas in 1800, the outlying shanties, rebels in their way against the urban constraint of the town proper," one chronicler wrote in 1880. "The skyline of shantytown is dotted with bird-houses. The roofs are bestuck with them. They sit acock of the gables, and atop of lonely poles . . .

The airy colony does its courting, its mating, its setting and its nursing, and all the other duties of life, in perfect quiet and content."

As in Brooklyn, they had distinct communities. Dutch Hill (or Corcoran's Roost), was built on the rocky banks of the East River from 39th to 40th streets. A smaller squatter outpost bordered what was then called Grand Central Depot on East 42nd Street. Goatville covered the Upper East Side and reached into Harlem. The West Side had Ashville, Dutchtown, Shanty Hill, and Wallhigh, with thousands of shacks lining the bluffs from 50th Street to 100th Street. Squatters populated the land that became some of the city's major parks, including Central Park in Manhattan and Pelham Bay Park in the Bronx.

A century ago, the city's illegal communities bore a great resemblance to the squatter regions of the Third World today: chaotic and cacophonous but also lively and commercial.

"The shanty architect revels in unevenness," journalist H.C. Bunner wrote in 1880. "He finds no two feet of surface on a level, and he adapts his structure to the condition of the site . . . There are bits of wood from the docks, burnt-out city houses, from wrecks of other shanties; there are rusty strips of roofing tin, sheets of painted canvas; the foundations are of broken bricks, neatly cemented, and the top of it all is tin, slate, shingle, canvas and tarred paper." Newspapers turned up surprising facts, like the squatter who amassed a fortune of $30,000.

New York's squatter communities had their own stores and bars. A squatter saloon on Eighth Avenue and 78th Street served German fare and homemade *kummel* (a caraway seed and fennel liquor). The Terrace, a grocery at the corner of Eighth Avenue and 67th Street, across from Central Park, was a squatter general store that newspapers likened to Dickens's Old Curiosity Shop. And beer halls dotted the hills of these shanty districts. A contemporary journalist described a visit to a squatter saloon:

> You climb up a shaky flight of steps and you enter a woeful lit-
> tle strip of a room—perhaps eight feet by fifteen. At one end
> are the bar and the German brigand who owns it; at the other
> several young local loafers . . . Meanwhile, glance through
> the door at the back. You see a huge empty room, dark except
> where light creeps in around the edges of the shutters, and
> shows the faded pink and blue fly-paper on the ceiling; the
> plain benches against the walls, and the kerosene lamps in
> iron brackets screwed to the side-posts. This is Shantytown's
> ball-room; where a fiddle or a banjo or peradventure a cracked
> piano, leads some queer revelry in the winter-time.

Shanties were so common in New York that Harrigan & Hart, the leading vaudeville duo of the age, memorialized them in a musical called "Squatter Sovereignty," which premiered at the Globe Theater on Broadway on January 9, 1882, and ran for 168 performances: an unbelievably long run in an era when most stage shows lasted less than a month. Writer Edward Harrigan undoubtedly drew on his own knowledge of the shanty areas in the revue. Although born poor, his vaudeville success made him a rich man. By the 1880s, Harrigan had a townhouse in Greenwich Village, a vacation home upstate, and an investment property on Madison Avenue, next to one of the city's large squatter villages.

Manhattan's squatter outposts were full communities. One West Side environ called Ashville (centered at what today is W. 81st Street) had its own school house, schoolmaster, priest, and chapel. Just off Ninth Avenue, nestled among the squatters near Central Park, was the Chapel of the Church of the Transfiguration. (The chapel is long gone, but the church remains: its base of operations still exists on E. 29th Street, where it is known by the friendly moniker The Little Church Around the Corner.) The Bloomingdale Reform Church, Rev. Carlos Martyn, pastor, was hidden among the shanties at Ninth Avenue and 71st Street. The Paulist Fathers (their presence remains on the West Side in St. Paul's Roman Catholic Church at 59th Street and Ninth Avenue) also ministered to the squatters. One priest, Father O'Gorman, was glad to speak with an inquisitive reporter in 1880. "There is but little vice or crime among the people of Shantytown," the journalist reported after his conversation with the clergyman, who noted that the squatters were not the destitute bums they were made out to be by real estate developers—but had disposable income and could "afford to be generous to us" by contributing to the collection plate.

The squatters were also tied into the city's democratic machine. They were dedicated voters. From the 1860s through the 1880s, the four densest squatter blocks of the Upper West Side accounted for half the votes in the 19th Ward—almost 700 ballots—meaning that anyone who wanted to win local office had to pay attention to the illegal residents. Most often, it was the Tammany Hall Democrats who won the majority of the squatter ballots. This drove *The New York Times* crazy. "In one ward," the newspaper sniffed in 1864, "they combined a year or two ago, in sufficient numbers, to control the elections for Aldermen and Councilmen." In 1867, the newspaper again weighed in with a nasty editorial:

They are conspirators against the order of society; and their ability to defy the law is referable primarily—solely, we may say—to the fact that the male adult portion of them are invested with the right of citizenship, or succeed generally in voting at elections, whether they have the right or not. They are universally courted by office-seekers of high and low degree; and their votes are held sufficient, by the ruling class in the City, to be a full equivalent for the immunity from rents, taxes, and licenses, which they enjoy.

Throughout the 1880s, the newspaper claimed, without providing any evidence, that the only reason squatters were able to resist landlords and block ejectment efforts was that they had the protection of John Kelly, leader of the Tammany machine. It is true that the city's Buildings Department, which was controlled by Tammany, granted occupation licenses to many of the shack-dwellers. However, New York's politicos never wholeheartedly weighed in on the side of squatters, which is why ejectments and evictions were so prevalent.

Indeed, the authorities hated the shantytowns. Where some saw industrious citizens or comic potential, the upper crust saw crime, pestilence and disease in these self-built communities.

"There are numerous shanties in the northern portions of my district, which are occupied by a shiftless, careless, filthy class of people, who ignore the commonest requirements of decency and cleanliness living in intimate association with and proximity to dogs, horses, pigs, geese, and other biped and quadrupeds, whose habits they assimilate and whose filth commingles with their own," a Health Department official wrote in 1876.

"It is next to impossible to do anything with these people, or to improve their sanitary surroundings. Complaints innumerable have been made by me, and orders by the score have been issued by the Boards against these shanties, but with very little permanent effect. Their occupants are an irresponsible set, against whom a legal proceeding would be worthless, and after a superficial cleansing of the Augean stables, they soon relapse into and wallow in their pristine filth. The only radical remedy for these nuisances is to drive the shanty population out altogether from their strongholds, an event which is certainly only a question of time."

Prodded by property owners groups, like the West Side Association, which represented speculators on the Hudson River side of Central Park, the Health Department avidly pursued the squatters. They prosecuted the squatters for health code violations, and threatened them with eviction if they did not hook their simple homes into the city's sewer system.

The local press piled on the criticism as well. "Squatters are in every land a terror and a scourge," *The New York Times* editorialized in 1854, calling their existence, "additional reason to pity the rich." Thirteen years later, the newspaper was still carping. Squatting, the paper lamented, "will go on just so long as the squatter population and their kindred are sustained with the idea that they are a strong and dominant political force among us." And again, 18 years on, *The Times* called for "a vigorous movement against these foul habitations." To *The Times* and most other newspapers, the squatters were godless criminals, a scourge, a nuisance, a horror.

In August 1867, *The Times* seized on an issue that would serve as a rallying cry against the city's squatters for decades: the possibility of disease. "In 1866," the newspaper reported, "the cholera broke out in twelve shanties of the Central Park—or East Side—settlement, carrying away its victims from each, and leaving four of these shanties tenantless. The statistics of the Board of Health show that nearly all the sickness in the Twenty-fifth Sanitary District was traceable to this same locality. Not only did the cholera make its first appearance there, but also scarlet fever and measles, and spread thence over the district." In 1885, *The Times* again cited the same health department report, claiming that cholera was "more fatal and more persistent" in the Central Park squatter village "than in any other cholera field within the limits of the metropolitan district."

The first report was an exaggeration. The second was sheer bunk. It was true that in 1866 the disease was particularly persistent in one of the four squatter villages that bordered Central Park, because residents did not have enough money to hook into the new Croton water system and the shallow wells they used were contaminated with the cholera bacillus. But the very report the newspaper quoted —the 1866 Annual Report of the Metropolitan Board of Health— makes abundantly clear that the principal area of cholera infection was in "the southwestern part of the city—in the Twelfth Ward—on a tongue of low land projecting into the bay." Anyone who knows New York geography—as any self-respecting reporter should— knows that this was not anywhere near Central Park. Furthermore, although the epidemic claimed 1,138 lives in Manhattan in just 4 months, only 15 people in the districts near Central Park died. By contrast, three small blocks in Chinatown—Mulberry, Mott, and Baxter streets—accounted for 117 deaths: 10 percent of the terrible total. According to the statistics, the tenements, not the squatter shanties, were the real incubators of the disease. As the report *The Times* cited concluded, "the first and at all times the most prolific cause of disease was found to be the very insalubrious condition of most of the tenement-houses."

Indeed, a close reading of health department reports shows that the squatter communities were relatively free from egregious violations of the sanitary code. The city's sanitary officials had the power to inspect and, if things were particularly bad, to issue complaints against the offending structures. And here, the shanties excelled. Between 1872 and 1876, inspectors visited 2,318 squatter shanties, but only cited 4.8 percent of them, or 112, for follow-up action. That compares with 19.1 percent of the private homes they inspected and almost 20 percent of the tenements. The clear conclusion: shanties required much less health department action than any other kind of dwelling in the city.

Only one of the city's health inspectors showed compassion for the squatters in his district. He understood their hardships instead of blaming them. "The shanties, of which there are about eight hundred (800) in all, are placed in German or Irish groups at every conceivable point of the compass, separated here and there by passageways," wrote S.D. Wadsworth, the sanitary inspector for portions of the West Side and northern Manhattan. "Their occupants are an industrious people, and many make their homes very comfortable by a skillful thatching of tin, oil-cloth, or other material, and the insides of their dwellings are generally lathed and plastered. During the droughts of the past summer there was much suffering among them on account of the great scarcity of water. Their 'wells' and 'springs' were nearly all dry."

As one free-thinking architectural journal noted, the shanty-towns may not have been beautiful, but, because of the light, air, and well-ventilated chimneys in most of the dwellings, they were in many ways preferable to the overcrowded blocks of tenements being thrown up by developers (including some of the same developers who were trying to evict the squatters from their properties).

Anyone who took the time to enter the shanties, and could free themselves from the dominant biases about the squatters, found well-tended homes occupied by people who were so busy scratching for money and food they had little time for idleness. On occasion, these favorable reports found their way into the newspapers. "The dwellers in this New World edition of Petrea are not outlaws in any sense, and by common admission of the landlords, there are no thieves or bad characters among them. They are simply very poor people, as respectable as possible in a country where nominal respectability so closely infringes on the question of money," *The Daily Graphic* reported. Even *The New York Times* conceded in a few reports that shanties were not all bad. In late 1880, after landlords vowed to smash the squatter shanties on the West Side, a *Times* editorialist commented that, "were such a thing to be done in Ireland under the prompting of a landlords' league, it would be called 'brutal eviction.'" The writer added that "the comparative ease with which pigs and poverty are made to give way to brown-stone mansions suggests that next to a perfect despotism a perfect democracy is the type of government which lends itself most easily to the strong method of enforcing the law." In a follow-up later that year, *The Times* admitted that "the health of the 'shanty population' compares favorably with that of those living in the lower class of tenement houses to which they would naturally gravitate if driven from the shanties." And, the newspaper acknowledged that the most bitter invective against the squatters came not from health officials but from people "whose property is depreciated by their presence."

The real estate lobby, however, was relentless. In 1870, it successfully pressured the state legislature to liberalize the ejection laws, making it easier to push squatters from their homes. Later in the decade, West Side property owners petitioned the health department to move on the squatters, because it was easier and cheaper than going to court. As *The Commercial Advertiser*, one of the leading newspapers of the time (and also a mouthpiece for local real estate interests), commented, "the Health and Building Departments have more arbitrary powers to remove the shanties," leaving squatters "no remedy at law."

What the real estate interests concealed, of course, was that some landlords who wanted to make some money on their vacant properties were actually responsible for the growth of squatting around the city. "The first comers were really squatters," an observant reporter noted in *The Times*. "Later on rent was charged and collected, and the rates have steadily risen of late years. The ground rent for a shanty ranges now from $20 to $100. These are 'open leases,' still, the dwellers are lessees of property, and citizens." In other words, the landlords who complained so bitterly about the squatter scourge were actually making decent money from their occupants.

But the landlords had the ear of City Hall. The Board of Health, in particular, embarked on a drive to rid the city of squatters. In April 1881, it pushed long-term squatters out of 67th Street near Lexington Avenue on Manhattan's East Side even though the property was owned by the city. Mount Sinai Hospital coveted the property, and so the squatters had to go. The eviction was a show of force, as 75 policemen guarded the phalanx of city workers who took axes to the delicate homes and smashed them to the ground.

"While the workmen were engaged in pulling down the framework of an unusually small shanty, a woman was seated on an old worn-out sofa in the yard," the *Tribune* reported. "She was bareheaded and held a baby in her arms. The furniture and other articles that had been taken from the home were piled around her in great confusion." The woman complained that she and her mother had been living in the house for 18 years, and had been paying rent to the city all that time. She accused the city of "enticing her into the house and then turnin' her out." Ultimately, the city's show of force was not necessary. "There was little resistance, and only one of the policemen remained," the newspaper noted.

Of course, the hospital did not use the property for long. It soon moved to more spacious quarters further uptown. Today the squatter site is the home of Hunter College, part of the City University system. Interestingly, this was a perfect test for *The Times's* theory that squatters had the protection of Tammany Hall. Here, squatters were being evicted from city property. A review of the minutes of the Board of Health clearly show that the Tammany Hall bigwigs who sat on the city's Sinking Fund Commission, the behind-the-scenes board that actually controlled all property owned by the city at the time, pushed the Health Department to go after the squatters. Either this was an incredible sell-out, or *The Times* was way off base about squatter power. The newspaper covered the eviction, but took no notice of the Tammany Hall angle in its columns.

Over the next 20 years, squatters came to understand that it was only a matter of time before city wrecking crews would made short work of their shanties. "A lawyer told us that they couldn't tear the roof from over our heads, but they have," said John Bhernes, a squatter at Tenth Avenue and 79th Street. "Our boards are all broken up now and not good for building again. They don't seem to give the poor people any show. We couldn't sleep in the streets and had no place to go to. We've worked hard for over seven years to build this house." One West Side owner bragged that he had invaded a cabin, tied up the squatter, and forced him to watch from afar as his shanty was ripped down.

And the health board found a new wrinkle. In addition to push-ing for expensive hookups to the city's water system, it ordered squatters to tie into the city's sewer system as well. Eugene Schatz, who lived for more than a decade in a squatter settlement on Madison Avenue in the 90s, was proud of his home. "A man can live much more comfortable here than he can in a flat," Schatz told a *Tribune* reporter when the city ordered him out of his home. "I'd sooner have this than the finest flat that was ever built." But he and other tenants knew what they faced: "We can't build no sewer. We haven't got money enough."

Lawyers for landlords had a grab bag of tricks for displacing squatters. Here's what they did to the single family that occupied Sandy Gibson's Rock, sometimes called Mill Rock: a small island in the East River across from 97th Street. Gibson started living on the rock, which varied in size from 2 acres to 8 acres depending on the tide, in 1860, when he bought a run-down shanty there from a pre-vious squatter named John Clark. Gibson and his wife Caroline raised five children on their island. They made their money fishing and ferrying people across the river. After a few years, Gibson rec-ognized that the location of his outpost in the center of the busy East River made it a lucrative perch. He sold the right to advertise to a local capitalist, and soon his rock was festooned on all sides with brightly painted billboards, making it a kind of maritime Times Square. With his newfound riches, Gibson tore down his shanty and built a solid frame house.

Sandy Gibson died in 1872, and Caroline in 1875. But their son Tyler and his two sisters, Jane and Violetta, continued on in the house.

In 1885, a state property commission determined that it owned the rock and decided to sell it to raise money. William Byrnes, who bought it, quickly flipped it to a lawyer and real estate speculator named Cecil Campbell Higgins. And he brought suit to eject the Gibson family. Tyler Gibson claimed adverse possession, but Higgins found a novel way to rebut him. Although a period of 20 years establishes adverse possession of privately owned property, it takes 40 years to establish adverse possession on state property, which Mill Rock was until Byrnes bought it. So, Higgins argued, adverse possession couldn't apply. In 1886, Justice McGowan of the Ninth Judicial Circuit agreed. Higgins didn't know what to do with the island he had just bought, so he leased it to the United States Dynamite Company, which stored a ton of explosives there. The Gibsons remained on the rock until January 1887, when Higgins paid them $10 to leave the property that had been their family's home for 27 years.

Even nonprofit organizations got into the act. The New York Historical Society, where today you can find some of the papers of the West Side Association, and records of some of William Beard's real estate dealings, built its home on the west side of Central Park in 1901. To clear the property, the Society drove out two elderly squatters who had maintained a shanty and cultivated peach trees on the site for decades.

After the 1898 merger into New York City, Brooklyn too began expanding the tactics available to muscle squatters out. In 1902, the city used eminent domain to push out a group of squatters along Brooklyn's Eleventh Avenue who had occupied the turf for a 25 years. The city took the land to install sewers and grade the area for streets. "As days go, it was a sad and mirthless one for the community of squatters," *The Brooklyn Eagle* commented. "The memories of 25 years were being blotted out—and all for two new streets and a sewer."

When Louis Heineman died in 1904, he was probably 87 years old, at least according to what he told a census bureau enumerator in 1870. But his relatives told *The New York Times* that he was 104— born, they said, in 1799—and thus had lived in three centuries. And why not? To his family, the wizened immigrant who remembered shooting waterfowl and fishing on the Red Hook shores must have seemed like a relic. The waterfront Heineman had known— indeed, the city Heineman had known—was gone: Slab City. Tinkersville, Kelsey's Patch, Cuba, Texas, Smoky Hollow, Gowanus Beach. All eradicated. Even his old nemesis, Billy Beard, was more than a decade cold. Across the East River, Corcoran's Roost had been obliterated 20 years before, and the dirt had been hauled across the river and used to fill Jackson's Hollow. The old aeries of the Upper East and Upper West Sides had been smoothed over and apartment blocks were on the rise.

The same year Heineman died, the last of the squatter settlements near Central Park—a small community called Sunken Village, on W. 64th Street between Central Park West and Broadway—was finally torn down. "It was more than 30 years ago that a laborer named Joyce built a little shack in the hollow west of the park," the *Tribune* reported as the residents packed their possessions. "The streets were graded up on three sides, and apartment houses presently closed in the fourth. As the surrounding property was claimed squatters moved their shacks and little frame houses into the pit. The roofs of the most pretentious story and a half houses did not come to the level of the pavement." By this time, no health department order was necessary. The real estate firm that owned the land served the eviction notices on September 6. All but one of the residents had moved by October 4, slinking off without any protest. Although the residents thought they were being pushed out because of imminent development, the sad truth was that the real estate firm said it had no immediate plans to build. "The squatters were ousted simply because the present is as good as any other time for that purpose and because, if there was to be trouble in getting rid of any of them, the company wanted to have it now rather than on some future occasion when it might hold up a building operation."

Over the first two decades of the new century, even more outlying squatter areas would be cleared. Crow Hill would be dug up for development, replaced first by a golf course and then by orderly lines of townhouses. Pigtown, a central Brooklyn squatter area, would be pushed out too, and in its place a ballpark would arrive: Ebbets' Field. There was a sad irony in the construction of the baseball stadium. In the 1870s, an amateur team from Slab City won the state baseball championship. Forty years later, their fellow squatters halfway across the borough were pushed out to make way for a professional team.

In 1903, a Brooklyn alderman complained that the city was letting squatters occupy land worth $1 million and demanded action to remove them. In February 1911, the Brooklyn Institute of Arts and Sciences (today called the Brooklyn Museum) successfully pressured the city to pull down Goat Town, a small squatter settlement that adjoined its property and the Botanic Gardens. By 1913, essayist Djuna Barnes profiled an area she claimed was Brooklyn's last squatter community. Her article, although tough on the squatters, got the feeling right: "It was quite out of the question to sympathize with them, for they got what we did not—something for nothing—and yet, go out to them, stand beside the hut, and watch the line of cars twisting along, watch the hurry of the people who work for their rent, and somehow there creeps into your heart a mad desire to place your foot on the earth and claim it as yours by the inalienable right of birth."

A few isolated squatters hung on in less developed areas. Through the 1920s, Marion H. Laing managed to outwit authorities and remain on her squatter perch on an island off the shore of the Bronx. To most people, Hog Island was little more than a few boulders, some tidal salt bogs, and, in season, gently waving grasses. But Marion Laing called it home. She moored a houseboat and lived there year-round. She collected driftwood, which she burned for warmth in the winters. She fished the East River, dug for clams, and supplemented her take by buying other items from a friendly resident of nearby Hunter Island. For a time, in the 1920s, Hog Island became a bohemian hangout, and a dedicated group of sunbathers and beachcombers joined her there in the warmer months. But, by the end of the decade, the New York State Park Commission sued to remove most of the people who were occupying shanty colonies along the waterfront. The sunbathers left, but Marion Laing withstood their eviction efforts. After her death, a bronze tablet appeared on the island's eastern shore, facing the sun. It read:

MARION H. LAING
Died September 12, 1930
"This island was her paradise"

No one stepped forward to take credit for the memorial. But for three decades thereafter, someone—no one knows whether it was the same admirer or admirers who installed the metal memorial or whether others joined in the homage—braved the icy waters and tricky currents to place a wreath on the spot every New Year's Day. The tradition, it's sad to say, seems to have ended.

In 1941, the city evicted Vincenzo Aurichio, who had built himself a shanty in 1926 on what was a garbage dump in Astoria, Queens, and lived there for 15 years, tending a prize-winning garden and expanding his shack into a three-room house. In a decision that would not have pleased Solomon, the judge allowed the garden to stay, but ordered Aurichio's home torn down. When the squatter pleaded for more time, the judge gave him two weeks.

The squatters were people whose communities defied the rigor of square blocks, whose dwellings rolled with the landscape rather than flattened it. They were people who dared to dream of a home: and then dared to build it in a place they didn't own.

"The shanty is the most wonderful instance of perfect adaptation of means to and end in the whole range of modern architecture," a sympathetic journalist wrote. "Nothing is prepared for it, neither ground for material. Its builders have but an empirical knowledge of the craft they practice. They scorn a model, and they work with whatever comes to hand."

That writer marveled at the simple beauty of squatter homes: "The gallery railings are painted a bright green, and enriched with iron scroll-work from some ruined villa-wall; the front porch is surmounted with a neat cornice, a well-tended vine clambers about the queer, rough corners, turkey-red curtains deck the irregular windows, and the stones and clam-shells that border the alley path shine with whitewash." Inside, the reporter continued, was even better: "Five children; all clean; and money in the bank. This is the kitchen—also the dining room. Good stove; dresser; bright pots and pans; white stone-china. Yankee clock on shelf. Old-clothed table. Doors right and left. Through left we see white bed, and crib with patch-work quilt. Right, best room of house; horse-hair sofa, chromo, fancy clock, sewing-machine and—a sofa-bed. This is luxury. Who wouldn't live in a shanty?"

Why didn't New York's squatters rebel? Why didn't they organize resistance to the evictions? Why didn't the city legalize its squatters, as San Francisco did under the Van Ness ordinance? Perhaps because New York's squatters didn't carry guns. Perhaps because the real estate interests in New York were entrenched, old-world, powerful, while the squatters were recent arrivals from Ireland and Germany and didn't know how to use the power of their vote or their brawn. In California, by contrast, almost everyone was a recent arrival, and so an aristocracy had yet to develop. Perhaps New York's squatters accepted leases because they were agrarian immigrants who were used to leasing property. Those leases proved to be their undoing, because courts have ruled that adverse possession claims must be adverse all the way; if you pay rent to anyone, you are clearly not occupying the property with the appropriate adverse intent.

New York's squatter neighborhoods were haphazard and rough, but also cozy and stable. There was a special spirit in those communities. "Taken as an architectural totality, they look as though they had been constructed by crazy poets and distributed by a whirlwind that had been drinking," The Daily Graphic commented. "They are not blessed with all the modern improvements, but nevertheless make comparatively cozy homes for those whose bank accounts do not as yet enable them to command brown-stone fronts or French flats."

During the Depression, temporary settlements of squatter shanties ("Hoovervilles" in the parlance of the day) were common around the city. But these encampments were home to economic refugees. As the New Deal lifted the economy, and the Depression receded, the temporary villages disbanded without a trace. More recently, in the 1970s, scores of landlords walked away from old tenement buildings. Many buildings slid into vacancy and rot. By the 1980s, squatters took over many of the structures in fringe areas such as Alphabet City (Avenues A to D) on the Lower East Side, and in certain areas of the Bronx and Brooklyn. In Brooklyn, squatters were organized by the community group Association of Community Organizations for Reform Now (ACORN) as a tactical move to put pressure on the city to rehabilitate smaller buildings. In Manhattan, these illegal occupants tended to be younger, better-educated, and more radical than the squatters of old. Still, they braved terrible conditions as they worked to fix their buildings. And they had to fight to stay. The city dispossessed hundreds of squatters, sometimes mounting massive paramilitary attacks on their buildings. In the end, 12 squatter buildings survived, and they outlasted official resistance. In 2002, 11 of those buildings were sold to the squatters as low-income cooperatives (the odd building out opted not to go legal; it remains in stasis: owned by the city and occupied by squatters). The squatters—the hardy few who remained—had won.

In a city of 8 million, a dozen buildings may seem like a statistical blip, an aberration, as meaningless as a dozen bagels. Still, as Popeye, one of the squatters on Avenue C, told me, "For whatever reason, the city made a mistake. We slipped through the cracks in this place that abhors what we are. Being here, in a mundane and tiny way, is committing treason." Popeye takes comfort in the fact that, whatever else is going on in this ever-more-expensive city, "this little place that ain't like the rest of the world will go on. As long as this little thing is here, this kind of spirit will persist in Manhattan."

There was a moment, years ago, when that spirit persisted all over New York. Squatter families—the crazy poets—ruled much of the city's available real estate. It's not possible to say what kind of city New York would have become if they had won, if the shanty dwellers of the Upper East and West Sides had held out against the landlords, if Corcoran still ruled his Roost, if Crow Hill and Slab City and Tinkersville had survived, if Red Hook had remained a Louis Heineman outpost rather than a William Beard development. But isn't it fun to wonder?

Issues on the
Way Forward

CHAPTER 7

The Habitat Fantasy

A cage went in search of a bird.

— Franz Kafka

A world away from Kibera across the Kenyan capital, in a building surrounded by well-watered undulating lawns, lies the complex that houses the world headquarters of the United Nations Human Settlements Programme: the agency called UN-HABITAT. From this tranquil outpost—so green and quiet that you almost feel like you have been transported into a parallel universe—the UN studies the neighborhoods it calls slums and I call squatter communities. Its job, in a sense, is to end the medieval character of these 21st century medieval cities.

Habitat has been in existence for 25 years. It promotes a global agenda of good government, adequate housing, healthy cities, and social empowerment. In addition to its headquarters in Nairobi, Habitat has regional offices in Japan and Brazil; liaison offices in New York, Geneva, and Brussels; and information offices in Budapest, Chennai (India), Beijing, and Moscow. The agency sponsors conferences around the world every year, and huge meetings every 10 years, like the one in Istanbul in 1996. Habitat also funds a variety of studies and promotes what it calls "best practices": the best governmental programs and interventions in the squatter areas.

But despite its undeniably good intentions and the useful research it conducts, some Habitat staffers admit that their actions don't have much relevance to squatters. "In actuality, most local agencies don't need us at all," one veteran Habitat official confided to me. "Maybe they consider Habitat a tool to use to put pressure on their governments. But they don't really need us for anything else because we don't have money. What we can do is only inform both regionally and internationally about what others are doing."

This longtime staffer was speaking of Habitat's relevance to local social service agencies. Down on the mud streets, where the people Habitat wants to represent actually live, the agency has almost no relevance at all. The people working for the agency are dedicated to the cause. But they are most comfortable talking to themselves or people like them. Most Habitat workers wouldn't know what to do if suddenly confronted with a squatter. They are great when discussing theory—the ideas of how to mobilize and improve the lives of the squatters—but they are sorely lacking on the practicalities.

At one point it seemed that Habitat was ready to change that.

In the 2003 *Global Report on Cities*, Habitat executive director Anna Kajumulo Tibaijuka emphasizes "the great potential for improving the effectiveness of slum policies by fully involving the urban poor."

Yet, on the ground, Habitat seems unwilling to put her words into practice. The agency, after a dismal 25 years of inaction and sloth regarding conditions in the mud hut cities in the city where it has its headquarters, announced in 2001 that it would work with the Kenyan government to organize a demonstration project to build new homes for people living in Nairobi's worst shantytowns. After the election of the new government in December 2002, the effort picked up speed. Raila Odinga, a prominent and ambitious member of parliament whose district includes part of Kibera, announced that the project would occur on his turf, in a portion of Kibera called Soweto Village. Over the past year, the rumors flew. According to one, Soweto residents would be evicted and relocated miles away to a town called Athi River while construction was taking place. It took months before Raila finally announced that this would not happen.

At the same time that rumors were flying in Kibera, I visited the Habitat headquarters and asked Chris Williams, one of the staff there, whether the UN had an actual plan for what would happen in Kibera. He had a one-word answer: "No."

To be fair, Williams was one the people at Habitat who believed the agency had a responsibility to move beyond studying squatter communities. He has long pushed the agency to get involved on the ground in making conditions in existing communities better. Williams understood the stakes involved in such an action. "If this project fails, we will live with the failure," he told me. "This is a very messy line of work." And, he added, he understood the danger of working only with the government and not the community: "Maybe a deal has to be cut between the government of Kenya and Habitat about what the project is. But at a certain point. Raila's going to say we're just going to do it, because if we plan forever we'll never do it." If that happened, he suggested, "the casualty will be the community."

With the agency that proposed the program admitting that it had no program and the politicians not quite sure what to do, unscrupulous people found opportunities. Already, while I was in Kibera, people told me that some operators were traveling the mud lanes collecting money (1,000 shillings per family) so that they would supposedly be registered as eligible for housing the UN development. These operators told the people they spoke with that they had been authorized by the provincial administration to do this census. "This whole game was a pure promotion of corruption," complained Geoffrey Peter Mwindi, who told me of the scheme.

A year and a half after the Kenyan election, despite Tibaijuka's words, the UN has yet to involve Kibera people (regular people, not the nonprofits or the provincial administration, or the cadre of skilled outsiders: lawyers, planners, advocates) in pushing forward the project that is supposed to pave the way to redevelopment of the entire community.

And even if Habitat did have a plan and had involved the community, there's another issue: the nuts and bolts issue of being able to make things happen. You have to manage construction. You have to ride herd on your contractors to make sure the job gets done.

"I personally don't think that Habitat has the capacity to do an on-the-ground project," said Japheth Mbuvi, of the Water and Sanitation Program, a multilaterally funded nonprofit that is hosted in Nairobi by the World Bank.

Mbuvi knows a thing or two about failure. His agency, working with the city council and the World Bank, attempted to install water mains in Kibera between 1998 and 2000. It was a $500,000 project, a cost of approximately $1 per Kibera resident. And it was a total failure and embarrassment: the contracts were signed, some of the work was completed, but as of today not one drop of water has flowed and many of the pipes that were installed stayed inactive for so long that people finally ripped them up and sold them for scrap.

Bad management. Bad preparation. Bad accountability. No transparency. And no attempt to instill awareness or pressure from people inside Kibera to keep the heat on the Council to get the work done.

"How honest are we as development agencies?" Mbuvi asked, critiquing his own efforts as well as Habitat's. "We pretend that it's all in the public interest. But there are very radical decisions to be made. There are going to be losers in this, and not everyone will be satisfied at the end of the day."

In Mbuvi's opinion, land—who holds it, controls it, maybe even winds up owning it—will be a major issue for the UN to confront. "Land ownership: that, to me, has been a very big challenge in moving development forward. Who do you engage? If you engage the residents, who benefits? If you improve an area, does it end up being an incentive to the structure owners to raise rents? If so, the residents could get thrown out, and they were the ones who were used to improve the area." And, he added, if the UN attempts to redistribute land, that will have fallout as well. "Reallocating land means people who have been making money for years will lose their income. They're not going to take this lying down. The land issue, I'm telling you, is not easy. There are tough trade-offs that have to be made."

People in Kibera understand this. Bernard Nzau, who has lived in Kibera since 1963 and whose sole income comes from the 20 mud huts he owns, fears that the UN project will not include him. If Kibera is redeveloped, he said, "those who have no money, like me, will sell. And no one from Kibera will wind up staying here." He pleaded for the UN simply to provide loans and expertise. "Why don't you give money to me and show me how to build," he said. "I can do this. If it is something that is good for us, we can agree, because everyone wants development. What we refuse is the people from outside getting the benefits."

Dorcas Mogaka, a community leader from the Kianda neighborhood of Kibera, suggested that there should be a kind of seniority system established for people participating in the project. "Landlords living here should get the first priority [to build]. Then landlords not living here. Then tenants who have been here for more than 15 years."

That's not to say that Dorcas or Bernard should have the final say or that their ideas would satisfy most Kibera residents. They are both landlords and they worry about losing what little stake they have in the community. Still, their comments indicate that they are willing to talk. So are Kibera's tenants. Almost everyone I asked said that they would be willing to pay a bit more for better housing. But how much more can they afford? Few are willing to answer this hypothetical question until the UN actually comes clean on the plan. The point is, only Kibera's tenants can define how much of a cost increase is too much.

And how about Kibera's absentee owners? The UN will most likely have to speak with them, since they are the ones who have the most to lose.

Nothing good will come of the UN plan if it is not thoroughly talked through with the people who ultimately must live with it. And to do that, the UN has to get into the community. This will be a time-consuming and frustrating process. But it is necessary. No outsider can make the tough trade-offs. Only Kibera residents can. "Change does not come easily," Joachim Maanzo told me. "It does not come on a silver platter. Opposition will be there. We should not compromise the interests of a large number of people in Kibera just because of a few who are amassing wealth."

And if Habitat doesn't take the time to talk things through with Kibera, it doesn't have to travel far to see what will happen. Across town, in Mathare, another mud hut shantytown, a local Catholic parish tried to rebuild part of the community, replacing mud blockhouses with permanent concrete homes. But, afraid to replicate the division between landlords and tenants, the church decided to retain ownership of the buildings. Thus the church turned dozens of owners who joined in the plan into tenants. What's more, although the new homes are certainly an improvement on decaying mud houses (they are made of brick and have water taps located near almost every doorway), the rooms are smaller than in the old mud buildings, and people still only have one room per family, with no possibility of expansion. Later, confronted with charges of cronyism, the church hired an outside management company to run the units. But that company, too, had a history of favoritism and corruption. Things got so bad that rowdy protesters torched several of the new brick homes, and they remain unfinished shells to this day. As one of the original participants told me, only partly tongue in cheek, the church project has certainly done one thing: it has united everyone. All the different tribes, landlord and tenant, businessman and thug: everyone now opposes further upgrading of the community.

The other side of Mathare boasts another failed attempt to remake the mud hut city. Here, in what is called Mathare North, the city handed building rights to some locals, who then flipped them to developers for a quick profit. The developers, in turn, built without getting permits. If you visit the structures they erected, you will find that they are already seriously decaying less than a decade after they were built. Although they are concrete high-rise structures, and although many of my friends living in mud huts consider them akin to paradise, in any city of the developed world these buildings would be considered dilapidated and unfit for habitation.

Another issue facing the UN is whether working on a tiny piece of Kibera can ever be seen as successful. Mbuvi suggested that the less sexy approach of working on infrastructure (paved roads, water pipes, sewers, etc.) could be more meaningful than simply building a few new houses. "What benefit does it make to have Soweto top class while the next area there is in complete filth?" Mbuvi asked. "Whether it's 100 meters away or 10, hygiene is a problem. Soweto is actually downstream—so all the bad stuff flows down there. I believe personally that remaking one settlement in Kibera—like Soweto—is just like what has been done over the last 30 years with no tangible benefits."

Again, there is a precedent for this, and it's right next to the neighborhood Habitat wants to fix. There, you can find a 1980s development called Nyayo Highrise. This complex—a score of four- and five-story buildings—replaced a portion of Kibera, and, in return, the local residents who were displaced were supposed to get the apartments there. But, political conniving and payoffs, combined with Kibera's leadership being completely unprepared for the sell-out, led to the buildings becoming a middle-class enclave. Not a single Kibera resident gained a home at Nyayo Highrise. The smallest apartments there cost 8,000 shillings a month: far beyond what Kibera residents can afford.

In early 2004, the UN faced a test of whether it would put into practice its own rhetoric about involving squatters in decision making. The government of Kenya started evicting people and demolishing huts in Kibera as part of three projects: a road that would come blasting through the community, clearing people from a wide swath around the train tracks, and clearing people from underneath electrical lines.

Some community leaders approached Habitat to intervene, and push for a negotiated solution that would give Kibera people some power over their lives. But Habitat remained silent.

In 2003, Habitat titled its annual compendium of statistics on the world's cities, *The Challenge of the Slums.* One previous report was entitled *A World Without Slums.*

But, based on the achievements of the squatters in some countries, Habitat might want to rethink its emphasis. The true challenge is not to eradicate these communities but to stop treating them as slums—that is, as horrific, scary, and criminal—and start treating them as neighborhoods that can be improved. They don't need to be knocked down and built new, because in most cases this will only produce housing that is not affordable to the people who are living there. If the UN wants to make a difference in these communities, it has to work with the squatters. Squatters are interested, hard-working, and responsible adults. They can make decisions for their communities. They can define the trade-offs that will be acceptable. And without them, any work to upgrade their communities will be doomed to fail.

CHAPTER 8

Are Squatters Criminals?

A mistake, King, is hated more than an enemy.

— John Berger

was big in Bombay.

For a brief moment, the idea of a New York journalist living in the squatter community captivated local newshounds, and I became the center of a minor media circus. Newspapers, magazines, radio and television stations called me daily. They seldom bother with squatters. But suddenly it was important to have face time with a strange nonsquatter who had chosen, temporarily, to become a squatter.

At first I was excited. I spoke rapidly, like a coffee fiend. I told *The Times of India* how safe I felt in all the communities I had lived in, how the vast majority of squatters I had met were amazingly giving and generous. Here's what came out in the paper: "Several things are common in squatters all over the world. High crime rate, congestion, neglected kids, and refusal of the residents to move out."

There were two things wrong with this. First, I didn't say it. And, second, the only true thing in it is congestion.

So the next time I spoke with a reporter, I tried to be much more precise. I told the reporter that, of course, there was some crime is squatter communities. But the communities I had lived in were safe—and I felt more secure in them than I felt in many legal neighborhoods. And in Mumbai, I never felt threatened, never saw any crime, never even saw anything that I felt might be potentially criminal. This is how I was quoted: "There is high crime in slums, certainly."

Each time I spoke with a reporter, I felt like I was entering a twilight zone where journalists had no compunction about bending the facts to fit the mold they thought their editors or readers wanted.

The reporters were all nice people. But it seems that many in the elite, newspaper-reading and -writing population in Mumbai have had it drilled into their heads for years that squatters are neglectful and criminal and intransigent, and attempts to tell a different story don't get heard—or, at least, don't get printed. These opinions persist although these are the very same squatters who are driving them to work and cleaning their houses and hauling the materials for a new building rising next to their homes and, even, cooking for them, washing their clothes, and taking care of their kids.

But the spurious facts get repeated no matter what. Squatters and crime. Squatters and crime. Squatters and crime. And if you repeat something enough, it comes to seem true.

"Onde voce mora?"

Where do you live?

The gun was an automatic, and the cop had it pushed in the crevice under my rib cage.

This was my second day in. Everything was new. It was raining—the kind of rain that isn't really rain but more like 100 percent humidity, like thick ooze emerging spontaneously from every object. It was dusk and the cars, the people, the stalls selling pirated merchandise in the Passarella, even the noise from everything and everyone around me seemed glazed and far away.

"Onde voce mora."

I hardly understood the question. I didn't know where I lived. I had just arrived. I couldn't speak the language. Although I had rehearsed my Portuguese before I left, my brain shut down: I didn't know a goddamned thing.

The cop pushed the gun harder against my chest. It was a modern handgun. The plastic barrel wasn't cold against my skin. I didn't have a sense of imminent death. I didn't experience any film noir clichés.

"Onde voce mora?"

I looked over at Paul, who was on the other side of the bus shelter. I hardly knew the guy—but he had been living in Rocinha for a while and seemed comfortable there. He, too, had a gun against his stomach. He was standing like a scarecrow, arms straight out and the cop was shouting at him and jabbing the gun in his gut.

"Onde voce mora," my cop shouted again.

My brain started slowly. Be polite. Show respect. Use the third person singular. "Com voce," I croaked.

It was instinct. Pure fear. Blind. And totally wrong.

"Com eu?" the cop asked.

"Sim, com voce?" I said again.

I wish I could say it was intentional. I wish I could say I knew what I was doing. "Where do you live?" the cop was shouting. And I had answered this way: I live with you. With you, motherfucker. With your mother.

He didn't pull the trigger. Instead, his eyes changed and it seemed that a little light went on in his brain. He finally realized that this strange gringo with a shaved head who was walking out of the favela was most likely not a *viciado*, or drug addict, not a *traficante*, or drug dealer, but most likely simply an incredibly stupid white man.

"Não com voce. Com ele." He corrected me, still angry. Not with me. With him. He waved his gun at Paul.

The cops kept us there for 20 minutes. They made Paul recite the names of the people he knew in Rocinha. He went through dozens of names until he mentioned someone they knew: Josevaldo, the driver for the city's regional administrator. That was when they put away their guns and let us go.

I realized then that there were a dozen people waiting in the bus shelter to avoid the rain. They were all standing within a few feet of us. None of them said or did anything. They didn't even move away from the guns. And it occurred to me: this, for them, was normal, average, ordinary, simply a fact of everyday life—and it is why many favela-dwellers don't like the police.

Dusk. I walked down to the base of Rocinha. It was Saturday, and there had been a street fair along the Caminho dos Boiadeiros, one of the main shopping streets of the favela. Now, most of the merchants were packing up. The road was greasy with trampled lettuce leaves and the leavings from various butchers who were hosing down their cutting blocks. It was a pleasant night, and the streets were crowded. At the bottom of the hill, in a wide space known as Largo dos Boiadeiros, opposite a Catholic Church, a kid was outlined in the half-light. He stood next to a man who had set up a hibachi and was selling skewers of grilled meat.

He was skinny, with long blond hair, and he was wearing baggy Bermuda shorts, flip flops and no shirt. Across his shoulders was a long strap that ran down across his concave hairless chest. The strap was connected to an AK-47. He wore it low, like a rock star, right over his pelvis.

In Rocinha, the guys with guns come out at night. Some stand as solo sentinels; others congregate in packs of 10 or more. A few have pistols—sleek 9 mm jobs that are light enough for kids to stick in the elastic waistbands of their Bermuda shorts—but most carry weapons that would make even a terrorist or revolutionary drool with envy: AK-47s, AR-15s (made by Colt), M-16s (old U.S. Army standard issue), submachine guns, even grenades.

You usually see them on the streets where the drug trade is active, in locations called *bocas de fumo,* or "mouths of smoke." Because of its size, Rocinha has many *bocas.* The main one is in the Valão: and there are dozens of guys with guns at the Friday night *bailes funk.* But there was another *boca* on the Via Ápia, one of the favela's main commercial streets, where young men often sell *papelotes:* little paper sacks of cocaine or marijuana. There was a *boca* high up the hill at Rua Um. And there was also a *boca* on my street in Cachopa. Here, gunmen appeared two or three nights a week.

When you see them for the first time, the weapons don't look real. They seem like cartoon killing machines, with oversized, bent-billed bullet clips hanging off absurdly tiny barrels. And the comic book image is enhanced when the guns are clutched by pimply adolescents or moon-faced teenagers who silently watch as families return from church or children run by kicking a soda bottle soccer ball. But these are not caricatures. These guns will pierce a bulletproof vest at a great distance.

Valéria Cristina, who owns a jewelry and eyeglasses emporium, came to Rocinha because of the guys with guns. She used to live and work in Rio's ritzy Flamengo neighborhood. But after armed robbers assaulted her store and cleaned out her entire inventory, she closed up shop and relocated to the favela. Valéria Cristina was frank about the reason she fled the legal city. "I wanted a more secure location," she said cheerfully as she sat amid the mirrors and stylish designer frames in her bright new store. In the rest of the city being assaulted was always a risk, she explained. Muggings and robberies were common. Thieves had even been known to pull knives and guns in broad daylight on the city's buses and to beat up tourists on the crowded beaches for their backpacks and valuables.

But in the squatter communities things are different. "If someone broke in or tried to rob this store," she said, smiling broadly, "they would die."

Rio's favelas are ruled by three drug gangs: The *Comando Vermelho* (CV: "Red Command"), the *Terceiro Comando* (TC: "Third Command"), and *Amigos dos Amigos* (ADA: "Friends of Friends"). In the early days, these posses were little more than bands of friends with a few handguns and a *jeito* ("talent") for selling marijuana. Now they are big businesses: highly structured, impeccably led, and well-armed. The CV controls most of the drug trade in Rio and Rocinha is part of its empire. The gangs operate on a massive scale. In the past, the government has estimated that as much as $15 million in drugs (3 or 4 tons of cocaine and 7 or 8 tons of marijuana) move through Rio's favelas every month. Only 20 percent of it stays local. The rest is destined for Europe and the United States.

The dealers offer a trade-off to favela residents: accept our presence in exchange for a crimefree community. And they are one of the reasons why the asfalto businesses (business from outside the community) feel safe coming to the favelas. The trade-off is good for business: accept the proliferation of hard drugs and men with guns in exchange for security and freedom from crime.

"There is no risk doing business in the favelas," Daniel Pla, the proprietor of film-developing company Deplá, assured me. "You have more risk with a store in Ipanema [a well-off beachfront neighborhood] than in Rocinha. Because in Rocinha we have no robberies. In Ipanema, we have problems almost every three months. In the favela, the community protects itself."

He conceded that it is strange to see heavily armed men stalking the streets of the neighborhood after dark. But, said Pla, that is not unique to the favelas. "As a citizen, of course, it's a shock," he said. "When you see it yourself, it's incredible. It's very difficult to live with that. At the same time, if you go to the authorities, you know corruption exists and the problem will not be solved. All big cities live with these problems. It's not only a problem here in Brazil. It exists in Chicago, New York, and Los Angeles, too."

But Deplá has a closer relationship with the traffickers than most businesses in Chicago, New York, or Los Angeles. For instance, in the favela called Pavão-Pavãozinho the owner of the Deplá franchise is invited to parties thrown by the chief drug trafficker. Other merchants report similar encounters. The manager of a supermarket just outside Rocinha that caters mostly to favela residents says that Rocinha's *traficantes* call him regularly to find out how things are going and ask whether any customers are giving him problems.

Dante Quinterno, from TV Roc, Rocinha's cable television company, must deal with the traffickers every day. In order to string the cable to each of his 30,000 customers in the favela, he had to create maps detailing every *beco* in Rocinha. A few of the maps are taped to the walls in the meeting room in the TV Roc office in São Conrado, just opposite Rocinha. He said his company never had a problem with the traffickers: perhaps because he is providing a service for the community. But when I asked him if I could get copies of those maps, he declined. "If I gave you a map, word would get around quickly. You might be with the police." I laughed, but he remained serious. "These are the rules if you want to work well in this situation. I don't need to explain them to you or give you a book. They're not written anywhere. But if I give you a map, I will get a call saying 'Be careful.'"

Washington Gonçalves Miranda Ferreira, a teenager who has spent half his life in Rocinha, also understands the trade-off. He has witnessed shoot-outs. He has seen the smugglers—his word for the drug traffickers—beat a man, douse him with gasoline, and dump his burning body onto the highway near Rocinha at the height of rush hour. Washington is extremely moral. He has never used drugs and refuses to participate in the illegal economy—he won't even buy a pirated CD. Yet he insists that he feels most comfortable in the favela.

"I feel safe here," Washington said. "I only feel scared when I go to the rest of the city. You can't fight in Rocinha. If you have a fight, you can get, well, not necessarily killed, but hurt. Because if you fight you might bring the police. And the smugglers don't want that.

If you leave your knapsack somewhere, people will return it. If you leave a bucket of money, if you leave your wallet in a restaurant, people will return it to you. If you lose your wallet in Copacabana, forget about ever seeing it again: it's gone."

Early in my researches, I hired Washington to help translate for me. He had learned English from listening to Iron Maiden albums (some Brazilians aren't huge fans of Brazilian music) and then studied it in school.

After a few days, he confided that his mother was worried about him working for me. I figured that his mother might have wondered where he got the money for his latest Iron Maiden purchase, and that she might have some fears about whether I was an honest man.

But it wasn't that at all. She was worried that he might get in trouble with the drug dealers because he was working for me.

I asked Washington what he thought.

He paused for a minute, then said: "I think the smugglers know who you are. They know your name though you have not talked with them. They know what you are doing here. When you go talk with someone, the *aviãozinhos* follow. They watch and they report. Maybe they even talk with the people you are talking with. The smugglers know what you are doing."

He said that if they had not tried to talk with me or pressure me to stop, then they must be OK with what I was doing.

This taught me a new and valuable lesson. Protecting the *bocas* takes more than guys with guns. It takes eyes. It takes knowledge. It takes social control. And that's where the *olheiros* and *vapores* and *aviãozinhos* (the "watchers," "steamboats," and "little airplanes") come in. The *olheiros* sit at strategic locations: on rooftops or at important intersections or on rock outcroppings or, like the guys on my corner in Cachopa, in a strategically placed abandoned car. If anything the least bit suspicious went on, they blew off firecrackers, warning whomever might be involved in the drug trade that something was up. The *vapores* bring buyers to the *bocas*. And the *aviãozinhos*—often little kids, who tend to run all over the favela—are paid simply to keep their eyes open.

I experienced their operation firsthand. One day not long before I left Rocinha, I took two international researchers on a walking tour. They were planners, in town for a conference held at one of the luxury hotels in Ipanema. I met them at the bus stop at the bottom of Rocinha and took them up through the *becos*. We started our trip in Valão. One of them was interested in the way sanitation is handled in the favela. He asked if he could take a picture of the open sewage channel in the Valão. After a quick look around to make sure no one was wrapping any *papelotes*, I let him take a snapshot.

Three hours later, we were near Rua Um, at the top of the favela, a world away from Valão, when a scar-faced guy emerged from the crowd at a bus stop, grabbed my friend by the shoulder, and said, "Why were you taking pictures of my house?"

My friend didn't speak Portuguese, so I stepped in between them. He repeated his question in a more menacing tone.

I had never seen the man before. He was tough-looking—with a weathered face that probably made him look much older than he actually was—and dressed in the typical Rocinha style: Bermuda shorts, a tank top, and flip-flops. He had tattoos on his arms and was wearing dark sunglasses, so I couldn't see his eyes.

"Why were you taking pictures of my house," he said again.

I introduced myself and my two friends. I explained that they were researchers. I told him they were studying the infrastructure of the favela. I don't know your house, I said. Where is it?

"Alli em baixo," he responded, Down there. Down in the Valão.

I explained again that we didn't know his house, that we were simply interested in infrastructure. I told him that I was living in Rocinha, in Cachopa, although most likely he knew that already.

At length he calmed down and, without words, shook my hand and disappeared back into the throng.

That's how the message was sent: we know what you are doing and wherever you are we can find you. It was simple and devastating. For a few days, I wasn't relaxed wherever I went in Rocinha. And, although I took dozens of snapshots before I left the favela, I never even brought my camera to the Valão.

The cop who is a killer is a small man, a family man, a disciplined man. He doesn't drink or smoke.

He is the son of a preacher. Now in his 30s, he lives with his wife and three children in the same neighborhood where he grew up: a rundown section of Rio far from the famous tourist beaches. He told me he never wanted to be a cop, that he didn't like the police when he was young. He joined the force simply because he needed a job.

He doesn't defend what he does. He's matter-of-fact. After all, it's not that he likes it. He knows that the people he kills are not responsible for crime. He knows that the true culprits lie higher, outside the favelas, in the upper echelons of society.

But the cop who is a killer can't waste time with these thoughts. One false move, one hesitation or distraction, even for a fraction of a second, and he could be dead. So he'd better be ready to kill.

He asked that his identity be protected, so call him Jorge. Jorge has been on the force since the mid-1980s and now commands a *patamo* —a motorized tactical patrol vehicle—that conducts raids on drug dealers in the favelas.

Jorge does not see police work as public service. For him, it's more self-protection. "Traffickers kill police. And what gives them that power is guns. And what gives them guns is money. And how do they get money? Selling drugs." His job, as he sees it, is to interrupt that pattern.

And this allows him to justify things that to an outsider seem absolutely incomprehensible. For instance, Jorge has killed 13 people during his raids on favelas. He has a hard-core attitude. "It's a war. If I'm a warrior, I'm a man who combats another force. I won't tell you I am good and he is bad. I'm a warrior. There is a war. Forget bad or good. They are the other side and it's my job to fight them."

This, he told me, is the credo that has kept him alive: "If you have a gun and you shoot at me, I will kill you. If you take out your gun, it's sufficient for me: I will kill you. But if you don't, if you surrender, then I will not kill you."

But he freely admits he has broken that rule. He was leading a patrol into a favela where two drug gangs were battling for turf. High up the hill, his team got into a shoot-out with one of the gangs. After a lengthy exchange of gunfire, there was a lull. "We injured the chief of that group," Jorge recalled. "He took a bullet to his leg and fell to the ground. He threw his weapon forward and said 'Hey. We can talk now. There's money here. There are guns. Let's work this out. Let's talk.'" Jorge took a slow sip of soda, then continued. "I said 'You want to talk? Here's how we'll talk.'" He pantomimed a series of gunshots. "We killed five guys. Each of the cornered bandits. We killed in a barbarian way." He insists he has no regrets about this massacre. They were *bandidos* ("bandits," the bad guys) and they were trying to kill him. Jorge says he has also marched into favelas and beaten people up in order to prove his toughness to the dealers, and has even seen innocent people wounded in crossfire. In one case, a 6-year-old girl was seriously wounded during one of his gun battles, and although she recovered fully, he says the sound of her pleas for help plague him to this day.

Jorge admits that many cops are on the take. In the most dangerous favelas he says the cops are actually in league with the drug commands. Here's how Jorge explains a 1991 massacre in Vigário Geral, which left 21 residents dead, executed by the police: five cops who were on the take decided to extort more money from the local drug dealers. The dealers then executed the cops as they sat in their car. In response, the police raided the favela and killed indiscriminately. He doesn't defend this action, but he understands it. "When you are trading shots and you see a friend of yours wounded and all the blood, when the mission stops, you have to control yourself not to take revenge," he said. "It is very difficult."

"Seventy percent of cops are corrupt," Jorge said, meaning that they are willing to take money to void an arrest. "And 15 percent are involved in big corruption," meaning that they are in league with the drug dealers. Vintém, for example, is a north-end favela run by *Amigos dos Amigos*, the smallest of the city's three drug gangs. *Amigos dos Amigos* is run by Celso Luís Rodrigues, known on the street as Celsinho. Celsinho is an unusual drug dealer, because his posse has an unwritten rule not to kill cops. Instead, he bribes them. "In the 14th district, almost all the cops receive money from him," Jorge told me. "It's not a secret. Everyone knows it. It's been in the newspapers and on TV. When Celsinho needs to leave the favela, he calls the cops, who send a *patamo*. He puts on a police uniform and goes wherever he wants to go, transported by the cops." What's more, Celsinho has community values. He funds the local samba school and sports programs for kids.

Still, Jorge says the current environment is too restrictive on the police. He recalls with joy a former governor who inaugurated a policy he calls *"recompensa far west,"* which gave extra money to cops who brought down drug dealers. Jorge received one of these "far west" incentives. It raised his pay by 30 percent. And the pay raise lasted forever. "This was a good policy," Jorge said. "When he did that the drug traffic started to stop." He derides most current politicians as being beholden to the drug gangs for votes. And he laments the government's recent gun amnesty, in which favela dwellers were asked to turn in weapons without fear of repercussions, because several hundred high-powered weapons were crushed and melted down. "Why didn't they give those guns to us," he asked. "We need more firepower."

Despite this hardcore attitude, Jorge believes that the people he is trying to kill (and who are trying to kill him) are not the ones who control the drug trade. "Our country is dominated by traffic. Our federal government, our state government, everything is dominated by traffic. All of this may sound like theater to you. But it's true." Jorge believes that the true leaders of the drug gangs are not the drug dealers in the favelas but people in high positions in society. "When we go to favelas and we find an arms stockpile," he explained, "we see boxes from the air force, army, navy. They are very new weapons. The military is very serious about making sure all weapons are accounted for. How can three or four boxes of grenades, pistols, and rifles simply disappear from the military and reappear at the favela? I am almost certain that the guys that really run the drug commands are big military guys from the army, air force, and even politicians."

These days, to rival the community-minded dealers, the police are trying to make a community statement too. Instead of raiding the favela every night and engaging the drug dealers in shootouts, the police are trying a new tactic in Pavão Pavãozinho, which borders Copacabana and was once one of the most dangerous favelas in the city's Zona Sul. Today, 100 specially trained officers walk the beat in the favela and are working with the residents rather than fighting against them.

Still, it's hard to convince favela residents that the police are not the bad guys. "It's a very fragile model," said Pedro Strozenberg, a lawyer with Viva Rio, a nonprofit organization that helped spawn the community policing program. "The first problem we face is to convince people that there is a problem. The second problem is for people to speak out."

Jorge, who has engaged in many shootouts in Pavão Pavãozinho, was initially dubious about this effort. But he's become a convert to community policing. "It really works," he said. "The violence has been greatly reduced. There is still drug traffic. But it is very small."

But Jorge remains cautious. "The community still hates the police," he says. "They don't trust us at all. The program's working, but it depends on everyone working together. It depends on the government and on the community sticking to it when things get tough."

Still, Jorge doesn't have a positive view of human nature. "For me, everyone is born bad," he told me as he took a sip of his second bottle of Coke. "The strength is to control your bad instincts, control your impulses. Human beings are very bad."

Given a choice between the cops and the criminals, the people in the favelas will take the criminals: for at least they fund community projects. On a sunny midmorning I journeyed up the hill in Dona Marta: the favela above the middle class community of Botafogo. The police were opening a new substation, high up the hill, and I wanted to see it. It was an odd ceremony. The military police band set up on a rooftop across the *beco* from the new outpost and played lugubrious marches. A priest from Botafogo sprinkled holy water on the building, which had once belonged to the family of Marcinho V.P., the local *chefe do trafico* ("chief of drug trafficking"). Col. Wilton Suarez Ribeiro, head of the military police, made a speech. "With this office," he told the few reporters and police brass present, "the problem with security will be solved." Not a single local resident—not one, not even the people who lived next door, not even the head of the local residents association—attended the ceremony.

As one city official later told me, he'd rather work with the dealers than the cops because they are more honorable.

I tell these stories of crime and drug trafficking not to be lurid and not to impugn favela dwellers. Although there are criminal gangs in the favelas, and although people who live in the favelas must regulate their lives around the gangs' activities, most favelados are not involved in the drug trade. Indeed, criminologists have estimated that only 1 percent of the residents of the favelas are actively involved in the drug trade. What's more, the gangs only exist because the Brazilian government—local, state, and federal— ignored the favelas for decades, allowing the criminal element to establish itself unimpeded. The drug gangs are, essentially, an opportunistic infection.

But it's important to understand that these criminal enterprises are part of the reality of the favelas, and that the danger is real. Sometime in April 2004, around Easter, a trafficker named Eduino Eustaquio de Araujo (Dudu, for short) jumped bail and evaded the police who tried to catch him. Dudu had once had power in Rocinha, and he decided to challenge Luciano Barboso da Silva, or Lulu, the new *chefe* in the favela. The resulting war, involving gangs from Rocinha, an adjacent favela called Vidigal, and two others that are not far away, killed 12 people, including several innocent residents who were simply caught in the crossfire. The police responded by occupying Vidigal and Rocinha, pouring 1,600 heavily armed officers into the favelas. Lulu, just 26 years old, was shot dead in one raid. Dudu, as of this writing, is still at large. Raids on other favelas have turned up caches of weapons including, as the police officer I call Jorge suggested, a trove of hand grenades and land mines that were clearly stolen from the military.

Of course, that's if we can believe the police and the press. Because sometimes they can conspire to make the favelas and the drug gangs look particularly bad. Here's an example of how the press can spin and sustain misleading stories.

The *Piscinão* of Ramos is a giant puddle in the sand. It's a saltwater pool, created because the beach in Ramos, on the Bay of Guanabara, the only beach in Rio's crowded, working class, unglamorous Zona Norte, is badly polluted: so badly polluted that it's dangerous for people to go in.

The *Piscinão* (the word means, simply, "big pool") was the brainchild of Anthony Garotinho, former governor of Rio. It was financed, so I was told, by the government of Japan. There are plans for other *piscinoes* in other far-flung neighborhoods.

This was the initial *politica* ("politically motivated dispute") about the *Piscinão*: It was an effort to divert the poor residents of the Zona Norte favelas away from the favored Zona Sul beaches because upper-class people from Copacabana and Ipanema and Leblon and the Barra de Tijuca think there are too many dangerous types invading their neighborhoods.

This was the second *politica* of the *piscinão*: It was a misguided attempt to paper over the real problem: raw sewage being dumped into the bay. Ramos sits on the lip of Guanabara Bay, at a narrows with little current and little clean water. The beach is still there, 20 yards from the *piscinão*, and it is dirty. A shroud of bottles and cans and shreds of plastic and filmy-looking oil cover the bubbly, cloudy, snot-green sea.

The *piscinão* really is a clay-lined hole in the sand and a treatment plant. The treatment plant takes the dirty water of the bay, purifies it, and dumps it into the hole. At the other end is an evacuation pump, which removes as much water as the treatment plant pumps in and dumps it back into the bay.

So, the argument goes, channels of raw sewage from all over Rio still dump into the bay. Many kilometers away in Jacarezinho, for instance, people build their wooden *barracas* right at the edge of the stagnant rivulets covered with brown algae that give off a stench you wouldn't believe: a stench you feel in your mouth, not just in your nose, for hours after you pass by. Those streams run to the ocean, but, rather than take on the real problem, the government buys people off with the promise of a few cheap hours in the sun at the *piscinão*.

This was the third politica of the *piscinão*: It's dangerous. In order to give adults maximum swimming pleasure, the *piscinão* was 8 feet deep. But two kids drowned within a month of its opening. So it was shut, drained, filled in a bit, and reopened with a maximum depth of only 5 feet.

This was the fourth politica of the *piscinão*: It is built in a community that is the epicenter of a gang war. There are several large favelas running up the coastline: Maré, Ramos, Parque Uniao. And there are others inland, on the hills just across Avenida Brasil, for instance the dangerous zone known as Complexo Alemão ("the German complex").

Ramos is contested turf, and two drug gangs are battling it out: the *Comando Vermelho* and the *Terceiro Comando*. A street in Maré shows the scars, because it is the boundary line: the houses on both sides of the street are flecked with the telltale pockmarks of automatic gunfire.

This war—a low-level, occasional conflict—has been known for years. But right after the *piscinão* opened, this news item hit the papers and television: the *Terceiro Comando* had decreed that no one was to wear red—the CV's color—to the *piscinão* or they would be shot.

I was there the day the ban was supposedly issued. It was a hot day and it seemed that all of Rio was heading to the *piscinão*. On the bus that morning, the driver sped through his route, shouting at each stop: "Piscinão, piscinão, piscinão de Ramos," and watching happily as more and more people piled on.

There were 70,000 people at the *piscinão* that day. There was music and arts and crafts and dancing. The local beauties—men and women—strutted their stuff. Along the perimeter of the artificial beach, people set up stalls, working as makeshift merchants, selling fried fish or cold beer or grilled meat. And there were plenty of people wearing red. There was no fear. No violence. No nothing except people hanging out in the sun. How do you explain this, I asked my friend Robson Umbelino, who lives in Maré and works for Viva Rio, a nonprofit active in almost all the favelas in Rio.

He had a one-word answer: "Politica" "Politics."

Every day, there was another story about the *piscinão*. Until the drug gangs embarked on their own guerrilla marketing campaign.

Members of the *Terceiro Comando* spent one night spraypainting slogans along Avenida Brasil and the nearby Linea Vermelho highway. They even painted one on a local police station. It said: "It's OK to wear red to the piscinão. Lies of the press."

The grabber was already streaking across the road and disappearing onto the dark dirt pathways of Kibera. All we saw was the back of his bright red shirt illuminated for a moment in the bright bounce of an oncoming headlight.

When he stopped running and opened the plastic bag he had stolen, he would curse his bad fortune. All that was inside was a traditionally woven straw bag worth maybe 150 shillings—or about $2.

Crime exists in all the shantytowns of Nairobi. In the darkness of the mud hut cities, almost all my friends had been victimized. Nicodemus had been held up at knifepoint several times. John Kasyoka Maluku, a man with a ready smile, can-do attitude, and enthusiasm for life, has been attacked by men with *pangas* on several occasions, only escaping because he was willing to run through the sewage to get away. He was unemployed, and had nothing to give the thugs, but still he ran. Having nothing to hand over, he told me, can be even more risky than having a roll of bills in your pocket. But, he insisted, he understands why the criminals take to the streets. "The cause of crime is unemployment," he told me. "If you are unemployed and want to eat or to feed your family, you are forced to meet someone on the road."

The gangsters come from within. Reuben Sambuli told me he knew all the gangsters in his little alley. "The thugs from this area are good neighbors here," he said. "They go to other areas to be thugs. They are thugs at night, but neighbors during the day."

But you can't complain to the police, because they are known to be thugs, too. Joachim Maanzo recounted the story of walking home at nine o'clock one night when he was accosted by several cops. "They asked for ID," he told me. "Woe unto you if you don't have any ID with you. They took my money. You don't protest. Because they may end up planting things on you. They gave me back my ID and my empty wallet." Another time, the cops fabricated a charge that he was drinking *chang'aa* (a dangerously strong, illicit liquor that is often chemically enhanced with methanol that has been known to make people blind and even to kill). "I pleaded guilty to drinking chang'aa and was sentenced to two days of community service at the hospital. I was powerless. I had to plead guilty. If you say you are innocent, you will stay there [incarcerated at the police station or the courthouse] for two weeks or even a month."

It's odd to hear Joachim talk so openly about Kenya's corrupt legal system, for he is trained as a lawyer. In Kenya, all schooling is expensive (in January 2003, the new government fulfilled a campaign pledge and decreed that public primary schools would be free). But secondary school (the equivalent of American high school) is still beyond the means of many families. Going to university is even more expensive: an entitlement that belongs only to the rich. But Joachim was lucky. A strong student, he received a scholarship to an exclusive secondary school and partial funding for university. He completed his law degree, but didn't have the money to pay off his debt to Nairobi University, and therefore cannot get his diploma. So he works nights at a bakery and lives in Kibera with his wife Rose, a teacher, and their young son, Kennedy. "We know that the police are the custodians of law and order in this country," Joachim told me. "They are supposed to make sure every citizen is secure. But contrary to that, they have been so corrupt that they are just interested in their own selfish game. Sometimes it's better to confront the thugs because they will negotiate. If you have 200 bob [200 shillings: about $2.50], they may take 150 and give you back 50 and say: 'Go buy some *sukuma wiki* [collard greens] with this.'"

A few of Kibera's most crowded commercial strips have come up with their own indigenous security forces. These are Masai: high-plains herdsmen who have migrated to the city from the area near the Tanzanian border. Every evening, merchants pay them 10 or 20 shillings per kiosk to patrol the shopping street at night. The Masai are not necessarily big, and they don't necessarily have better weaponry, but they are known as good fighters. Julia Wangari, who owns two small bars in Kibera, explains the way they work. "When there were no Masais, the thugs came in and stole everything. These kind of people—Masai—they stay outside at night. They are paid something small, perhaps 20 shillings per day." Although no one I spoke with could explain why, there's a belief that Masai cannot be attacked. "If you are with a Masai," Julia continued, "even the police cannot arrest you." Recently, freelance Masai have started hanging out late at night near the major bus stops. For 20 shillings, they will escort you home.

Despite all the tales of violence, the shantytowns are actually no less safe than the rest of the city. Cell phone snatchings and other robberies are everyday occurrences in downtown Nairobi. I know this firsthand, for on my third day in town I was mugged by seven street kids about 10 minutes after sunset next to Jivanjee Gardens downtown.

The biggest kid got me in a chokehold around my neck. Another grabbed my feet. I was off the ground before I knew what was happening. A bunch of desperate hands rifled through my pockets. They tore at my shoulder bag. They ripped my vest in half. Then they put me down and started to untie my shoes. That was when I got angry. I shouted and the kids ran. They scored a watch, a pair of glasses, a shoulder bag, a few notebooks, a dictionary, half of my vest, and about 2,000 shillings ($25).

A good haul.

I went to the police station, which was just two blocks away. The officers wrote down everything I said. When they finished, they signed the paper and gave it to me.

"What am I supposed to do with this?"

"Take it to your embassy. They will reimburse you for everything you lost."

I could only laugh.

"Don't you need a copy?"

"No."

"But how will you know if you find my things?"

"We will remember."

Back at my hotel, two businessmen from Uganda were hanging out in the lobby. They listened politely to my story. "Oh that's nothing," one of them said. "When we were here last year, we were carjacked at gunpoint, stripped of our clothes, and left in our underwear in the bush five kilometers from town."

But whether it be drug gangs in Rio or thugs and streetkids in Nairobi, violent crime can be controlled when communities and government work in partnership. But there's another form of crime that's rampant in the developing world. It's much more insidious and much harder to control.

Corruption.

There's competition over corruption. Every country I visited took a perverse pride in the deep corruption of its public officials.

"No other country steals like they do here," a Brazilian told me.

"We have maximum corruption," an Indian argued.

"Everything depends on bribes," a Turk said.

There's no doubt that all of these countries are corrupt. But none of them can compete with Kenya.

I can't talk about the big-time looting, although the Kenyan newspapers are full of stories about quasi-governmental agencies (what they call "parastatals") that have been bankrupted or fleeced by the people paid to manage them.

But I can talk about communities like Kibera, which seem to exist principally because of corruption.

Kibera is actually ruled by a form of civil service that is a holdover from British colonial times: the provincial administration. The British set up the provincial administration as an African civil service that it could use to oppress Africans. When Kenya won independence, Jomo Kenyatta, the country's first president, never dismantled the provincial administration.

I interviewed scores of people—landlords, tenants, even academics—who all told me the same story: anything that you want to do in the community, from constructing a dwelling to making a serious repair, the civil servants from the provincial administration (known as district officers, chiefs, assistant chiefs, and village elders) insist on payoffs. If you don't pay them off, they will knock down anything that you have built or call in the police to inspect your business. The going rate for someone who wants to build a new mud hut is 2,000 or 3,000 shillings: equal to the average Kibera worker's monthly pay.

One resident who was able to buy his hut lives with a plastic tarp strung underneath this rusted-out metal roof, because he said it would cost too much in bribes to fix. "To repair the roof, first I would have to see the chief," he told me. "It would cost 2,000 shillings there. Then the village elders. Maybe 1,000 to be distributed among them. So I'm better off leaving things the way they are."

Another person, a Kibera landlord who asked not to be identified, said bribery was a way of life. "If you want to survive you have to cooperate with the provincial administration and the police department," he told me. "Let's say if you profit 100,000, almost 40,000 goes to them. If you refuse, your business is history. A person like the district officer has the power to withdraw licenses. He will say robbers are hanging out there or that the construction was not right. If you think it's a joke, he will send 10 men to search your house. So you are ready to give even 100,000 to make them stop this rubbish."

The police, this landlord said, shake down all the local businesses. They take a cut of the profits from the bars. And they use their power to squash people who refuse to pay.

The chiefs even shake down local schools. One small school was overcrowded and wanted to build a new classroom. They designed it to be temporary and made of mud. But still they had to bribe the chief. "First, the chief took 2000 shillings," the school administrator told me. "Then he wanted another 10,000 in an envelope. He said if we didn't give him the 10,000, there would be no building. We gave him 5,000 and hoped he would forgive the other half. He gave us a document with a stamp and a letter with his stamp, but no stamp from the district officer. He told us we need to pay another 5,000 to get the full approval."

The project had a budget of 46,000 shillings—and the school spent almost one-third of that (13,500 shillings) in bribes.

This is the way things work in Kenya. People will ask you for *kitu kidogo* ("something small," although in reality the bribes are pretty big), for shoe polish, for any of the going slang names. It all amounts to the same thing: a bribe.

The provincial administrators denied that any bribery occurs.

"There is no official payment involved" for anyone to improve their buildings in Kibera, Abdi Rabi, the district officer at the time, told me. "If anyone is soliciting on his own, it is a private thing that amounts to corruption. I am not aware of anything like that. Anyone who is soliciting any payment is doing that illegally."

Similarly one of the chiefs who administer Kibera, who asked not to be identified, denied that he or any of the others solicit payments from owners who want to improve their huts. "That is not the case," he said emphatically.

It's his word against the words of scores of residents from Kibera and other shantytowns, who told me how the system really works.

And the corruption flows downward to the community. Many residents contend that the nonprofit organizations that claim to be doing so much in Kibera are simply scams to make money.

As I traveled around the community, I interviewed many people at nonprofit entities. Almost without exception, they were all focused on making a profit. First, I visited people at the Kenya Water for Health Organization (KWAHO). They were promoting a Scandinavian system that used sunlight to purify water—a worthy goal—and they had hundreds of plastic bottles and reams of literature. But all they did was hang out at their office and drink tea; I never saw anyone in Kibera using their water purification system.

I bumped into a brand new organization concerned with acquired immunodeficiency syndrome (AIDS) that seemed the same. Instead of being out doing outreach, the five members of the group—all of whom insisted they were not being paid—were hanging out at the office. There wasn't a person with AIDS in sight and, from the questions I asked, none of the volunteers seemed to have any knowledge about AIDS or how to counsel people who might be sick.

Even the biggest AIDS organization in Kibera—the Kibera Community Self-Help Program (Kicoshep)—seemed questionable. The group started as a voluntary counseling and testing clinic in Kibera and, after opening several facilities among the mud huts, moved its headquarters to a comfortable air-conditioned home along Kabarnet Lane just outside the shantytown. Even worse, the community was abuzz with gossip that the agency had been buying off-road vehicles. These rugged four-wheel-drive vehicles may be useful around the city, but not in Kibera, which has no real roads. Most people—particularly the people with AIDS whom Kicoshep is supposedly serving—live down narrow alleys, across pathways sodden with raw sewage that are not accessible by car, even if it is a four-wheel-drive vehicle. A health organization in Kibera does not need cars, outraged residents told me. It needs doctors. Yet there is not a single physician practicing in Kibera. In India, doctors were working in many of the larger squatter areas. I even met a physician who had set out a shingle in the extremely deprived squatter community in Borivali National Park, a controversial place subject to a continuing threat of demolition. But in Kibera, a city of at least 500,000 people, there was not a single doctor.

I went into the Kicoshep youth education and drop-in center inside Kibera. There certainly were teenagers hanging out although they all said they were from outside Kibera. Most revealing were the massive stacks of condoms—a whole wall full of them. But they were in an inner sanctum and behind a desk. The best thing for preventing the spread of AIDS was there, but no one would know unless they asked.

Another outpost for AIDS counseling and testing, funded by the Association of Medical Doctors of Asia, opened inside a clinic called Frepals. Frepals was famous around Kibera because it had an ambulance that was always parked just outside the community. I never saw that ambulance do anything (although a friend once saw it parked downtown, outside a restaurant.) It's good that the community has an ambulance, I suppose, but what is the point of having an ambulance when it cannot go into the community. People still have to be hauled out of Kibera in wheelbarrows to get them to the main road, where they can get the ambulance to take them to the hospital.

Freda F.C.O. Enane, a registered nurse, and her husband Paul, a travel agent, started Frepals in 1995 (the name is an amalgam of Freda and Paul). Like most health clinics in Kibera, it is a for-profit entity. Adults pay between 350 and 600 shillings for a checkup with a registered nurse. Children pay between 150 and 250 shillings. Although these amounts (approximately $5 to $8 for adults and $2 to $3.25 for kids) are similar to copayments people in the United States might pay, they are huge by Kiberan standards.

In addition to her health facility, Freda and her husband own 32 rooms in nearby mud huts. Each tenant pays 800 shillings a month, giving the couple a total of 25,600 in income every month.

Freda explained that the ambulance that was never used in Kibera was a gift from the Netherlands embassy in Kenya. In 1998, it seems, thieves broke into the clinic, and the robbery was reported in one of Nairobi's daily newspapers. "The ambassador from the Netherlands wanted to do something to help us," she told me. "I mentioned to him the problem that in the slum there is no ambulance. Patients are taken in wheelbarrows to the nearest bus stop. They don't fund vehicles, but they found an ambulance that he bought and gave us."

While her story may be true, it made me wonder: Freda is middle class. One of her children is a lawyer, another is studying computers, and a third is in university. She is not so awed by an ambassador that she couldn't tell him that the vehicle is useless. And if it is, why not sell it and use the money for something that can benefit the community more—like bringing a doctor to her facility?

Everyone—even the good people like my friends Mercy Kadenyeka and Nicodemus Mutemi—were periodically seduced by the idea that they could get rich by starting a nonprofit. The income seems to come first, the doing good is secondary.

Then there are the schools. Until early 2003, when the government instituted free primary education, the only way a family from Kibera could get their children educated was at one of the dozens of private schools that had sprung up in the community. The schools charged around 300 shillings per month. If a school had 100 kids, that's 30,000 shillings per month. The average salary for teachers was quite low: around 2,000 shillings a month. If a school rented six classrooms at 1,000 shillings each, and paid six teachers 2,000 each, the owner would pocket 12,000 shillings each month.

Given the possible profits, some of the schools were little more than warehouses. At one school, I opened a classroom door and found hundreds of children stuffed into a large room with no light and few notebooks. Some were squatting on the mud floor, others hunkered down at the few available desks. Wherever they were, they bent low over their notebooks because there was so little light in the room that they could hardly see. There's no question that the overworked staff was trying to teach. But I question the values of the administration when the school doesn't spend anything on conditions conducive to learning.

A blackboard certainly costs money, but when someone is making 12,000 shillings a month, I think he or she can afford to buy a few.

I tell these stories of crime and corruption because they are part of life in these communities. It is also true that they exist everywhere. In Nairobi, the legal neighborhood of Eastleigh is the center of gun dealing and is more dangerous than many squatter areas. In Brazil, as the British parasailor Mick found out in his brief stay in Copacabana, things can be much more dangerous in the legal city than in the illegal one.

Squatter communities may be illegal, but that doesn't make them criminal.

CHAPTER 9

Proper Squatters, Improper Property

Pity the meek, for they shall inherit the earth.

— Don Marquis

So what would happen, I asked Armstrong O'Brian, Jr., and his roommates, if the government offered you a title deed. There was no hesitation: All four of them agreed that the government should never offer title deeds.

Hilary Kibagendi Onsomu explained. "We are four of us in this house and we will all want it," he said. "It will never work. People will start fighting. So we will just have an exchange of grabbers.

And the new grabbers will be us." A title deed, Hilary said, would upset their amity, thus destroying the community in the name of helping it.

Similarly, in Kibera, I asked Nicodemus Mutemi and Geoffrey Barasa Wafubwa what would happen if the residents were given title deeds. They almost spoke in unison: "There would be war!"

Aristotle would have understood these Kenyans well. "In the opinion of some," he wrote in the *Politics*, "the regulation of property is the chief point of all, that being the question upon which all revolutions turn." Aristotle was on the side of stable governments, and against the restive masses. But his thought—that people who have less access to property have a greater tendency to revolt—is not all that different from Malcolm X, who declared, "Revolution is based on land. Land is the basis of all independence. Land is the basis of freedom, justice, and equality."

Malcolm X thought revolution was necessary to achieve property and real independence. Aristotle, by contrast, advocated a kind of mass amnesia. He rejected the ideas of Phaleas of Chalcedon, who proposed equalizing wealth by compelling the rich to give huge marriage dowries to the poor, in a kind of primitive redistributive communism. Aristotle suggested that such leveling legislation would not work because humans are by nature acquisitive and competitive. "The beginning of reform," he argued, "is not so much to equalize property as to train the nobler sort of natures not to desire more, and to prevent the lower from getting more; that is to say, they must be kept down, but not ill-treated."

It's a shocking vision of social justice—as shocking as Malcolm's call for violent revolution: convince the rich not to seek more and hoodwink the poor into believing their deprivation is for the best.

The Kenyans would have understood Aristotle, too. His solution —or at least the second half of it, about keeping the poor down—is similar to the current reality in Kenya.

What is it about property? It's the basis of the modern Western system that has undeniably grown wealth and material comfort, but it's an incredibly divisive thing. No one's been able to come up with a convincing justification for it.

John Locke came closest. He's the great modern theoretician of property on whose philosophical wizardry much of the American political process is based. Locke proposed that the right to property was forged through labor: "Though the earth and all inferior creatures be common to all men, yet every man has a 'property' in his own person. That nobody has any right to but himself. The 'labour' of his body and the 'work' of his hands, we may say, are properly his. Whatsoever, then, he removes out of the state that nature hath provided and left it in, he hath mixed his labour with it, and joined to it something that is his own, and thereby makes it his property."

Thus, if a person works a field, his or her expenditure of labor grants a right: it allows that person to enclose the land and claim it as his or her own. Locke even alludes approvingly to squatters: "I have heard it affirmed that in Spain itself a man may be permitted to plow, sow, and reap, without being disturbed, upon land he has no other title to, but only his making use of it."

It's a wonderful theory: workers make land into property through sheer effort. But once you delve into it, things fall apart.

After all, what is labor? By Locke's reasoning, the former slaves who established their *barracas* on Morro da Favela and the first intruders who created farms in Rocinha deserved to own the property. Fine. But what if there was a carpenter who helped build the houses, yet didn't build one for himself: shouldn't he get a stake? And what about the person who cleared the land for that initial *roça* in Rocinha? And what about the family member—a cousin, perhaps —who worked in a factory or as a maid for a nearby rich family, so the others could afford clothes and seed for the crops that first year. Which laborer gets the land?

Does the labor have to be done personally on the land in question for that land to become personal property? Can I gain a property right only by personally turning the soil with a pitchfork or personally erecting my own home? How about hiring someone else to turn the soil or build a house? How about turning the soil with an automatic tiller or buying and installing a prefabricated house? How about the interest of someone who worked four months on that little *roça* weighed against another who worked eight months: which is the property interest?

And how much effort does a person have to expend? Is planting a single fruit tree enough or do you have to plant a whole orchard? How about simply blazing a trail that leads to the field or across it? How about one man who built a stone house or another who created a crude hut—perhaps simply a bower of foraged branches leaned against a tree—a few yards away: Which one of them gets the property right? Does a person who builds a two-room hut deserve more land than a person who only builds a single room? What if a family that needs a two-room hut doesn't have enough wood or enough able-bodied family members to build that much?

And what if a lawyer from town put in 18-hour days so that she could save enough to buy part of Rocinha, fence it in, and hire a contractor to build a vacation home? Hasn't she labored?

Locke also seeds his theory with an escape clause: "As much as any one can make use of to any advantage of life before it spoils, so much he may by his labour fix a property in, whatever is beyond that is more than his share, and belongs to others." So, according to Locke, the original land invaders who developed the first farms in Rocinha should gain a legitimate property right. But if those same people cleared space for a second field that they didn't specifically need, they should not gain the right to own that land.

Of course, need, too, is subjective. Everyone needs what they take: or at least says they do.

Anyway, why on earth should labor be what counts? Isn't existing enough? Why should anyone be denied land simply because he or she hasn't tilled it? After all, a person may have labored at something else: boatmaking or fishing or selling *cafezinhos*, like Márcio; or waiting on tables, like Maria; or, for that matter, writing. Each of us still needs a place to live.

Whatever the ultimate coherence of his theory, Locke's 1690 treatise was quickly appropriated by the British aristocracy to justify the land grab that has come to be called enclosure, in which the rich fenced in and grabbed much of the land that had historically been held in common throughout England, Scotland, and Wales. They didn't worry about laboring on the land. They did their labor with the sword and the law.

Perhaps no one saw the conflicts inherent in property more clearly than Jean-Jacques Rousseau, in the *Discourse on the Origin of Inequality*, published in 1755.

> The true founder of civil society was the first man who, having enclosed a piece of land, thought of saying, "This is mine," and came across people simple enough to believe him. How many crimes, wars, murders, and how much misery and horror the human race might have been spared if someone

had pulled up the stakes or filled in the ditch, and cried out to his fellows: "Beware of listening to this charlatan. You are lost if you forget that the fruits of the earth belong to all and that the earth itself belongs to no one."

It's a wonderfully contradictory statement, for even as Rousseau argues that private property institutionalizes inequality and outright violence, he also credits it with being the root of civic interaction and the foundation of society. According to Rousseau, then, civilization implies inequality, and property is its big enforcer.

Even Adam Smith, the sage of laissez-faire capitalism, was resoundingly blunt in his famous tome *The Wealth of Nations* about the role property plays in keeping the poor poor and the rich rich: "Civil government, so far as it is instituted for the security of property, is in reality instituted for the defence of the rich against the poor, or of those who have some property against those who have none at all," he wrote.

My friends in the developing world would understand this, too: because all the laws in their countries seem to be on the side of the rich.

Even Karl Marx, apostle of propertyless communist revolution, had this to say about property:

> The expropriation of the mass of people from the soil forms the basis of the capitalist mode of production. The essence of a free colony . . . consists in this—that the bulk of the soil is still public property, and every settler on it therefore can turn part of it into his private property and individual means of production, without hindering the later settlers in the same operation.

In a sense, squatter communities function like colonies without any people being colonized. The bulk of the soil starts out available for free. Problems start when access to land becomes limited. Indeed, following Marx, it might be that the future problems that may occur in squatter communities and shantytowns may arise from this limit. In Rocinha, for instance, there is no more freedom to build. The community is expanding through rentals—and, like my friend Washington and his family, tenants have different interests than landlords. This is also being seen in Kibera, where owner–occupants such as Dorcas Mogaka express different interests than the tenants who are the majority. Likewise in Bombay, where Laxmi Chinnoo must live under a roadway overpass because she was a tenant, and therefore couldn't qualify for replacement housing given free to all structure owners. As space becomes limited, class distinctions grow, and the communal values inherent in squatter communities break down.

The typical polemic on property in the Western philosophical tradition is like a battle of tired heavyweights swinging mightily but not able to bring each other down. In one corner are the free market absolutists. They say, with Nobel Prize-winning economist F.A. von Hayek, "The system of private property is the most important guarantee of freedom, not only for those who own property, but scarcely less for those who do not." In the other corner, pontificating with identical weight, are the idealists and socialists. They say, with British analytic philosopher Bertrand Russell, "Private property in land has no justification except historically through power of the sword." The discussions seldom go beyond what Rousseau sketched out. The absolutists focus on property as the origin of civic interaction. The idealists focus on property as setting the stage for inequality.

A few thinkers have gone further. American critic and literary theorist Kenneth Burke noted that one of the important losses in the transition from feudalism to capitalism was the end of traditional right of the peasantry to use the land. Burke pointed out the irony implicit in enshrining property rights as the bulwark of freedom. Calling the idea a "liberal one-way system of apologetics," he argued that American triumphalism over private property ignores

> the fact that the history of emancipation in Europe shows the integral relation between freedom and alienation. In "binding" the serf to the soil, feudalism also bound the soil to the serf, matching his "duties" with "rights" that were protected by custom. The liberal revolution "freed" him of his "duties" by alienating him from his "rights." Hence, for great numbers of people, "freedom" functioned simply as "dispossession." Conversely, you cannot "repossess" without a corresponding pattern of obligations. "Freedom" is a truncated concept, an unintended caricature of human relations.

In feudal times, a serf had, at least, some right to use the soil for his or her own benefit. The great liberal revolution freed the laborer from the duty to work the land for the benefit of the lord, which was undeniably a good thing. But at the same time it wiped out the serf's right to continue to use the land to grow his or her own food, which was certainly a hardship. Thus, the emancipation of serfs, which arguably was the start of our modern liberties, also dispossessed them—and by extension all of us—from our customary right to provide for ourselves and our families.

Hannah Arendt extended this thought to practical politics, noting that the propertied class retooled government to protect its newfound monopoly. "Society, when it first entered the public realm," she wrote in *The Human Condition*, "assumed the disguise of an organization of property-owners who, instead of claiming access to the public realm because of their wealth, demanded protection from it for the accumulation of more wealth." Thus, according to Arendt, modern society defrauds the poor twice. First it deprives them of any claim to land; then it organizes government to prevent any regulation of the new order of property.

Still the heavyweights slog it out. Property rights theorists debate whether common property regimes—land held in common for use by a group of people—can work without denuding and exhausting the soil, and whether economic growth can be attained without strict adherence to private property rights. The debate is framed according to the polemic: are you for private property or against it? And it is set in purely economic terms, as if people only act for their economic benefit and as if maximizing profit is a human universal. No nuances are allowed.

My friends the squatters—who have had to live the nuances almost their entire lives—would find solace in the theory of Pierre-Joseph Proudhon, a French socialist who in 1840 published a manifesto called *What Is Property?* His answer—"Property is robbery"—probably sounds more scandalous today than it did when he wrote it. But Proudhon's argument is more refined than the three-word sound bite. He suggests that there's a difference between property and possession. Property turns land into a commodity: people own land not to use it or because they need it for survival, but simply as an investment. Possession guarantees personal use and control rather than profit. For Proudhon, property, not money, is the root of all evil:

Individual possession is the condition of social life. Five thousand years of property demonstrates this. Property is the suicide of society. Possession is within right; property is against right. Suppress property while maintaining possess, and by this simple modification of the principle, you will revolutionize the law, government, economy, and institutions; you will drive evil from the face of the earth.

And my squatter friends would also take comfort in the homegrown analysis of American egalitarian theorist Henry George. "Private property in land is a bold, bare, enormous wrong," he wrote in his most famous work, *Progress and Poverty*, published in 1879. George differentiated between private ownership of things and private ownership of land. Simply put, he argued that the things of the world were truly created by labor and could be bought and sold, while land was created by nature and therefore should not be turned into an economic value. "The equal right of all men to the use of land is as clear as their equal right to breathe the air," George wrote. "For we cannot suppose that some men have a right to be in this world and others have no right."

Journalist Ambrose Bierce adopted both Rousseau's and George's thoughts when he defined property in his *Devil's Dictionary:* "The theory that land is property subject to private ownership and control is the foundation of modern society," he wrote. "Carried to its logical conclusion, it means that some have the right to prevent others from living."

Ahmet Kutluk bought his house in Paşaköy in 1998. A Kurd originally from the southeastern region of Turkey, he came to Istanbul to work because his hometown was being ripped apart by the long-running war between the Turkish government and Kurdish separatists. At first he lived in Eminönü, the historic and crowded portside district hard by the Golden Horn on the European side of the city. Later, seeking more room, he moved his family to the center of Sarigazi, on the Asian side of Istanbul. But Sarigazi's rutted streets and the thick crowd of buses that passed every day churned up dust that made his wife sick. So he decided his family would move again. He found what he wanted in Paşaköy: a single-story three-room house on an ample plot of land, a place that got good breezes because it was on the top of a hill. This house was for sale, not for rent, so he considered the matter and then decided to make the investment.

He paid 3 billion Turkish lire for the house and the land: this would be better than $19,000, a fairly stiff price. He was willing to pay so much because the real estate agent assured him that the property was legal and had what is called *ifrazli tapu*: a private title deed. The realtor even dragged him down to the regional property office in the seaside neighborhood of Kartal to review the paperwork.

"When I bought the house, I signed all the papers in Kartal," Ahmet told me. "All the official paperwork was in order. Now they tell me I do not own the land. They treat us like invaders. But we are not invaders. We paid for our land."

His neighbor Omer Akyuz, joined in: "I paid 10 billion for my land and then it turned out it was government land. I was tricked."

The game works this way, Omer explained: Real estate agencies and unscrupulous owners make lots of photocopies of old title deeds. And they sell the fakes as if they are real. They're Turkey's version of the *grillos* of Brazil.

This particular portion of Paşaköy faces a particularly complex situation. The neighborhood is actually part of the Istanbul municipality of Kartal. But these residents are far from the center of Kartal, more than 5 kilometers away, down on the coast, along the Sea of Marmara. Indeed, Sultanbeyli, an entirely independent city, stands between Paşaköy and Kartal. Sultanbeyli is so close that some residents list their addresses as Sultanbeyli. It is Sultanbeyli that provides garbage pickup to these Paşaköy residents.

Although Kartal does not recognize their ownership, the residents here must pay taxes nonetheless. Some people, however, thought that since they get no services from Kartal while they got some from Sultanbeyli, they were supposed to pay Sultanbeyli. This was a mistake. Sultanbeyli kept the money and Kartal will not credit it. "Sultanbeyli could give the money to Kartal, or at least report that people paid, but it won't," Omer complained.

Kartal has already sent letters to some residents saying that their houses must be destroyed. Others claim to have papers saying that their houses cannot be knocked down. Those who paid taxes to Sultanbeyli now face a kind of double jeopardy. They may be evicted and their houses demolished, and they may also face foreclosure for nonpayment of taxes.

"That's the way it is in Turkey," Ahmet Kutluk said with a sigh. "Many times you buy property over here and you have a title deed but it is really for property somewhere else. We didn't know these things before. We were naïve. But now we are learning. After bitter experience we have learned we have to check these things."

Still, what gets Paşaköy's residents really steamed is that they attempted to be honest and bought their homes thinking they were legal. Yet they have no water and had to chip in together to install a rudimentary sewer system. Half a kilometer away in Sultanbeyli, everyone knew they were occupying the land illegally. But the big city government is installing services and paving roads. "Sultanbeyli," one of the people I spoke with in Paşaköy said, half humorously and half enviously, "is not part of Istanbul. It is part of Ankara." Meaning that there are enough voters in Sultanbeyli that it gets its advantages straight from the national government.

Sultanbeyli's gains illustrate another problem facing these residents of Paşaköy. Under Turkish law, even though no one in Sultanbeyli owns the land, the people were able to apply to the federal government to be recognized as an *ilçe* and a *belediye*. But Paşaköy is dominated by people who were relocated 80 years ago from Salonika (Greece), after Turkey's war of independence. They were farmers then, and farmers they remain, and they don't want to lose their farming lifestyle. So they have refused to incorporate as an *ilçe* or a *belediye*. Without that status, it will be difficult for people to gain the services that their neighbors in Sultanbeyli already have.

I joined Ahmet Kutluk and his family for a cup of tea. We sat in the sparse shade of a brick pile in his front yard. He told me he bought the bricks in 1999, to build an addition to his house. He wanted to create a second-story apartment for his son, who was planning to get married. But the lack of a title deed and planning permission from Kartal has stymied this plan. Others have ignored the rules and built their additions—and then the military has come to demolish what they have constructed. So, for the past five years, the 10 members of his family have been sharing three small rooms. And the week before I visited, his son finally got married. His son's new wife has now joined the crowd living in their overstuffed house.

Ahmet Kutluk pointed at the flag flying from a corner of his house. He is a Kurd but he proudly displays the Turkish flag.

"I am thankful for this we have, because we could have nothing. But still . . . " he said, his voice trailing off. "We didn't want to come here. We had our villages in the East. But the villages were burnt down. And when we came here, we preferred to live in the center. But this is where we can live. No person can kick me out from this. We are not invaders. We are citizens."

Ahmet Kutluk is caught in a dilemma. He does not have a title deed and he does not have any political rights. The combination is fatal to his desire to have a bigger home. But it is the lack of political rights and planning approval that is holding him back. If his home were 500 yards away, across the border in Sultanbeyli, he would build, *tapu* or no *tapu*.

Ahmet Kutluk (second from left) and friends, at the teahouse in Paşakoy.

When it comes to squatters, intellectuals seem to get ideological dyslexia: the left is sometimes on the right and the right on the left.

For instance, progressive urbanist Peter Marcuse is suspicious of self-help housing—people invading land and building for themselves—because, he has written, they are essentially individualists clawing to get ahead rather than working to change society. And Peruvian free market absolutist Hernando de Soto, in his recent book *The Mystery of Capital*, endorses squatting and argues that governments should reward self-help builders with titles to their land so as to liberate what he calls the dead capital inherent in their constructions.

Marcuse has provided 10 reasons why squatting will not work. As I understand them, these are his objections:

1. Squatters will not provide enough resources to handle the immense problem.
2. Squatters are individuals and cannot deal with a host of issues that require centralized decision making.
3. Squatters only produce temporary solutions to their immediate needs.
4. There is no evaluation mechanism and no way to replicate the success stories to allow squatting to be transformed from individual action into a program.
5. Squatters are inefficient and do not make use of economies of scale.
6. Squatters are economically regressive because they are not redistributing wealth.
7. Squatters lower housing standards.
8. Squatters are politically reactionary; they shield the status quo from anger that should be directed at it.

9. Squatters are socially divisive: the more aggressive squatters get more while less aggressive squatters get less.
10. Squatters are exploitative: they are forced to exploit themselves.

Marcuse is skeptical about squatting because it violates his ideology. He sees it as fundamentally conservative: a kind of self-exploitation that buys into the fundamental class biases of the capitalist system. What's more, he has suggested, it promotes a kind of "I've got mine" mentality, through which squatters become politically passive once they have achieved their own security.

However, it's possible to agree with all of Marcuse's objections and still endorse squatting. It's certainly true that squatters are no bold band of brothers and sisters. They may have taken a great risk when they first entered land illegally, but once they feel secure, they lose interest in anyone else's land battles. When I was living in Rocinha, the army was enforcing a major squatter eviction in Brasilia. It was all over the newspapers and TV, but none of my neighbors seemed to care. Their solidarity did not extend much beyond their street. And in Turkey, Kenya, and India, squatters often presented themselves as needing a handout rather than courageously battling a society that ignored them.

But who says squatters should be courageous? They are squatting not out of ideology but out of necessity. They are trying desperately to make ends meet, to make a future, in a society where money and good contacts are what gets the power structure to pay attention.

Squatters are often politically incorrect. They often are conservative (indeed, many of the people I have come to be close with in the course of my research identified themselves as conservatives). Their communities may be massively inefficient (that is, they don't achieve economies of scale, and, because they start by building single-family huts with small private gardens, they do not use scarce acreage efficiently). Certainly, their homes start off as little more than hovels, and it may take years for them to develop the money and skills to build permanent structures. Also, since squatters bear all the costs and burdens of their constructions, while developers get bank financing and often receive government assistance, it's no wonder that Marcuse and others on the left believe that the squatters are exploiting themselves.

But the squatters are building their own homes at a price they can afford, which is a form of efficiency. They are holding back the tide of gentrification. They are staking a claim to the city, to certain areas of the city, and to a level of participation in politics. They may not know they are doing these things, but that's hardly a legitimate complaint. Theirs is an unconscious, insurgent critique: challenging the power structure while participating in it.

On the other side, De Soto is right that if squatters gain legal title to their land, they can be a creative and energizing force in their economies. And it's undeniable that most squatters, like Ahmet Kutluk, would not turn down a title deed. Still, many also know that one of the reasons they are able to survive is because their neighborhoods are illegal. The profit margins of their businesses, for instance, depend on the special status of being located in an in-between area. Many of them don't pay taxes. They don't have to meet zoning or labor laws. They run cash businesses: and they get to keep all the cash.

Granting titles certainly can be part of the government's bag of tricks in working with squatters. But title deeds will not work well in all areas. In Peru, where de Soto did much of his fieldwork, and in some of the gecekondu areas of Turkey, squatter communities seem to be built on the suburban model—each hut on its own chunk of land—and this can lend itself to dividing the land into individual parcels. But how do you allocate titles within the dense fabric of Rocinha or Kibera? Who should get title to each parcel? The family that built the house? The woman who bought it from them? The tenants who rent there? How about if there are many individuals sharing a home, or if the builder sold off rooms in the squatter version of a cooperative apartment house? And what of someone like Francisco Breszara Loyola, a pleasant, plump, gray-haired man who spends his days sitting by his candy stall in the crowded Passarella in Rocinha? He owns his two-story home, but sold his roof rights to a friend, who built two stories and sold his roof rights to someone build an additional two stories above his. Indeed, de Soto's belief that the old fashioned profit motive will save the squatters ignores all sorts of other human factors.

The people in Sanjay Gandhi Nagar, where I lived in Mumbai, had the opportunity to buy their land 10 years ago. They did, but not with individual titles. They own the property as a cooperative association.

This, it turns out, has been a wise decision. When they moved to Goregaon, it was a sparse jungle area, and conditions were tough. But as Mumbai has sprawled, development has overtaken Sanjay Gandhi Nagar. Goregaon (a 45-minute train ride from the center of the city) has become desirable, and a scores of high-priced towers have been built. Developers would clearly love to get their hands on Sanjay Gandhi Nagar's three acres.

If the residents held separate titles, some would take the money and run. They would, most likely, get less for their homes than they could if they were truly savvy and played the market. Like most poor people, they would probably spend the windfall quickly, and, when the money was gone, join a new squatter encampment farther from the center of town. Of course, if families sold out one by one, and towers encroached on the neighboring homes, those that remained in Sanjay Gandhi Nagar would be under greater pressure to sell as well. So here, cooperative ownership has kept people in their homes as the neighborhood has improved around them.

Sanjay Gandhi Nagar may be an exception. The neighborhood has been organized for more than a decade. People there have been through eviction wars, and have come to trust each other. So cooperative ownership seems natural to them.

But in more competitive places—where the collective feeling of a community has not been built over time—creating a cooperative is more difficult. Indeed, I recently met some South African squatters who have assured me that nothing but a title deed would satisfy them. After years of being brutalized by the government, they want the piece of paper that entitles them to their land.

For a poor person, a title deed can be a wonderful symbol. It says: I belong, I have something incontestable, I can never be pushed out ever again, I have my very own estate, no matter how modest.

De Soto asserts that title deeds will liberate people's economic power. A house without a title deed, he argues, is dead capital, because the builder cannot use it as collateral to get a loan. Granting a true title will allow people to get mortgages, giving them the power to get cash and credit on the strength of their illegal construction. Unfortunately, this ignores one of the basic unknown truths about squatter communities: that people are building capital every day. In Rocinha, people buy and sell squatter houses, advertise apartments and stores for rent, start businesses, expand them, and sometimes close them. There is an active market, but it's informal. It flies beneath the radar of banks and government agencies. Even in Kibera, where everything built is temporary, people are opening businesses, investing in their own futures, creating capital. It may not be much, compared to the capital produced by multinational corporations, but it is economic activity. As one squatter storeowner in Rocinha told me, "Why should I be legal if nobody here is legal? If I am illegal, things here will be cheaper than if I have to pay taxes, electricity, water. So for things to be affordable, I have to be illegal."

And there's another problem as well: I'd challenge de Soto to name one bank that would willingly write a mortgage secured by a tiny patch of land covered by a 10-by-10 mud hut with no water, sewers, or electricity.

De Soto backs his claim that full-fledged title deeds are the only way towards economic integration of the squatters into society by citing the squatter history of the United States, particularly the history of westward expansion, which was hastened by the Preemption Act and the Homestead Act. Both of these essentially made squatters' rights the law of the nation.

But de Soto takes a broad-brush approach to history and misses some important details. First, much more land was handed to corporations and wealthy speculators under a series of railway, timber, and mining acts than was given to squatters through preemption and homesteading. This was antidemocratic and led to huge land monopolies in the west, but it certainly did build wealth—which de Soto seems to think is central. Second, preemption and homesteading were never put to use in the cities. They were agrarian laws, not urban. And, of course, the natives who were on the land prior to the European spread through the areas that became the United States were almost completely expropriated and, at times, exterminated.

I am not arguing against the squatters who were legalized through preemption and homesteading. I am arguing that land in cities is different: to protect and empower squatters there often requires different tools than title deeds.

In the end, it doesn't matter whether we are hypercapitalist or ultraleftist. The point is to look at the facts. Not one government in existence is successfully building for the poorest of the poor. So the poorest of the poor are building for themselves. That may not fit into any great ideological category, and it is certainly illegal according to current law. But it is sensible, patriotic, and worthy of a true citizen. In answer to Marcuse, I'd stress that the squatters, through their illegal act, are tacitly calling into question social and economic norms that don't serve the mass of people. In reply to de Soto, I'd note that squatters build and rebuild and build again without a title deed. They don't need one to secure their future. They simply need a sense of control over their homes and a guarantee that they will not be arbitrarily evicted.

The legal instrument is not important. The political instrument is. By which I mean that two laws that have nothing to do with property rights—the "built overnight" or gecekondu law, and the law allowing squatters, after amassing 2,000 people, to create a government—are what has enabled squatters in Turkey to have real staying power. Not title deeds. The fact that no one else really wanted the hilltops and muddy river bottoms that the favela dwellers seized in Rio de Janeiro is what gave them staying power.

Even without *ifrazli tapu*—the "private title" that Paşaköy residents want—the bulk of Turkey's squatters have successfully built gecekondus and improved them over time. Without any legal right, the favelas are fact in Rio de Janeiro and people are using Jorge's forms to buy and sell their homes. And, as the novel nonprofit that is working with the electric company to install real service and meters throughout the major favelas continues its work, the houses they are selling and buying are gaining even more permanence: all without any title deeds. Sartaj Jaipuri and the other residents of Squatter Colony in Mumbai have likewise built permanent houses with upper floors, lofts, and utilities inside their buildings. And they have done this without any pieces of paper conveying title to the land. They hold nothing except the belief that their neighborhood is permanent.

Security, stability, protection, and control are what's important.

It doesn't matter whether you give people title deeds or secure tenure, people simply need to know they won't be evicted. When they know they are secure, they build. They establish a market. They buy and sell. They rent. They create. They develop. Actual control, not legal control, is the key. Give squatters security and they will develop the cities of tomorrow.

Property is both necessary and inexcusable. It does seem to be part of human nature to want to feel that we have something that is ours, or at least under our control, particularly where we live. At the same time, when property becomes a commodity—simply a means of making money—we have begun the process that leads to homelessness and abandonment of the social contract to care for each other.

Property is not a priori. Land was not born as property. Property is a human creation and only one way of organizing the world. Before the system of privately held property became prevalent, people used to have a right that was so basic, so inextricably tied to living that no one thought to codify it. It was, as Walter Benjamin once labeled it, freedom of domicile.

There's still a vestige of that ancient freedom embedded in the Western legal tradition: a concept of the rights of possession. In countries ruled by the British legal tradition, this is called adverse possession. Under Roman law, it's called *usucapio*. Both offer a recognition that longstanding possession gives a person a claim to land: a form of squatters' rights.

Many people think that if you've lived as a squatter for a long time (most laws require 20 or 25 years) you can invoke squatters' rights and gain title to the property. But it's not so simple.

As some of New York City's squatters found out when they went to court, adverse possession is adverse because it must be hostile and antagonistic. This means that from the very beginning a squatter must intend to seize the land from the person, institution, or government that owns or controls it. This necessity makes it very hard for squatters to claim adverse possession because, for the most part, they do not begin their land invasion adversely. They begin, simply, because they are desperate for a home. And, since they always worry that they will be evicted, they tend to enter their illegally seized land surreptitiously: by building under cover of darkness or by hiding their houses in areas where most people simply won't look.

Yet as courts have interpreted the doctrine, to trigger adverse possession successfully, a squatter must start out intending to hold the land against any other person's claim from the very beginning of his or her occupancy. Even worse, courts have ruled that squatters must do this in an open, notorious, public fashion. Which means that the owner of a parcel—whether a private individual or the government—must somehow be put on notice that the squatter has taken over. Over the years, as courts have refined the concept, they've made it very difficult for most squatters to claim adverse possession.

Usucapio offers better protection for squatters. Under this precept, instead of the squatter having to prove his or her intent, the burden is on the title owner to show why the person in occupancy should not be given the land. Squatters can claim *usucapio* even if they don't know they are occupying someone else's land. The owner has to show that he or she took an interest in the land and made efforts to use it. In early Roman law, a person could establish *usucapio* on a piece of land after just two years.

Usucapio remains on the books in a number of countries. It is the law of the land in Brazil, for instance, where it is known as *usucapião*. Brazil's 1988 constitution even creates a special right of *usucapião* in cities after just five years of occupancy. Although courts have expanded the time period (jacking the residency requirement to 20 years, in some cases), squatters in a number of Brazilian cities have attempted to gain a secure title to their illegally seized land through *usucapião*. The procedure is cumbersome, however, and many squatters simply don't have the money to support the legal work necessary to prove their homes. Also, according to Brazilian law, squatters cannot use *usucapião* to gain title to publicly owned property. Since many favelas are on land that is nominally owned or controlled by government agencies, this makes it unlikely that large numbers of squatters can be helped by *usucapião*.

Still, it's significant that adverse possession and *usucapio* are on the books. These two pieces of property law show that, even in the modern world, we still recognize the tension between possession and property. We recognize that occupancy gives some kind of a right. Adverse possession and *usucapio* are the legal vestiges of the problem with property.

How far we go with private property depends on how we define our social and political impulse. If we see society as a mechanism for producing and protecting individual wealth, then it is only fitting that property be, as Blackstone intoned, an individual's "sole and despotic dominion" over land. (To be fair, Blackstone also wrote, "There is no foundation in nature or in natural law why a set of words upon parchment should convey the dominion of land.") But if we follow Aristotle, who argued that people can live alone but come into political association in order to live well, then government, laws, and the rest of the system can protect property or prune it, depending on what creates the most beneficial situation for the most people.

Today, we have crowned the market as the ultimate arbiter of our ability to dwell here on earth. The market will ensure that we all have adequate homes. The market will correct any deficiencies. In all things, we have made the market all-powerful. It is our civic religion.

Yet, when it comes to human necessities (such as having a place to live or enough to eat) the market doesn't seem to do such a good job. For as long as there have been humans on the planet we have needed shelter. Whether it takes the form of a cave, a grass hut, a room in a Bowery flophouse, or a massive private home with a three-car garage, we all need a roof over our heads. The market, however, does not provide enough roofs to go around, and certainly not at prices most people can afford. If the market truly worked, if supply met demand as it's supposed to in the classic fable of economics, we would not need government incentives to spur the production of housing. We would not need direct government investment in affordable housing. We would not need laws to force banks to make mortgages to low-income people. There would be no homeless. And there would be no squatters.

There is a problem of property. It's been with us as long as we've been on the planet. Today, the world's squatters are demonstrating a new way forward in the fight to create a more equitable globe. Without any laws to support them, they are making their improper, illegal communities grow and prosper. We don't need to crush their communities with our hard-nosed conception of property rights. Instead, we can learn from them how possession can trump property: how people with no right to any land can produce more housing than people who have a title deed.

To many philosophers, there is no life without a place to live. French philosopher Emmanuel Levinas put it this way: "Man abides in the world as having come to it from a private domain." For Levinas, dwelling, having a home, is prior to being. It is the grounding of our existence, both mental and physical. "Every consideration of objects, and of buildings too, is produced out of a dwelling. Concretely speaking the dwelling is not situated in the objective world, but the objective world is situated by relation to my dwelling."

In other words, without a home, there is no world.

The squatters, by building their own homes, are creating their own world.

Time Future

CHAPTER 10

The Cities of Tomorrow

It is recorded that at first their dwellings were humble, mere huts and shacks, built of wood gathered at random, the walls plastered with mud. The roofs came to a point and were thatched with straw. But now all houses have a handsome appearance and are built three stories high.

—Thomas More

There is no mud hut utopia. Even in the mythical city of Amaurot, capital of the island of Utopia, people had to build, struggle, work, and fight to achieve the republic of their dreams. It's the same in the real world. As I think about the time I spent in the four cities I have profiled in this book, I think of the hard work involved in squatting: The discipline required to improve your house one wall at a time, and sometimes simply one brick at a time. The love people have for their communities. The pride in creation. The hunger people have for their efforts to be taken seriously. The desire for government to wrestle with their issues. And the modesty squatters display about their achievements.

While I was in Mumbai, Haaris Shaikh, a writer for a Marathi-language news weekly, asked me an excellent question. We were talking about my experiences in the squatter communities and my feeling that squatters were maligned through bad press. He interrupted to ask: "But aren't squatters the enemy of civil society?"

For once, I was prepared.

Think about it, I said: Squatters make up half the population of Mumbai. If they organized and pooled their votes, they could control the communities. If just 1 in 10 squatters organized to demand city services and, when they weren't provided, decided to march on the central business district, the crowd would be 600,000 people. They could paralyze downtown. They could outnumber the police. They could take over the city for a time. They could run civil society, or at least win whatever demand they were articulating at the time.

But they don't do this.

No, squatters aren't the enemy of civil society. They are the most law-abiding people around. As Valeria Cristina told me in Rocinha, "People may be poorer here, but they pay their bills. In Flamengo, which has rich people, many didn't pay their bills."

If the rich and wellborn were treated as badly by governments as the squatters have been, there would have been a rebellion long ago. The miracle is that the world's squatters value civil society and want to find a way of working within the system. They are law-abiding outlaws, patriotic criminals.

I'm standing on a wasteland. Forlorn, empty, unhappy, the gloomy pilings of the boardwalk in the distance, the lonely roar of the ocean on the unkempt beach beyond. This is, still, Sprayview Avenue in New York. Slowly, now, developers are picking off the parcels here, taking them from the government and building market-rate housing.

How much more quickly things would have gone, and how many worthy people would have good homes, if we had learned from the squatters of the developing world and allowed Sprayview Avenue to be built according to their model.

The world's squatters give some reality to Henri Lefebvre's loose concept of "the right to the city." They are excluded, so they take. But they are not seizing an abstract right, they are taking an actual place: a place to lay their heads. This act—to challenge society's denial of place by taking one of your own—is an assertion of being in a world that routinely denies people the dignity and the validity inherent in a home. As Patrick Chamoiseau put it in *Texaco*, his richly imagined fictional squatter history of Martinique, "In City, to be is first and foremost to possess a roof."

For a time, thousands of squatters in the cities of the developed world possessed that roof. Their history—one of mistreatment and, ultimately, eviction from the land, which, in some cases, had been theirs for decades—is not simply a tale of woe. Understanding this squatter heritage means accepting that squatters exist and that their constructions are a form of urban development. Squatters have been extremely effective at clearing land and building on it. They've never had the might to defy the moneyed interests for long.

But their brief successes—even in a world that espouses ever more strict adherence to property rights—show that there's another way to look at land; one that values possession more than purchase, and that recognizes need as well as greed. For those moments when squatters succeeded, there was freedom of domicile in our cities.

In the middle of my stay in Rio, I met Sonia Rabello de Castro. She's a former attorney general in the Rio de Janeiro government who now teaches law at the state university there. I thought that, as a person who has spent her life applying and upholding the law, she'd be against squatters. But she had a different viewpoint. She said that the favelas are here to stay, that they have become permanent, and there's no sense in government opposing them. She'd like to see squatters empowered to run their communities. But, unlike many of the other progressive lawyers around town, she doesn't think squatters need laws or lawyers to achieve great things. "They already have enough laws to exercise their rights," she told me. "The solution lies within, not outside. They do not need title deeds. They simply need a few simple rules to create their own self-governing bodies."

She wasn't talking about politics, and least not politics in the electoral sense. She wasn't talking about bringing court cases, although that might be something squatters could decide to do. She was talking about old-fashioned grass roots organizing. People getting together, deciding what they want, and then figuring out how to get it. It's messy. It's time-consuming. It's frustrating. People will have to make mistakes and learn from them.

But it just might work.

Here's an example, from halfway across the globe.

Leonard Njeru Munyi and Samuel Njeroge grew up in Korogocho, a shantytown on the west side of Nairobi. Like many Korogocho kids, they were dump pickers when they were young. Nairobi's garbage dump is right next to Korogocho: a valley with a pall of smoke hanging over it because of the perpetual rubbish fires. Njeru and Njeroge culled the refuse every day, looking for items they could sell for a few shillings. It was simple survival.

Korogocho is tough turf—tougher, I think, than Kibera. Many of the people here were kicked out of downtown to make way for a real estate development, and they are still angry.

Njeru and Njeroge are still working together. Now they are social workers. When I met them, they were employed by the government to work with street kids. And their lives mirror each others. They both are married. They both have, as they call it, "micro families," meaning that each has just one child. They share a post office box. They share a mobile phone. They share, it seems, life.

Rocinha: sunset from my balcony.

We walked through the alleys of Korogocho and through the neighborhood called Kisumu Ndogo ("little Kisumu"), where vendors were frying fish on the street and selling chunks to the crowds coming home from work. Night was falling and we stopped in the gathering dusk to interview an *mzee* (a respected older man) who has lived in Korogocho for more than 40 years. As we spoke, a crowd gathered to listen. Eventually, the *mzee* tired of the discussion and wandered off. The others took over. We had what Njeru jokingly called a perfect focus group. I stopped asking questions and listened. The debate was between landlords and tenants. It was about people's rights. It was about how privileged people take advantage of others to grab land. Some of the younger folk were uncompromising: they wanted land reform now. Others said that you can't just take a man's land away from him, even if he doesn't officially own it, without giving him some consideration.

Someone—in the darkness I could no longer tell exactly who was speaking—told a story. Working together with a local school, the people in their part of Korogocho (a neighborhood called Grogan) built a toilet for the community. But after some payoffs to the local politicos, a man took control of the toilet. He turned each section of the toilet into a single room, and has rented them out to families. Thus the community lost a toilet to one man's greed.

There were no answers during that night of political education. There was shouting, laughter, hard words, anger, duplicity, sincerity, frustration, communication. But no answers.

But since when are there ever answers in a day? The way forward is not a straight line, and the questions raised by the squatters are not easy ones. How do you organize a community where property does not exist? Whose interests are most important? What kind of homes do people want? Where should any money that might be available be put: into buildings, into infrastructure, or into education? How much can people really afford to pay in rent? If they are renters, who should own the buildings? These are tough issues and require tough debate. The people of Korogocho clearly have the appetite, energy, and intelligence to step into the conversation. The question is why the UN, the Kenyan government, and anyone else who cares about these communities doesn't work with them to start it.

This is what Korogocho needs, what Kibera needs, and Rocinha and Sultanbeyli and Dharavi and Squatter Colony. More focus groups, more debate, more discussion, more conversation.

The squatters are ready.

Are we?

doors-leading-to, never doors-against; doors to freedom: air light sure reason.

—João Cabral de Melo Neto

Acknowledgments

Blanche Dubois was right: You can depend on the kindness of strangers.

In each country, scores of people who didn't know me welcomed me into their communities and their homes. I now have friends all over the world, and it was a privilege to get to know all of them, even briefly. But a few people not only went out of their way to help a strange fellow they didn't know, but also made me family. Without them, I would not have survived. I often ask myself: If a journalist from overseas came to my city to do a book, would I be as giving and welcoming? It is a humbling thought.

Paul Sneed, Washington Ferreira, Robson Umbelino, and Jose Geraldo Moreira were my family in Rio. Nicodemus Mutemi and David Mburu Kamau were my relatives in Nairobi. In Mumbai, Raju ("Soni World") Soni, J.F. Wadekar (and Manda, Aasha, Vijay, Rajkanya, Nisha, and Manisha), Anthony Dias, Aasif Sartaj, and

Vilas Jabade made me part of their families. My family in Istanbul included Tahsin and Zeynep Çağlayan (and their son Rafet), Turgut and Inci Akcağoz, and Zamanhan Ablak.

Among others who extended themselves incredibly: Edésio Fernandes, Christine Bodewes, P.K. Das, Şehnaz Layikel, Evrem Tilki, Mercy Kadenyeka, Seyhan Tüzün, Mithat Kahveci, Dilip D'Souza, Girish Menon, Samuel Njeroge, Leonard Njeru Munyi, Adem Karagöl, Catalina Trujillo-Hinchey, Ali Tayan, Amos Okoth, the team at the Shabana Azmi compound of *Nivarra Hakk Suraksha Samiti*, Ignatius Namenje, Smita Deshmukh, Sudharak Olwe, Satish Malavade, Sarah Karirah-Gitau, the whole crew of the Fundaçao Dois Irmãos, Sachin Heralkar, Devika Mahadevan, Irfan Merchant, Festus Kivunji, Sister Kusum (and Kalpana and Jonita) from Navjeet Community Center at Holy Family Hospital, the congregation of Christ the King Church in Kibera, Savaş Karamanoğlu, Raju Pangwani, Gavin O'Malley, Mukesh Mehta, Dietmar Starke, Joachim Maanzo, Sheela Patel, Sundar Burra, Márcio Ferreira, Naresh Fernandes, Chris Williams, Rachel Mrabu, the team from Koçlar Pastanesi, the gang at Karamanoğlu Iskender, Joseph the porter at the Parkside Hotel, the David Sassoon Library, Bruno (for changing the shape of my nose on the basketball court), Sam the blind man who begs on Moi Avenue.

Closer to home, many others helped make this book a reality:

Jan-Erik Guerth, my agent, believed in the power of this work almost before I did. And yes, Jan, it did change my life.

The John D. and Catherine T. MacArthur Foundation awarded me a research and writing grant that made many things that seemed impossible possible.

Dave McBride, at Routledge, took a chance on squatters, and on me.

Ernest Barteldes, Başak Dedeoğlu, Elif Ozmenek, and Karen Austrian worked valiantly to stuff languages into my unwilling brain. Great teachers all.

My parents, Marilyn and Frank Neuwirth, and my brother Dave and his family, were supremely supportive and involved in making this book a reality. My aunt, Helen Melnick, enabled me to extend my research to India—and I will never get a chance to thank her.

Among friends, Seth Robbins helped spawn the original idea, back in 1996. Brian Connell, Ben Maurer, Vinny Spinola, Shqipe Malushi, George Garneau, and Donna and William Hooker all listened to my stories and put up with my bouts of invisibility and self-doubt. Brian read an early draft of the manuscript. Ben clued me in to Woody Guthrie's radical side. William invited me to read some of my attempts at the Bowery Poetry Cafe.

My colleagues Annette Fuentes, Maria Laurino, and Linda Ocasio heard my first fumblings with this project and encouraged me to follow through.

Three publications deserve honorable mention. *City Limits* magazine and its editor, Alyssa Katz, helped immensely, with assignments and encouragement. *NACLA Report on the Americas,* and its editor at the time, JoAnn Kawell, had me do a piece on drug gangs in Rio. *The Nation* magazine, editor Karen Rothmyer, and the Nation Institute, sponsored one of my early works on squatters, in 1999.

Through it all, beyond words, as always: Andrea Haenggi.

Finally, though I mentioned him before, I have to again, as a memorial:

Nicodemus Kimanzi Mutemi

1974–2004

All errors, omissions, sins, stupidities, and acts of bad faith are the exclusive property of the author.

Sources

TIME PRESENT

All the reporting on Brazil, Kenya, India, and Turkey is my own. I did consult some valuable books and papers for background and history:

Casé, Paulo. *Favela*. Rio de Janeiro: Relume Dumará, 1996.

Durand-Lasserve, Alain, and Lauren Royston, eds. *Holding Their Ground*. London: Earthscan, 2002.

Fernandes, Edésio, and Ann Varley. *Illegal Cities: Law and Urban Change in Developing Countries*. London: Zed Books, 1998.

Furedi, Frank. "The African Crowd in Nairobi." *The Journal of African History* 14, no. 2 (1973).

Goulart, Jose Alipio. *Favelas do Distrito Federal*, Ministerio da Agricultura, Rio de Janeiro, Estudos Brasileiros #9, 1957.

Hardoy, Julio, and David Satterthwaite. *Squatter Citizen: Life in the Urban Third World*. London: Worldscan, 1990.

Hoy, Michael, and Emmanuel Jiminez. "Squatters' Rights and Urban Development." *Economica*, Feb. 1991.

Institute for Research and Study of the Market. *The Mental Life of the Favelados of the Federal District.* Rio de Janeiro: 1958.

James, Preston E. "Rio de Janeiro & São Paulo." *Geographical Review,* 23, no. 2, April, 1933.

Levine, Robert M. "'Mud Hut Jerusalem': Canudos Revisited." *Hispanic American Historical Review,* 68, no. 3, Aug. 1988.

Nascimento e Silva, Maria Hortensia do. *Impressions of an Assistant Working in Favelas.* Rio de Janeiro: 1942.

Nunes, Guida. *Rio, Metropole de 300 Favelas.* Petropolis: Vozes, 1976.

Parsons, Timothy. *"Kibra is our Blood:* The Sudanese Military Legacy in Nairobi's Kibera Location." *International Journal of African Historical Studies,* 30, no. 1, 1997.

Payne, Geoffrey. *Land, Rights & Innovation.* London: ITDG Publishing, 2002.

Robinson, Richard D. "Turkey's Agrarian Revolution and the Problem of Urbanization." *Public Opinion Quarterly,* 22, no. 3, Autumn 1958.

Secretaria Geral do Interior e Segurança. *Censo das Favelas,* Rio de Janeiro: Prefeitura do Distrito Federal, Departamento de Geografia e Estatística, 1949.

Sharma, Kalpana. *Rediscovering Dharavi.* New Delhi: Penguin Books India, 2000.

Sultanbeyli Belediye Baskanligi. *"Sultanbeyli Bulteni,"* Sayi:5, 2002.

Varma, Gita Dewan. *Slumming India.* New Delhi: Penguin Books India, 2002.

UN Habitat. *The Challenge of Slums, Global Report on Human Settlements 2003.* London: Earthscan, 2003.

UN Habitat. *Nairobi Situation Analysis Supplementary Study: A Rapid Economic Appraisal of Rents in Slums and Informal Settlements.* Nairobi, 2002.

Water & Sanitation Program. *The Water Kiosks of Kibera.* Nairobi, no date.

Some fine works of fiction about squatters and land issues also provided inspiration.

Berger, John. *King: A Street Story.* New York: Pantheon, 1999.

Chamoiseau, Patrick. *Texaco.* London: Granta Books, 1997.

Gébler, Carlo. *How to Murder a Man.* New York: Marion Boyars, 1999.

Tekin, Latife. *Berji Kristin: Tales from the Garbage Hills.* London: Marion Boyars, 1993.

THE 21ST CENTURY MEDIEVAL CITY

Bayly, Mary. *Ragged Homes and How to Mend Them.* Philadelphia: American Sunday School Union, 1859.

Braudel, Fernand. *Civilization & Capitalism, 15th–18th Century,* vol 2: *The Wheels of Commerce.* New York: Harper & Row, 1982.

Carcopino, Jerome. *Daily Life in Ancient Rome.* New Haven, Yale University Press, 1940.

Clark, Peter, and Bernard Lepetit, eds. *Capital Cities and Their Hinterlands in Early Modern Europe.* Scolar Press, 1996.

Clark, Peter, and Paul Slack, eds., *Crisis and Order in English Towns 1500–1700.* London: Routledge, 1972.

Dupont, Florence. *Daily Life in Ancient Rome*. Oxford: Blackwell, 1993.

Finley, M.I. *The Ancient Economy*. London: Hogarth Press, 1985.

Geremek, Bronislaw. *The Margins of Society in Late Medieval Paris*. Cambridge: Cambridge University Press, 1987.

Hardy, Dennis, and Colin Ward, *Arcadia for All, The Legacy of a Makeshift Landscape*. London: Mansell, 1984.

Hollingshead, John. *Ragged London in 1861*. London: Smith, Elder & Co., 1861.

Jones, David J.V. *Before Rebecca*. London: Allen Lane, 1973.

Knight, Charles. *London*. London: Henry G. Bohn, 1851.

Lu, Hanchao. "Creating Urban Outcasts." *Journal of Urban History*, 21, no. 5, July, 1995.

Reddaway, T.F. *The Rebuilding of London After the Great Fire*. London: Jonathan Cape, 1940.

Sharp, Buchanan. *In Contempt of All Authority*. Berkeley: University of California Press, 1980.

Slack, Paul A. "Vagrants and Vagrancy in England, 1598–1664." *Economic History Review*, August, 1974.

"Social Condition of the People in Skye," *Times* (London), Sept. 3, 1851.

Stow, John. *Survey of London Written in the year 1598*. London: Whittaker and Co., 1842.

Stubbes, Phillip. *The Anatomie of Abuses* (1583; reprint ed., Arizona Center for Medieval and Renaissance Studies, 2003).

Third Report of the Commissioners Appointed to Enquire into the State and Condition of the Woods, Forests and Land Revenues of the Crown, June 3, 1788.

Ward, Colin. *Cotters and Squatters*. Nottingham: Five Leaves Publications, 2002.

Whittaker, C.R. *Land, City and Trade in the Roman Empire*. Brookfield, Vt. :Ashgate Publishing Co., 1993.

Williams, David. *The Rebecca Riots*. Cardiff: University of Wales Press, 1955.

Leader, *Times* (London), July 1, 1864.

American History

Aron, Stephen. *How the West Was Lost*. Baltimore: Johns Hopkins University Press, 1996.

Ford, Amelia Clewley. *Colonial Precedents of Our National Land System As It Existed in 1800*. Madison: University of Wisconsin Press, 1910.

Gates, Paul Wallace. *History of Public Land Law Development*. Washington, D.C.: U.S. Government Printing Office, 1968.

Harris, Marshall D. *The Origin of the Land Tenure System in the United States*. Ames: Iowa State College Press, 1953.

Hening, William Waller. *The Statutes at Large Being a Collection of the Laws of Virginia from the First Session of the Legislature in the Year 1619*. New York: R&W&G Bartow, 1823.

Sakolski, Aaron M. *Land Tenure and Taxation in America*. New York: Robert Schalkenbach Foundation, 1957.

Minneapolis/St. Paul

Atwater, Isaac, ed. *History of the City of Minneapolis Minnesota*. New York: Munsell & Co.,
    1893.
Hudson, Horace B., ed. *A Half Century of Minneapolis*. Minneapolis: Hudson Publishing
    Company, 1908.
New York Times, May 15, 1889.

Sacramento

Dart, Dennis M. "Sacramento Squatter Riot of August 14, 1850." *Pacific Historian*,
    Summer 1980.
Eifler, Mark A. "Taming the Wilderness Within." *California History 79*.
"Forbes 400." *Forbes Magazine*, 1996.
Gates, Paul Wallace. *Fifty Million Acres*. New York: Atherton Press, 1966.
"Letter from California." *Brooklyn Eagle*, October 12, 1850, p. 2.
McClatchy Co. filings with the Securities and Exchange Commission.
Robinson, Charles. *The Kansas Conflict*. New York: Harper & Brothers, 1892.
Thompson and West. *A History of Sacramento City* (1880; reprint ed., Berkeley: Howell-
    North, 1960).
Wooldridge, J.W. *History of the Sacramento Valley*. Chicago: Pioneer Historical Publishing,
    1931.

San Francisco

Pioneer, or *California Monthly Magazine,* July, 1854.
Brooklyn Eagle, July 10, 1854, p. 2.
Soulé, Frank et al. *The Annals of San Francisco*. New York: D. Appleton & Co., 1855.
California Chronicle, May 16, 1855, May 31, 1855.
San Francisco Herald, April 11, 1860.
"Golden Gate Park," *Overland Monthly,* Dec. 1913.

Chicago

Ballard, Everett Guy. *Captain Streeter, Pioneer*. Chicago: Emery Publishing Service, 1914.
Chicago Tribune, "'Sparrow Cop' Routs an Army," May 27, 1900; "The Streeter Rebellion,"
    May 28, 1900; "True Bills For Capt. Streeter," Feb. 1, 1902; "Grand Jury Lashes
    Streeter," Feb. 2, 1902; "District Battle Ends in Murder," Feb. 12, 1902; "Alderman
    Who Figures in Streeter Case," Feb. 13, 1902; "One Shot in Streeter Raid," Nov. 15,
    1915; "Streeter's Wet Oasis Dries Up," Nov. 16, 1915; "'Ma' Streeter Fights On as the
    'Cap'n' Dies," Jan. 25, 1921.

New York Times, "Rifle Battle in Chicago," Feb. 12, 1902, p. 1; "Chicago's 'Oasis' Raided by Police," Nov. 15, 1915, p. 8; "Chicago Claimant Dead," Jan 25, 1921, p. 7; "Streeter's Odd Land Fight Continues After 39 Years," June 8, 1924, p. XX6; "Squatter Rights Upheld," Sept. 25, 1925, p. 25.

New York Tribune, "Squatter in Lake Michigan," Sept. 29, 1899, 11:4; "Chicago's Squatter War," May 27, 1900, 1:5.

Sherman, J.D., and Samuel S. Sherman. "The Lake Front War." *Frank Leslie's Popular Monthly*, April 1901.

"This Land is Your Land" ©1956 (renewed 1984), 1958 (renewed 1986) and 1970, TRO-Ludlo, BMI.

Robinson, W. W. *Land in California*. Berkeley: University of California Press, 1948.

SQUATTERS IN NEW YORK

Louis Heineman/William Beard

Brooklyn Eagle, "The Cholera," July 30, 1866, p. 2; "From the Basin's Brim," July 19, 1891, p. 9; "Life Among the Squatters," June 24, 1900, p. 17.

New York Times, "Red Hook Patriarch Dead," April 3, 1904, p. 20.

"Abstract of the title of William Beard and Others to Land on and Near Gowanus Bay," Beard and Robinson Papers, 1849–1902. New York Historical Society, New York.

Brooklyn Land Records.

Michael Cooney/Patrick Kinglety

Brooklyn Eagle, "A Shanty Siege," June 7, 1888, p. 6; letter, June 10, 1888, p. 15.

Brooklyn Land Records.

Corcoran's Roost

New York Times: "Dutch Hill," March 21, 1855; "Local Intelligence," July 15, 1867; "A Raid on Squatterdom," August 16, 1867; "James J. Corcoran Dead," Nov. 14, 1900, p. 9; "Exit the New York 'Character,'" Feb. 1, 1925; "Location of 'Corcoran's Roost,' Letter to the Editor," Feb. 26, 1926; "Corcoran's Roost to Change Again," March 32, 1926, p.X20; "Tudor City Development Occupies Property where 'Squatters' Lived in Civil War Era," Feb. 15, 1942.

New York Tribune: "Outlaws of Dutch Hill," Sept. 16, 1880, p. 8; "Shooting Two Policemen," August 25, 1887, p. 2; "Riot at 'Corcoran's Roost,'" Sept. 11, 1899, p. 14; "Founder of 'Corcoran's Roost' Dies," Nov. 14, 1900; "'King' Corcoran," November 18, 1900, p. 6.

Other Newspapers

"Red Hook Point," *Brooklyn Eagle*, March 1, 1851, p. 3.

"City Squatters," *The New-York Daily Times*, July 12, 1854.

The Sanitary Condition of the City," *New York Times*, Aug. 22, 1856, p. 6.

"Homes for the Poor: Jackson's Hollow and the People Who Live in It," *New York Times*, February 24, 1858, p3.

"The Charter Election—A Crying Evil," *New York Times*, Nov. 21, 1864.

"The Ruling Classes," *New York Times*, June 20, 1867.

"Misgovernment," *New York Times*, July 11, 1867, p 4.

"Among the Shanties," *New York Times*, Aug. 29, 1867.

"Red Hook Point," *Brooklyn Eagle*, Dec. 2, 1872, p. 4.

"Sanitary Sketches," *Brooklyn Eagle*, June 18, 1873, p. 3.

"South Brooklyn," *Brooklyn Eagle*, Aug. 1, 1873, p. 2.

"Crow Hill," *Brooklyn Eagle*, Aug. 14, 1873, p. 2.

"Criminals. Their Haunts in South Brooklyn," *Brooklyn Eagle*, Aug. 16, 1875, p. 2.

"Red Hook," *Brooklyn Eagle*, Aug. 3, 1877, p. 2.

"The West Side Squatters, City of Shantytown, Island of Manhattan," *The Daily Graphic* Thanksgiving Week Supplement, Nov. 29, 1879.

"Stopping the Way," *New York Commercial Advertiser*, Dec. 4, 1879, p. 3.

"Driving Out Squatters," *New York Tribune*, Dec. 15, 1879, p. 2, col 3.

"Ten Thousand Squatters," *New York Times*, April 20, 1880.

"John Kelly's Squatters," *New York Times*, April 29, 1880.

"Editorial," *New York Times*, Sept. 7, 1880, p. 4.

"Getting Rid of Squatters," *New York Times*, Nov. 10, 1880.

"Moving Against Their Will—Squatters Driven from their Homes," *New York Tribune*, April 17, 1881, page 7, col. 3.

"A Horrible Death Scene," *New York Times*, Aug. 2, 1884.

"The Shanties," *New York Times*, April 26, 1885.

"In the Second District," *Brooklyn Eagle*, May 9, 1885, p. 1.

"Sandy Gibson's Rock," *New York Times*, July 15, 1886, p. 2.

"Squatters on Mill Rock," *New York Tribune*, July 15, 1886, p. 5.

"Undisturbed by Dynamite," *New York Times*, July 16, 1886, p. 2.

"City and Suburban News,"*New York Times*, Jan. 9, 1887, p. 5.

"Slab City and its Mayor," *Brooklyn Eagle*, Oct. 27, 1889, p. 7.

"Wiping Out Crow Hill," *Brooklyn Eagle*, Nov. 24, 1889, p. 11.

"Funeral of Inspector Reilly," *New York Times*, July 2, 1895.

"Hard Days for Squatters," *New York Tribune*, June 1, 1896.

"Jamaica Bay Squatters Must Pay Rent," *New York Tribune*, June 5, 1901.

"A Bit of Old Color Gone," *New York Times*, Oct. 6, 1901, Sunday Magazine, p. 16.

"Squatter Shanties Sold for a Pittance," *Brooklyn Daily Eagle*, June 5, 1902, p. 1.

"Wants to Oust Squatters," *New York Tribune*, May 6, 1903.

"Manhattan Sunken Village Squatters Out," *New York Tribune*, Oct. 4, 1904, p. 6, col. 1.

"Gone the Sunken Village," *New York Times*, Oct. 4, 1904, p. 5.

"Who's the Last Squatter," *Brooklyn Daily Eagle*, Nov. 2, 1913 (reprinted in *Djuna Barnes's New York*. London: Virago Press, 1990).

"Progress Catches Up with Queens Squatter," *Brooklyn Eagle*, Oct. 2, 1941, 26:1.

"Islet Lore: Soldiers, Prisoners, the Rich, the Dead and, Perhaps, the Devil," *New York Times*, Jul 9, 1995. p. CY 8.

Other Sources

Brooklyn Land Records.

Bunner, H. C. "Shantytown." *Scribner's Monthly*, Oct. 1880.

Campbell, Helen, Knox, Thomas W., and Byrnes, Thomas. *Darkness and Daylight*, Hartford, CT: Hartford Publishing Co., 1897.

City Directories, Brooklyn and Manhattan, various years.

Cutting v. Burns, 57 App. Div. 185 (1901), p. 190.

Harrigan, Edward, and David Braham. *Collected Songs*, Jon W. Finson, editor. Madison, WI: American Musicological Society, 1997.

Hemstreet, Charles. *When Old New York Was Young*, New York: Charles Scribner's Sons, 1902.

Hill, C.T. "The Growth of the Upper West Side of New York," *Harper's Weekly*, July 25, 1896.

Joseph v. Whitcombe, 279 A.D.2nd 122 (1st Dept. 2001).

Metropolitan Board of Health and Board of Health of the Department of Health of the City of New York, Annual Reports, 1866–1876.

Minute book of the West Side Association of the City of New York, 1879.

Minutes of the meetings of the Health Department of the City of New York, March 8, 1881.

U.S. Bureau of the Census, 1860, 1870, 1880, 1900.

PROPER SQUATTERS, IMPROPER PROPERTY

These books influenced the overall argument:

Adorno, Theodor. *Minima Moralia*. New York: Verso, 1978.

Arendt, Hannah. *The Human Condition*. Chicago: University of Chicago Press, 1958.

Aristotle. *The Basic Works of Aristotle*. New York: Random House, 1941.

Benjamin, Walter. *One-Way Street*. New York: Verso, 1997.

Bierce, Ambrose. *The Devil's Dictionary*. New York: Dover Publications, 1958.

Blackstone, William. *Commentaries on the Laws of England. Ehrlich's Blackstone*. New York: Capricorn Books, 1959.

Bloch, Ernst. *A Philosophy of the Future*. New York: Herder and Herder, 1970.

———. *The Principle of Hope*. Cambridge, MA: The MIT Press, 1995.

Brewer, John and Susan Staves, eds. *Early Modern Conceptions of Property*. New York: Routledge, 1996.

Brueggemann, Walter. *The Land.* Philadelphia, PA: Fortress Press, 1977.

Burke, Kenneth. *Attitudes Toward History.* Boston: Beacon Press, 1961.

Canetti, Elias. *The Voices of Marrakesh.* New York: Farrar, Straus and Giroux, 1984.

Carruth, Hayden. *Asphalt Georgics.* New York: New Directions, 1983, 1984, 1985.

Cioran, E. M. *History and Utopia.* London: Quartet Books, 1987.

Cline, Ann. *A Hut of One's Own.* Cambridge, MA: MIT Press, 1997.

Cortazar, Julio. *Around the Day in Eighty Worlds.* San Francisco: North Point Press, 1986.

de Soto, Hernando. *The Mystery of Capital.* New York: Basic Books, 2000.

Ely, James W., Jr. *The Guardian of Every Other Right.* New York, Oxford University Press, 1992.

Galeano, Eduardo. *Days and Nights of Love and War.* New York: Monthly Review Press, 1983.

George, Henry. *Progress and Poverty.* New York: Robert Schalkenbach Foundation, 1997.

Glissant, Edouard. *Caribbean Discourse.* Charlotteseville, VA: University Press of Virginia, 1989.

Gorringe, Timothy. *A Theology of the Built Environment.* Cambridge: Cambridge University Press, 2002.

Habraken, N.J. *The Structure of the Ordinary.* Cambridge, MA: MIT Press, 2000.

Hayek, F. A. von. *The Road to Serfdom.* Chicago: University of Chicago Press, 1956.

Kafka, Franz. *The Great Wall of China.* New York: Schocken Books, 1970.

Kolakowski, Leszek. *Modernity on Endless Trial.* Chicago: University of Chicago Press, 1990.

Lefebvre, Henri. *Critique of Everyday Life.* Vol. 2. New York: Verso, 2002.

Levinas, Emmanuel. *Totality and Infinity.* Pittsburgh, PA: Duquesne University Press, 1969.

Locke, John. *Two Treatises of Government.* London: J. M. Dent & Son, 1966.

Lynch, Kevin. *What Time Is This Place?* Cambridge, MA: MIT Press, 1972.

Malcolm X. *Malcolm X Speaks.* New York: Grove Press, 1966.

Marcuse, Peter. "Why Conventional Self-Help Projects Won't Work." In *Beyond Self Help Housing,* edited by Kosta Mathéy. London: Mansell Publishing, 1992.

Marx, Karl. *Capital.* New York: International Publishers, 1967.

Mayne, Alan. *The Imagined Slum.* Leicester, UK: Leicester University Press, 1993.

Mitchell, John Hanson. *Trespassing.* Reading, MA: Perseus Books, 1998.

More, Thomas. *Utopia.* New Haven, CT: Yale University Press, 2001.

Mumford, Lewis. *The City in History.* New York: Harcourt, Brace Jovanovitch, 1961.

Pejovich, Svetozar, ed. *The Economics of Property Rights.* 2 vols. Cheltenhyam, UK: Edward Elgar Publishing, 2001.

Pierre-Joseph Proudhon. *What Is Property.* New York: Dover Publications, 1970.

Rousseau, Jean-Jacques. *The Basic Political Writings.* Indianapolis, IN: Hackett Publishing Company, 1987.

Russell, Bertrand. *Principles of Social Reconstruction.* New York: Routledge, 1997.

Rykwert, Joseph. *On Adam's House in Paradise.* Cambridge, MA: The MIT Press, 1981.

Singer, Joseph William. *The Edges of the Field.* Boston: Beacon Press, 2000.

Smith, Adam. *The Wealth of Nations.* New York: Knopf, 1991.

Turner, John F. C. *Housing by People.* New York: Pantheon Books, 1976–77.

Index

C

D

E

F

G